Also by Lindsy Van Gelder and Pamela Robin Brandt

Are You Two ... Together?
   A Gay and Lesbian Travel Guide to Europe

Lindsy Van Gelder
Pamela Robin Brandt

The

Into the Heart

Girls

of Lesbian

Next

America

Door

SIMON & SCHUSTER

SIMON & SCHUSTER
Rockefeller Center
1230 Avenue of the Americas
New York, NY 10020

SIMON & SCHUSTER and colophon are registered trademarks
of Simon & Schuster Inc.

Designed by Jeanette Olender
Manufactured in the United States of America

"Best Friend (The Unicorn Song)" by Margie Adam
© 1974 Labyris Music Co. ASCAP. Used by permission.

Six lines from the song "Manipulate" by Lynn Breedlove of Tribe 8
are reprinted by permission of Alternative Tentacles Records.

10   9   8   7   6   5   4   3   2   1

Library of Congress Cataloging-in-Publication Data
Van Gelder, Lindsy.
The girls next door: into the heart of lesbian America/Lindsy
Van Gelder, Pamela Robin Brandt.
p.   cm.
1. Lesbians—United States—Social life and customs.
2. Lesbians—United States—Identity.
3. Lesbians—United States—Sexual behavior.
I. Brandt, Pamela Robin.   II. Title.
HQ75.6.U5V35   1996   306.76´63´0973—dc20   96-7486   CIP
ISBN 0-684-81118-9

Acknowledgments

Our mandate from our editor was to find "the good talkers" in the lesbian community. Maybe it's all that notorious processing, but in the end, we contacted many more articulate women than we had room to quote. For their willingness to be grilled mercilessly about every detail of their lives and for invaluable background insights into countless aspects of lesbian culture all across America, thanks to Jennifer Akfirat, Dawn Aldridge, Lisa Anderson, Toni Armstrong Jr., Eva Blinder, Julie Bremer, Harley Broe, Ari Chagoya, Lisa Cox, Ruth Ellis, Elaine Felhandler, Leanne Franson, Shoshona Frieden, Gillian Gaar, Dr. Nanette Gartrell, Katherine Gibson, Willa Goodfellow, Rebecca Gorlin, Barbara Grier, Sherry Hicks, Crystal Jang, Laura Justice, Mallory Kates, Grace Lichtenstein, Deidre McCalla, Christina MacMullen, Cornelia Massolo, Billie Miracle, Sandra Mitchell, Lynda Montgomery, Guthrie Morgan, Lesléa Newman, Rhonda Palmer, Maryann Parker, Dr. Angela Pattatucci, Lessa Pow, Shannon Rose, Rene Rosechild, Diane Salvatore, Rev. Julia Seward, Kim Shaw, Cheryl Ann Spector, Sue Steeneken, Fawn Streeter, Chris Sweeney, Kay Turner, Mary Vasquez, Janis Walworth, Judy Wenning, Karen Williams, Sabrina Williams, Bren Yaklin, and many others (including those who were reluctant to let us use their names). Thanks as well to OWL Farm and Womanshare in Oregon, Spiraland in Kentucky, Something Special in Miami, and the Mount Holyoke College Lesbian Alumnae Association.

We're also grateful to Bret Israel of the *Los Angeles Times Mag-*

azine, who assigned the article on lipstick lesbians (*before* we were
chic) that prompted the phone call from Simon & Schuster that ultimately led to *The Girls Next Door;* to Linda Wells at *Allure,* who
let Lindsy take a leave of absence at a particularly crazed point in
the writing process; to Information Goddess Susan Krauss of
Krauss Research in Oakland; to Denise Roy at S&S; and to our
copy editor, Jolanta Benal, without whom we would go through life
misidentifying nipple hardware, among other faux pas.

    Donna Albino, Babs Daitch, the Daves (Nimmons and Fleysher),
J. T. Grimes, Laurie Holloway, Joe Miller, David Tuller, Thalia Za-
patos, and Helen Zia helped us find great women to interview all
over the country. Martha Barnette, Deb Clem, Sharon Kahn, Carla
Lupi, and Raquel Matas provided us with homes (and offices) away
from home. Helen Gallagher made our day by showing up at our
Michigan tent site with a cornucopia of junk food and very good
wine. Loly Carrillo served as our stringer at the 1995 festival.
Matthew Cope and Joan Friedman of CompuServe's WordPerfect
Users' Forum provided technical support when our incompatible
Mac and DOS computers proved that lesbian merger goes only
so far.

    For having their fingers on the pulse of the community during the
long months when our own fingers were glued to our keyboards,
we'd like to acknowledge the grassroots grapevine (i.e., the many
homespun lesbian-lifewire publications, local and national, that
subsist on a shoestring), including *Lesbian Connection, Maize,* and
Hikané. Thanks, too, to *The Advocate, Out, The Washington Blade,*
the far-flung lesbian and gay cyberworld (especially the Internet's
gay marriage newsgroup), and the newsletter of the National Center for Lesbian Rights. (In fact, thanks to NCLR just for existing.
We think everything should join up: Suite 570, 870 Market St., San
Francisco CA 94102.)

    Most of all, we want to thank the two people who made this book
happen: Becky Saletan at Simon & Schuster, for her wit, friendship,
and absolutely brilliant editing (a phrase that rarely leaves our tem-
peramental, "touch-one-comma-and-you're-dead" lips); and Barney Karpfinger, for being a great friend and a great literary
agent—in that order, even though he's the world's best literary
agent.

To real family values, and especially

to our own sibs and kids: Robert, Richard,

Lauri, Sally, Sadie, and Miranda

Contents

Were we all like the Sawhorse we would all be Sawhorses, which would be too many of the kind; if like Toto, we would be a pack of dogs; should we all become the shape of the Woozy, he would no longer be remarkable for his unusual appearance. Finally, were you all like me, I would consider you so common that I would not care to associate with you. To be individual, my friends, to be different from others, is the only way to become distinguished from the common herd. Let us be glad, therefore, that we differ from one another in form and disposition. Variety is the spice of life and we are various enough to enjoy one another's society; so let us be content.

The Cowardly Lion, in L. Frank Baum's *The Lost Princess of Oz*

Foreword

This book tells the story of a moment in time when it became at least marginally acceptable to be a lesbian in America. We hope we've told it well. But we don't pretend to have written *The Big Book of Everything That Ever Happened to All Gay Women.* We couldn't possibly cover the variety of lesbian experience, any more than a single work could encompass all of heterosexuality.

Still, we were painfully aware as we did our research that lesbians, so invisible for so long, have a hunger for the particulars of their individual stories to be acknowledged. We encountered many special appeals from those who knew we had a rare shot at reaching a mass audience. Surely we would have a chapter on lesbians and academia? Lesbians who are married to men? Lesbians who have suffered homelessness/cancer/abuse? Lesbians in cyberspace? Et cetera, et cetera. We realized that there are countless books—and songs, and plays, and movies—waiting to be written about countless lesbian lives. But we had to draw some lines.

In the end, we looked inside the lines, at the core experiences that are common to most lesbians. Love. Relationships. Sexuality, vanilla to hot fudge. The grab bag of connecting points known as the lesbian "community." Our title reflects the reality that lesbians can be found in any town, any office, any family. Unfortunately, it's precisely the normality of the typical lesbians next door that's most threatening to some of those who hate us. "I couldn't help but think that she's fifty-four years old and had been dating that woman for twelve years—isn't that sick?" a man who killed an Oregon lesbian couple in 1995 indignantly explained to the *San Francisco Examiner.* "That's someone's grandma, for God's sake. . . . Lesbo grandmas, what a thing, huh?" Although lesbians are more visible than we used to be, we're no less vulnerable. A powerful movement exists to deny gay people the ordinary, unradical, traditional life choices that other Americans take for granted, like marriage. But there are a lot of us in the neighborhood now—and we're not moving.

Though we live next door to mainstream America, we have our own subculture: lesbian bars, clubs, parties, festivals, guest houses, tours, teams, political organizations, professional networks, computer bulletin boards, bookstores, publications, arts and crafts, celebrities, and gossip grapevines. Not every woman who has sex with another woman is necessarily plugged in to all of this, but for most of us lesbianism is still about more than sex. We have unique ways of relating to each other, as lovers and as friends.

The two of us have homed in on a few large-scale tribal events that serve as windows into lesbian political, cultural, and social life. The story of the Michigan Womyn's Music Festivals of 1993 and 1994 is also about our feminist roots, our maddening tendencies toward political correctness, our rather admirable ability as a group to resolve disputes, the process of coming to feel like part of the lesbian community, and the sexual fluidity that makes it possible for some women to choose a lesbian identity. The 1994 LPGA Nabisco Dinah Shore Golf Tournament party circuit in Palm Springs is an entrée into the world of the lipstick lesbian, as well as a jumping-off point for talking about attraction, dating, sex, sex roles, body image, women's bars, and softball. The Austin, Texas, Lesbian Avengers' 1994 cross-country ride (leading up to the Gay Pride march commemorating the twenty-fifth anniversary of the Stonewall uprising in New York) is a perfect instance of modern ACT UP–style political activism. It's also a springboard for writing about the larger issues that concern us, from electing lesbian politicians to gaining the right to marry.

These three milieus represent wildly disparate slices of lesbian life, as different as Birkenstocks, high heels, and Doc Martens (which is not to say that any given woman might not have attended all of them). Gay Pride marches are always at some level a confrontation with society; the annual Michigan festival and Dinah are escapes from society—although women's music festivals were originally an escape from things like go-go dancers and whipped-cream wrestling that are now Dinah standards, and events like Dinah in turn are a reaction to the downward mobility and rigidity of Michigan. Most marches and political actions involve working with men; the festival bans them at the gates; Dinah relegates them to room service. Together this trio of events is a kind of lesbian Triple Crown for the nineties, raising ideas that we hope will resonate even for those lesbians who wouldn't be caught dead at any of them.

We've especially tried to focus on individuals and couples who simultaneously illuminate many of the deeper truths about lesbian lives and disprove many shallow stereotypes: that lesbianism is all about sex—or else not at all about sex; that lesbians are either all white middle-class professionals—or else all Dykes on Bikes; that lesbians have no families, hence no family values. (Although we admit we buy into some stereotypes ourselves. We're always surprised when we meet lesbians who don't live in multiple-cat households, for instance, or who have never lived up to the community joke about what a lesbian takes on a second date: a U-Haul.)

We drew heavily on the diversity of our community, interviewing well over a hundred women of all races and backgrounds, from the able-bodied to those in wheelchairs, from teenagers to women in their nineties, from separatists who live in the sticks and haven't seen a man (or a flush toilet) in ages, to urban lipstick "lesbians who sleep with men." Some interviewees were lesbian household words. Most were not. We found them through organizations, on-line services, newsletters, and friends of friends, and in some cases, by buttonholing interesting strangers. Our research took us all over the country, not only to obvious gay hot spots like New York and San Francisco, but also to heartland places like Pittsburgh, Indianapolis, and backwoods Kentucky. We spoke to carpenters, hospital workers, architects, musicians, stand-up comics, teachers, students, store owners, writers, doctors, farmers, a cartoonist, a sex-toy inventor, an electrician, a construction worker, an elected official, a minister who received us in her church, and a professional dominatrix who entertained us in her dungeon.

A caveat: Although we were looking for timeless insights, our interviews took place between 1993 and 1995. Life goes on, and individual lives have changed since then.

Finally, this is a book for readers of all genders and orientations. (We *have,* however, presumed a certain level of sophistication among our straight readers. People who really want to know which one of us is the boy will just have to keep scratching their heads.) Our inspiration throughout our writing lives has been the straight male journalist A. J. Liebling. In his columns for *The New Yorker* from 1935 until his death in 1963, Liebling wrote on a wide variety of topics—war, horse races, French wine, Louisiana politics, New York newspapering—but he was probably best known for his classic pieces on boxing. Way back when both of us were high school journalists who loathed sports in general and macho slugfests in particular, Liebling made us realize that there are ways of writing that can seduce even readers who could care less about any given subject into caring very much. Faced with tackling the topic of lesbian culture for a mass-market audience, the first thing we did was reread *The Sweet Science,* his witty and affectionate essays about the ringside subculture of fighters, trainers, sparring partners, gym owners, sportswriters, fans, and hangers-on. It knocked us out, all over again. We continue to try to learn from his example.

There have been many times in our lives when we've been exasperated with lesbian culture, God knows (or is that Goddess?). It can be insular, P.C., out to lunch, and as hatefully hurtful as your worst memories of sixth grade. This book reflects the reality that lesbians can sometimes be as wrongheaded as any other human. But we've also been strengthened by the very existence of the lesbian community. We're delighted to be able to share it with the rest of the world.

Icepicks
and Lipsticks:
The New
Visibility

In the spring of 1992, the premier fashion acces-
sory for the debonair lesbian-about-town was an icepick.

That, at least, was the inference the American moviegoing public
could have drawn from *Basic Instinct,* which opened in mid-March
and—despite a boycott by some queer activists—became an instant
box office smash. Rumors about the antilesbian content of the script
had set off fierce demonstrations during filming in San Francisco
the year before. What made *Basic Instinct* a hot ticket, however,
was its hetero content, particularly the beaver shot heard 'round the
world: the notorious scene in which Sharon Stone, minus panties,
flashed Michael Douglas and the rest of the police interrogation
team. The Stone character and her three female lovers were all variations on the basic ball-buster theme: slippery, voracious, kinky,
predatory, man-hating (but sexually available to—in fact fascinated
by—men), and, of course, criminally insane.

Still, if you rent the video of *Basic Instinct* today, just a few short
years later, it plays like a lesbian *Reefer Madness,* and it may be
hard to get a bead on why something so goofy upset so many peo-

ple. The answer is simple, although it's one that's probably difficult for even the most supportive heterosexual to imagine. At the time the movie was released, the parameters of lesbian life could be summed up in a word: invisibility.

For as long as the two of us can remember, to be a lesbian was to live in the social equivalent of a house without mirrors. Entire years could go by without us seeing ourselves reflected in any television show, on any billboard, in any mainstream magazine. Our lives had no context. Neither did our deaths: After the Northern California earthquake of 1989, newspapers and newscasts all over the world conveyed the dimensions of the tragedy with the image of a distraught woman whose "friend" was buried underneath the rubble of a collapsed coffee shop. Although the woman was openly gay and specifically asked reporters to make clear that she had lost a spouse, few did. While the same sort of "inning" can happen to gay men, lesbians seem to pass for straight more easily; in any case, after Rock Hudson's death from AIDS in 1985, gay men certainly ceased to be ignored by the media. The ensuing years were especially strange for lesbians, since "homophobia" no longer explained our absence. As recently as the 1992 Christmas holidays, a Philadelphia group called the Lesbian Visibility Project spent weekends holding hands in suburban shopping centers. "I just got tired of going to the malls and feeling like I was the only lesbian on the planet," the organizer of the group told a Reuters reporter.

Lesbianism was often erased even in liberal circles, where it was assumed that "gay" concerns were male and "women's" issues were heterosexual. Feminist Susan Faludi's best-selling 1991 tome, *Backlash,* didn't mention the L-word once. Stand-up comic Kate Clinton—the dean of a bunch of very funny women who have kept lesbians laughing ruefully for years—commented on this sexual-identity syndrome with a whole routine about "stealth lesbians." The shtick: We could have enormous potential as secret weapons, since nobody'd ever know we were there.

Hollywood overlooked lesbians, too, with only a few exceptions, most of them the work of foreign or independent filmmakers, like the 1986 *Desert Hearts.* On the rare occasions when we did appear, lesbian characters frequently ended up dead. Or undead, as vampires. Most lesbians were starved for the fluff that the rest of the world takes for granted: the basic story of two normal people who fall in love and live happily ever after. The popular *Fried Green Tomatoes,* which was released shortly before *Basic Instinct,* obliterated the lesbian relationship that, in the novel, existed between the two extremely sympathetic main characters. According to actress Mary-Louise Parker, she and Mary Stuart Masterson tried to play the parts as two women in love in spite of the direction and the script; as far as the L-word was concerned, Parker later told a reporter, the director "wasn't interested in delving into that." And tellingly, few moviegoers noticed that "that" was missing, although the result was surely as peculiar as a version of *Gone With the Wind* in which Rhett and Scarlett are just very good friends.

It seemed to be permissible to discuss lesbianism only when something was terribly wrong. Around the same time that *Fried Green Tomatoes* was playing in theaters around the nation, the two of us set up an online clipping service to earmark mentions of lesbians in the news. There weren't many, and the name that cropped up most often was that of accused serial killer Aileen Wuornos. For the overwhelming majority of women whose "lesbian lifestyle" consists of recycling the garbage and balancing the checkbook, *Fried Green Tomatoes* and *Basic Instinct* packed a familiar one-two punch: Our intimate lives were apparently too icky and weird for public consumption . . . unless we were homicidal maniacs.

Part of the problem, unquestionably, was that most lesbians weren't making themselves known; Martina Navratilova was for years the only openly lesbian celebrity in the world. But the issue went deeper. Gay men may be closeted, but for some time it's been apparent to all but the most provincial minds that queerness is at least a possibility when two unmarried adult males choose to live and/or spend all their time together. Women, straight or gay, are rarely presumed to be with each other out of choice; they're saving money as roomies, traveling together for safety's sake, out on the town "alone" because they don't have dates. At the same time, lesbianism is camouflaged by the fact that almost all women are publicly affectionate with their friends. Unless they're of different races, lesbian couples typically have had the experience of being asked if they're sisters. It happens to us all the time, although Pam is a blue-eyed, fair-skinned, prominent-featured redhead of part-Irish, part-Jewish ancestry, and Lindsy is a brown-eyed, dark-haired, small-boned WASP. There's a stunned silence when we reply that we're a couple—which we always do, since we prefer the possible danger inherent in being known for what we are to the humiliation of not being known at all. People often react as if they no more expected to encounter lesbians in their midst than Keebler elves.

The only corner of popular culture where lesbians could always be found was the straight-male pornography market. Here the problem was the opposite of the *Fried Green Tomatoes* syndrome: Two women could screw their brains out, as long as their sexuality was devoid of any emotional content or any real preference for women. The "lesbians" were invariably bored babes sporting black lace garter belts, not to mention fingernails that would make any genuine lesbian wince and cross her legs. Years ago, when Lindsy was covering the Times Square beat for a New York City newspaper, she asked a porn film distributor why the girl-on-girl action was so popular. "Simple," he explained. "The guy who's watching it doesn't have to get distracted comparing himself to an actor with a big dick. And he can fantasize that if he walked into the room, the girls would instantly drop each other and pay attention to *him*." Lesbian sexuality is a twice-the-fun warm-up act, unthreatening precisely because there is no penis; indeed, it's understood that what's going on is "foreplay." The girls with the garters are waiting for a penis to arrive on the scene, or posing for someone who has one.

Homophobia also plays itself out differently depending on the gender target. The taboo about sex between gay men *is* the sex. (How often have we heard straight men say that although they find lesbian sex a beautiful turn-on, they think gay male sex is gross?) In a culture in which women are inferior, men who allow themselves to be "used" as women (the way that the 'phobes see penetrative sex, which is also the only possible way they can imagine gay male sex) are traitors to their class. Homophobes get luridly, tonguewaggingly *upset* about the erotic possibilities between men, which is why the gays-in-the-military debate seemed absurdly focused on the plight of straight male soldiers bending over to pick up bars of soap in the shower.

But—except, perhaps, for lesbian-mother custody cases, which routinely involve grilling about how much the women hug and kiss in front of the children—sex between women doesn't scare the horses and shake the foundations of society. It's usually threatening only to the extent to which it excludes the men who are titillated by it. Early in our relationship, when we were still trying to get the hang of coming out gracefully, Pamela went for a routine gyneco-logical checkup. While she was in the stirrups, the doctor asked her about birth control. Pamela isn't a shy woman—she's spent a good part of her adult life playing in rock and country bands—but she took a deep breath as she haltingly explained that she was a lesbian. To her relief, the doctor smiled. Then he asked if the two of us would like to get together sometime with him and his social circle for a little hanky-panky. Not quite believing what was happening, Pamela sputtered that we were monogamous. The doctor spent the rest of the exam lecturing her that exclusive lesbianism was "im-mature." (No, we didn't report him, by the way, although we wished we had. A few years later he died in a plane crash.)

Plenty of people who might be threatened by lesbianism if they understood it better can't imagine What We Do in Bed, beyond serving as heterosexual hors d'oeuvres, and because of that, they doubt we exist at all. One of the greatest stereotypes about lesbians is that we just haven't met Mr. Right—less generously expressed as "All she needs is a good fuck." This mind-set is hardly limited to porno. Reviewing *The Children's Hour* for *The New Yorker,* Pauline Kael once snickered: "We're supposed to feel sorry for these girls because they're so hardworking, and after all, they don't do any-thing—the lesbianism is all in the mind. (I always thought this was why lesbians needed sympathy—there isn't much they *can* do.)"

The supposed crime of lesbians isn't same-sex sex but "man-hating." In our experience, the women who truly hate men are usu-ally those who live with one, but lesbians end up taking the rap.

Maybe because gender relationships today operate under so much tension, the idea of being a lesbian holds a kind of idealized charm for some straight women. Sharon Stone, of all people, remarked wistfully in an interview in *Vanity Fair* that she wished she could be a lesbian because "men can be annoying. . . . God! If I could get into it, it would be great." It's a line we've heard a zillion times. If straight men often assume that lesbian sexuality is a kind of holding pattern—something women do while they're waiting for a man— straight women take the opposite view: that lesbianism is something that exists across an abyss from their own sexuality, something that they could never, as Stone says, "get into" because of a basic attraction to men, however nasty they are. (What these ideas have in common, interestingly enough, is the inevitability of female desire for men.) Part of the appeal of lesbianism for straight women is the perceived freedom to hate men, without consequences. The two of us, and many other gay women we know, have often had the bizarre experience of hearing from an old friend at precisely the moment she's decided to leave a boyfriend or a husband. You can almost see the light bulb turn on: "I'm really pissed at him. Let's see. Who would be a good person to run all this anger by? Oh, *I* know . . ."

In truth, some lesbians do hate men, but ultimately, being a lesbian isn't *about* men. It's about loving women.

Heterosexual men often use "lesbian" as a kind of shorthand for "woman who refuses to defer to men," which is, of course, not the same thing as hating them. Again, there's a gender gap: When men spout rampant male chauvinism, it's never considered evidence, as radical feminism is, that they might be queer; woman-hating is seen as, at worst, a problematic form of normal male heterosexuality. But the equation of lesbianism with man-hating operates even in situations where the "lesbians" may in fact be unquestionably heterosexual. "Dyke" is the knee-jerk accusation made against a woman who doesn't want to sleep with some man, who bonds with other women, who puts women first, or who excels in a field that's been off-limits to women. (Which is why America's Cup competitor Dennis Conner reportedly referred to the rival, mostly female team aboard *Mighty Mary* as "the lesbo boat," and why gay-baiting slurs were spray-painted on the home of Shannon Faulkner, the first girl admitted to the Citadel.)

Paradoxically, the result of all these negative stereotypes is that antilesbian sentiment has tended to be relatively diffuse. Our "man-hating" is part of a pattern of behavior that nonlesbians may exhibit; and, thanks to porn, our sexuality isn't perceived as being far outside the realm of heterosexuality. Disliking lesbians is really just a variation on a larger misogynist theme of contempt for "castrating women" or "old maids." It's more like the air some people breathe than something requiring a specialized political movement, like the one trying to prevent Adam from getting it on with Steve.

And so, while gay men are despised for what they do in bed, lesbians are often just ignored. Except for those times when our man-hating explodes and we reach for those trusty icepicks, two women in love are, at worst, seen as merely pathetic—two zeroes trying to add up to the real thing. Inconsequential. Invisible.

Obviously a few things have changed, or we would not have written this book. But when lesbian chic began to ripple through the media around 1993, no one was more surprised than we. Throughout the Reagan-Bush era, the two of us frequently suggested lesbian-related articles to editors of the magazines and newspapers we worked for. Most often the reaction was embarrassment, as if we had proposed writing about something deeply personal, totally irrelevant to anyone but ourselves, and a little distasteful—like hemorrhoids, perhaps.

When the two of us first became lovers, Lindsy was hooked by the way Pamela strutted around onstage with her band, wearing her slinky clothes . . . while singing feminist lyrics. Pamela fell in love with Lindsy's teenage-brat personality, which she found oddly charming in a responsible thirtysomething.

We met at a time when both of us were thinking hard about the limitations of the closet, and each of us was attracted by the other's refusal to spend her life treading water in the Well of Loneliness. It was 1978. We had no idea how to live in the open (and there was certainly no issue of *Lesbo Cosmo* on the newsstand to give us "Ten Tips on How to Make the World Respect Your Relationship"), but we were determined to try. We often felt that we were inventing ourselves from scratch. For the first four years of raising two children together on New York's Upper West Side, for instance, we didn't know a single other lesbian mother. The only feedback we got on our intimate family life was the Woody Allen film *Manhattan,* in which the Allen character's ex-wife, played by Meryl Streep, is living with their son and her female lover. The running gag of the movie is Allen's fantasy about running the women down with his car.

Initially, we didn't have any cosmic notions about "lesbian visibility"; it was more a matter of simply not wanting to lie. Honesty began at home. We used to play a game—we still do—called "What Are You Thinking?" The question can be asked at any time, and the other person has to tell the truth, no matter what, even if she's thinking of something embarrassingly stupid, or about having sex with an ex. The game has major piss-off potential, and we did a lot of sulking and screaming during that first year. But we also ended up joined at the brainstem.

The concept of being "out" as individuals didn't have much currency in those days, even in the gay community, and plenty of people who were openly gay were only selectively so: They wouldn't be out to their parents or their children, for instance, or while walking down the street, or in the media. Fairly early on, we were all of the above. Sometimes the result was unnerving, like the time in a bar in rural New England when a good old boy who realized we were a couple followed us into the ladies' room, apparently convinced that we were about to Do It in one of the stalls. (Lindsy ended up throwing a wastebasketful of sanitary napkins at him.) Most of the time, being out was merely energy-consuming. We learned how to come out to new acquaintances naturally, dropping the bomb in a way that didn't come off as an apology, an "announcement," or a put-down. As we figured it all out, making mistakes and admiring each other's nerve, we felt as if we were inventing a new way to be in love: as partners in crime, two against the world. We became each other's lesbian visibility role models.

We had each arrived at this particular fork by rather different routes. Pardon us while "we" unmerge for a few pages.

Lindsy first:

I confess: I was pretty happily heterosexual. With the sex part, anyway. The guys in my life were often emotionally disappointing— either out of touch or out of control—but most of my friends had the same complaint. I'd been in love or at least deep lust with a half-dozen men before I ever seriously considered an affair with a woman. When I look back now on friendships with certain girls and women, I wish I *had* been involved with them. But at the time, the possibility simply didn't occur to me.

My first, brief, abstract, intellectual glimmer came one night around 1970 at a feminist consciousness-raising meeting. The group had invited several lesbians to explain their "lifestyle" to the rest of us. Poised to be tolerant, we were totally taken aback when the lesbians (led, as it happens, by a struggling young writer named Rita Mae Brown) challenged *our* sexuality. Why were we wasting time bitching endlessly about husbands and boyfriends? Why weren't we having sexual relationships with the people we felt closest to—i.e., other women?

We were hard pressed to defend ourselves. But lesbianism as the alternative? The requisite juices just weren't there. It was especially hard to envision all the qualities we loved in our female friendships—understanding, easiness, intimacy—in a hot sexual package. Would it be sexy? Would *we* be sexy? I remember wondering how on earth one could use "feminine wiles" on another woman without feeling ridiculous. A woman would see right through you, know what you were feeling, and know you knew she knew. You'd be as vulnerable as a baby. And yet, as the lesbians were quick to point out, emotional intimacy was precisely what we all said we weren't getting enough of from men.

This was food for thought, but at the time I was married and monogamous. I tucked the lesbian option away in some mental file cabinet labeled "Interesting, Worthwhile Things I Can't Conceive of Actually Doing"—like skydiving, perhaps. Then one night five or six years later, after the marriage had disintegrated beyond repair, an ostensibly straight, unhappily married female friend propositioned me. I had been aware for some weeks that there was tension between us, and that it felt oddly sexual. I couldn't imagine having sex with her—after a point, the picture in my mind would go blank—but the very fact that I was even thinking in sexual terms about her was a revelation. When she asked me if I wanted to make love, my response, to reduce a complex swirl of emotions to two words, was, "Why not?"

Although I probably never would have been the one to make the first move, the sex-and-romance aspect turned out to be a piece of cake. In sheer mechanical terms, it wasn't the best sex I'd ever had, but it felt surprisingly natural—and the emotional interplay put it over the top. I felt like I had just discovered a grand ballroom inexplicably hidden behind a screen in my apartment.

My lover was another story. The very next day, she began having anxiety attacks. "If only one of us were a man," she lamented, and continued to lament during the months of the affair. And yet the point—the exciting part, the part that seemingly should have been shouted from the rooftops—was that we were both women, equals who understood each other's emotional terrain. Or at least we always had before.

There was no shouting from the rooftops, or anywhere else. Worse, I had lost my usual confidante—her—and I couldn't turn to any of our friends. I was terrified that my ex-husband might try to snatch the kids from their suddenly "unfit" home if he got wind of us, but I also felt in my guts that I could fight any battle if my lover and I were at least on the same side. She, however, couldn't even say the word "lesbian" out loud. The thought of what we did, and of anyone finding out about it, made her sick, she said. She began desperately casting around for something, anything, that would put the relationship in a context she could accept. Pickings were slim, and mostly depressing or pornographic, but having been an English major, she glommed onto Emile Zola's *Nana,* a sleazoid novel about a bisexual hooker. She began sleeping with several men (aside from her husband) and reveling in the image of herself as a femme fatale with overflowing sexuality.

In the midst of all this suffocating secrecy I did learn some valuable lessons about myself. When my lover began to withdraw, I held on for dear life, like a little vampire bat. The same dynamic had characterized my marriage, and I had always blamed it on some never-the-twain-shall-meet stereotype about the way men and women interact. All of a sudden, I had to come face to face with the possibility that the problem was *me,* and the kind of people I fell in love with.

I developed sympathy for men who have to deal with some of the uniquely difficult barriers that women can put up in a relationship. Getting a woman into bed when she isn't sure she wants to be there is a far more convoluted process than seducing a man. Women are also the high priestesses of the mixed message: When we twist the knife in, we sugarcoat it, we cry, we sincerely want to be friends. We aim to wound places most men don't even know are there. I had done it all myself.

Not surprisingly, the relationship ended painfully. So did a subsequent fling I had with another closeted married woman, one of the few lesbians I knew, and therefore one of the only people I eventually did confide in. I realized the closet wasn't for me, and I didn't particularly relate to most of what I knew about open lesbian culture. By the time I met Pamela, I hadn't ruled women out, but I was dating only men.

Pamela's turn:

I had also done time clattering around with the hangers and the shoeboxes. During my senior year in college, I had, to my surprise, gotten romantically involved with my best friend, Helen. While hardly a heterosexual ball of fire, I'd had a number of genuine crushes on guys, a few majorly magical involvements, and no girls' locker room longings whatsoever. Given the absence of virtually any lesbian role models except *The Well of Loneliness*'s Stephen Gordon, a "Kick me again, world" loser who apparently emerged from her mom's womb with the shoulders of Mike Tyson and a lifelong genetic compulsion to wear boxy men's suits, as well as a lifelong conviction that she should have been born a man . . . well, let's just say lesbianism did not strike me as truly *moi.*

What did make sense about the attraction is that Helen and I were, together, the songwriting/creative leaders of an all-women's band. Budding feminist consciousness made 1969 an exciting time to be females in a very male-dominated profession; sure, we were fighting, but we were *alive* and fighting, rather than sitting in a stagnant pool of household cleansers in our two-child, two-car suburban "homes." Everyone was waiting for the 1970s to cough up its Elvis or Beatles, and Helen and I were certain women were the key. Namely, us. This made for a very deep emotional tie, though, for me, no physical connection.

But finally, a year and a half into our friendship, after yet another intense all-night talk session about our mutual musical dreams, I woke up at seven A.M. with the astonishing revelation that the odd fainting spells my professional partner had been having for the previous year—many of them, coincidentally, after I had stayed out overnight with a boyfriend—were perhaps not such a coincidence, nor, as everyone in the band had been assuming, attributable to typical sixties space-cadethood on her part; that this allegedly out-to-lunch lady was, perhaps, more in touch with her feelings, in at least one respect, than I was; that in fact, my own immediate feelings could be described as, "Oh, shit. I don't believe this."

A quick trip to the nearby general store in Bennington, Vermont (where the band was playing), for two quarts of Colt .45 took care of coming-out angst before ten A.M. And I confess that instead of immediately revealing my feelings, thus risking rejection (to this day, after twenty-five years as a lesbian, I have never gotten up the nerve to ask another woman to dance; how do straight guys do it every Saturday night?), I cleverly manipulated Helen into revealing what was bothering *her* by throwing her in the band van, driving north, and refusing to stop until she told me what was up. She caved just before the Canadian border.

However, there still remained the question: Just what do two women *do* in bed? Even today, it's embarrassing to admit I ever could have been so dumb as not to know. (And actually, our research for this book indicates that many straight men still haven't a clue.) Fortunately, it was college spring break time, so there was opportunity, before having to make a fool of myself in bed, to do research at the Upper Montclair, New Jersey, public library. What I, as a very recently straight girl used to thinking in "Did he get to first, second, or third base?" terms, naturally had in mind was finding a specific sexual procedure, *the* one secret act that surely must exist, in the world of sex between women, and that would replace intercourse as home plate.

But after checking the "L" and "H" sections of the card catalog, I finally found all the lesbiana filed under "P," for "Perversion, sexual"—and things didn't look good. From the runaway nonfiction best-seller of that year (1969), David Reuben's *Everything You Always Wanted to Know About Sex,* came this discouraging professional advice: "Like their male counterparts, lesbians are handicapped by having only half the pieces in the anatomical jigsaw puzzle. . . . No matter how ingenious they are, their sexual practices must always be some sort of imitation of sexual intercourse."

There were a few bright spots, though, such as the description (from the "Female Homosexuality: Women with the Souls of Men" chapter of Dr. Frank Caprio's 1953 book, *The Sexually Adequate Female*), lacking in technical details but nevertheless promising, of "Miss A" 's first perverted encounter: "Our homosexual relations consisted of mutual masturbation and cunnilingus which lasted approximately five months." Now *that* sounded like decent sex, and James B. Fairly agreed, fervently warning readers in his 1964 *Sex and the Coed* that "many of our young ladies, 15 percent or more of them, are latent Lesbians," but that "with luck, they'll never have that first, that fatal experience." I decided it sounded promising enough to wing the fatal plunge, technique-wise. The relationship lasted more than nine years.

Still, it was nearly a year before we met another lesbian couple. One of the pair, ironically, had been in our band the whole time, but was also closeted. We didn't even tell our straight male manager, although he figured it out when he continually tried to date my lover and was continually rejected. His reaction was nightmarish: He rigged a microphone in our room and taped us making love, then obsessively played back the tape. When I confronted him, he was clearly expecting to have his injured feelings soothed. This was the first time I'd ever discussed being a lesbian with a straight person, and it wasn't an experience I felt motivated to repeat often. (The next time I did give it a shot, another friend confided that he'd initially felt like vomiting, but had decided, tolerantly, to remain friends.)

It was more than four years before Helen and I even held hands in public, in the gay enclave of Provincetown. It wasn't until the relationship broke up that I came out to my parents, mostly as a way to explain why I was sobbing all the time.

Meanwhile our musical careers had taken off. Our band The Deadly Nightshade was signed, in 1974, to the RCA custom label Phantom, going on to make two albums and several singles, one of which was a semi-hit (Number 68 nationally, Top 10 in our current hometown of Miami). Was the three-lesbian band out? Not in 1975, not when you're signed to a mainstream record label and opening tours for Billy Joel. Every night we'd play our feminist-oriented music to a receptive but puzzled mixed-gender audience of several thousand "Piano Man" fans who didn't know feminism from botulism, pull ourselves out at the end of the set with a faster-than-light instrumental medley, and come offstage to hear record company reps deliver some version of "You know, with your musicianship you could really go far, if you'd just can this feminism thing and write *regular* lyrics." There was also considerable discussion of how the major record-buying group was adolescent females, who were very protective of adolescent males, who would not be *at all* happy to be sexually rejected; just look at what happened to the career of Dusty Springfield, the only mainstream female musician of the time who had the guts to admit attraction for other women: nosedive.

In confusing collusion, the message from the 1970s feminist movement was that lesbianism confused the feminism issue; one thing at a time, and it wasn't our time yet.

Come out as lesbians professionally? No way.

Tellingly, after I got together with Lindsy in 1978, and simultaneously decided that ready-or-not-here-I-come-out, I never had a bit of trouble in any of the straight venues I played, post-Nightshade, throughout the 1980s. And these places were mostly tough country-and-western biker bars. A typical response, from a trucker who'd asked me to dance and gotten the usual coming-out story in response, was, "Heck, that's fine. If I was a woman, I'd be a lesbian, too. Now, you wanna two-step?"

The year 1993 could have been the United Nations Year of the Dyke. But what most lesbians remember as a major opening volley occurred on October 23, 1992, when *20/20* broadcast a segment on the community in and around Northampton, Massachusetts, "the town that opened its door to a lesbian community," as the teaser before the segment noted. "Women are meeting, marrying, and raising families in the heart of New England!" Heavily promoted, the show ended up being the seventh most watched *20/20* program of the year.

And then suddenly we were everywhere: *Mademoiselle, Harper's Bazaar, USA Today,* the cover of *Newsweek* (which was taken out of the magazine aisle of a Maryland supermarket by an overzealous clerk who was shocked at the cover photo of two women hugging), the "Lesbian Chic" cover of *New York* magazine, even *Cosmo* (which sandwiched the dignified cover line "A Matter of Pride: Being a Gay Woman in the 90s" between "How to Make Your Man Better in Bed" and "Check Out These Super Hunks"). *Rolling Stone* named lesbians as the "hot subculture." *The New York Times Magazine* ran a fashion spread featuring two women doing a sultry tango. Lesbian subplots cropped up on *Seinfeld* and *Roseanne*. A cartoon in *The New Yorker* showed a Hollywood screenwriter, poolside, tapping his laptop and explaining to his companion, "It's a new take on 'Snow White.' The prince turns out to be a lesbian." *Doonesbury*'s Mark came out as a gay man—but, as his friend J.J. pointed out in the punch line of the strip, "Of course, it's much hipper to be lesbian."

Not all of the attention had to do with how chic we were. The right wing—which had previously limited itself to fulminations about "homosexuals spreading AIDS"—was suddenly targeting women like performance artist Holly Hughes, *Heather Has Two Mommies* author Lesléa Newman, and assistant secretary of Housing and Urban Development Roberta Achtenberg. But for the first time there were lesbian role models galore. Melissa Etheridge had come out. So had k. d. lang, both Indigo Girls, Amanda Bearse, Janis Ian, Dee Mosbacher (the daughter of George Bush's campaign chief), top editors at *Essence* and *Redbook,* and various supermodels and punk rockers. Angela Davis appeared to come out during a speech, although she refused to elaborate on it. Sandra Bernhardt came out and went back in, several times. To almost universal lesbian dismay, Camille Paglia came out, too.

A few lesbians who had been out (often out in left field) for years were meanwhile allowed to move to center stage—like Lea DeLaria, the first lesbian comic to make it to prime-time TV, on the now-defunct *Arsenio Hall Show.* Stalking out in a man's suit, at a frenetic 45-degree tilt, like a heavier and much butcher Groucho Marx, DeLaria screamed, "It's the 1990s; it's hip to be queer. And I'm a BIG DYKE!" In the eleven-minute routine that followed, she said "queer," "dyke," or "faggot" eleven times and told a totally offensive joke about Hillary Clinton ("Finally we have a first lady you could boink"). And she got asked back to the show, twice.

There were lesbians in ads for Versace and Banana Republic, lesbians in Madonna videos, lesbians on *Phil* and *Oprah. Esquire* listed "lesbians *everywhere*" as Reason Number 38 in a feature called "Sixty Reasons to Go On Living." Then there was the notorious August 1993 *Vanity Fair* cover showing a scantily clad Cindy Crawford lounging seductively over a barber chair, strop in hand, shaving a dapperly butched-up k. d. lang. An inside-the-book shot showed Crawford straddling lang while lang stroked Crawford's butt.

Of course, many lesbian celebrities, including ludicrously obvious ones, still remained in the closet. And a het/homo double standard—sometimes well-intended—continues to conspire to keep them there. Take a May 1995 letter to the editor from a male reader chiding the slick fashion mag *W* for raising the question of "Madonna gal pal" Ingrid Casares's sexual orientation in a previous issue's interview. (Casares declined to affirm that she is a lesbian.) "I, for one, do not read this magazine to know what goes on in a person's bedroom," he farumphed. In truth, magazines have routinely recognized the sexual identities and relationships of straight celebrities like, say, Joanne Woodward and Paul Newman, without once invading their bedroom with trusty headboard-mounted video camcorders; we see no reason why a simple characterization of Casares's sexual orientation calls for any follow-up revelations of her boudoir, either, unless the interviewer is from *Architectural Digest*. But the likes of this letter can be found in print every month.

Additionally, in an atmosphere where lesbianism appeared to be, for the first time, truly a growth industry, it was easy to overlook that many of us were still being overlooked. As Jewelle Gomez, a writer who has put in time in the Black Panther, feminist, and gay movements, notes, "Lesbian visibility is still really restricted to either someone in a Donna Karan suit who carries an animal-skin attaché case and is a lawyer, or someone who has multiple ear and facial piercings and looks like she's in the Madonna dance troupe. The larger majority of lesbians who go to jobs every day in factories, as secretaries, as health care providers, are completely ignored. It's easier for the larger society to see lesbians as clones of the upright systems or as a freakish entertainment factor. And most of us, certainly lesbians of color, don't fit in there at all." Neither, frankly, do most of the lesbians of festive but frumpy semirural Northampton, where the *20/20* segment left one question on everyone's lips: "Where the hell, in this town, did they find a couple of dykes with a Rolls-Royce?"

Still, for a subculture that was used to fanning itself every time Jodie Foster refused to answer questions from reporters about her private life, a media blitz like this was pretty hot stuff.

To be truly seen, and to see oneself being seen by others, is to have the world open up. We've met countless lesbians for whom the *20/20* feature or the *Newsweek* cover story became the medium through which they could talk to friends or families about their lives for the first time, without feeling as if they were raising an alien topic. Jane Neven runs what used to be the Northampton area's only all-women's bed and breakfast, in a classic Colonial farmhouse bordering the village green in a nearby town. She remembers well the day after the *20/20* segment. "The show was aired on a Friday night. On Saturday the phone started ringing. People were suddenly coming from everywhere." One couple called from Houston with their bags packed. Over the next few months, said Jane, "we had people who would walk the streets in Northampton and come back here and cry. They'd spend the weekend, off and on, crying, because they were so closeted that just to be able to walk in downtown Northampton with another woman, being perceived as a couple, and having people smile at them—not getting yelled at, not getting shot at—blew them away. A couple of women from Canada came and wanted to take home a lesbian video. They're schoolteachers, and it states right in their contract they're not permitted to be homosexual. I said sure, picked up the phone, called the local video store, asked them what lesbian videos they had. I thought these women were going under the sofa! I'd said 'lesbian' out loud."

The B & B business boomed; Jane had to quit her day job to handle the crowds, who were booking four to six weeks in advance. Dozens of lesbians came to the area with the explicit plan of moving there, just so they could be around other out lesbians. "The whole nature of the business changed," Jane said, "from 'Here's your bath, breakfast is at eight' to 'Here's who you speak to if you're interested in real estate. Here's who you contact if you're interested in practicing law here. Here are the people we know in the school system if you're a teacher. Here's where the sperm bank is if you're thinking of having kids.' "

Northampton and its surrounding Pioneer Valley region—like Provincetown, the Mission and Bernal Heights neighborhoods of San Francisco, parts of Oakland, Park Slope in Brooklyn, the Little Five Points area of Atlanta, South Beach in Miami, Capitol Hill in Seattle, the Dutch Hill area of Kansas City, Andersonville in Chicago, and numerous other college towns, resorts, and urban neighborhoods—had long been known among lesbians in the know. But, according to Jane, a lot of isolated lesbians didn't have a clue. "One woman from Connecticut who stayed here had been straight and had left her husband for a girlfriend. But she had no support, no one to talk to. She had a three-year-old son and she thought he would hate her forever." The woman had never met another lesbian mother before, and she peppered Jane with questions about how her children had reacted when she'd gotten involved with a woman. Jane, stocky and middle-aged, is a dead ringer for a straight, cookie-baking New England college professor's wife (which she was, for seventeen years—and she still makes a darned fine canapé). She snorted: "I told her, I'm not a New Age mom. It was like, 'Yeah, I'm with Gail—so? You want your dinner? Set the table.' But you know, she got me thinking: If you aren't in the women's movement or the lesbian movement, you don't know where to start finding information. And all of a sudden the *20/20* show said, 'You're not alone.' "

Probably the major beneficiaries of lesbian visibility are precisely those whom the right wing accuses the rest of us of "recruiting": the young. Amy Anderson lives far from Northampton, in Muncie, Indiana, the town that so epitomized Middle American Babbitry that, as "Middletown," it was the subject of Robert S. and Helen M. Lynd's landmark sociological studies in the 1930s. Amy looks like a tough elf (although she prefers the term "soft butch"), with sparkly eyes and dark blond hair cut into one of those flat-on-the-top/buzzed-on-the-sides dos that make teenagers' parents nuts. "I came out to my mom on April 19, 1993," Amy told us. She had just turned seventeen.

Although Amy had had a few crushes on boys, she had been primarily attracted to girls since she was six years old. She even joined a fundamentalist church in eighth grade in order to back-burner those feelings. "I felt so welcome there; I was this new little enthusiastic Christian girl. They adored me, because they didn't know. And I didn't want to know. I used the church to try to keep it down, and it worked. I wouldn't listen to rock and roll. I would not cuss. I quit smoking. The church taught me to witness to people—to tell them about Jesus and God and the Holy Spirit, and try to get them to come and get saved—so I was annoying. It was my mother I was most hard on. She was single at the time, and I'd be, 'You don't need to go out with these guys, you should come to the church.' She was just goin' out on a date, and I'd get on her. I was brainwashed. They really have an agenda. I mean, they say *we* do, but they really do.

"I think these talk shows and other stuff would have made a big difference to me, in terms of not feeling so isolated and alone, if they'd been happening earlier in my life," she said. "Because I didn't learn about gay culture until I came out. I didn't know we *had* a culture. I got some books about homosexuality at the library, but I felt funny about that; I said I was doing a sexuality project for school. And now this lesbian visibility is everywhere. It's also a big help to my family that they can see we're really out there and successful and like everyone else—that there are lots of us, all over the country and in other countries, not just some little group in San Francisco who had some weird chemical go over them. My mom and I are total talk-show queens. She sits and watches them with me, and we talk about them. But the communicating goes both ways, you know, because sometimes these shows deal with her— you know, when your man won't have sex with you or something, not just about gay issues. So it helps me understand her better too. It's neat. I feel very lucky now." From TV, Amy's mom also found out about a group for parents of gay kids.

Actually, Amy's mom wasn't completely stunned when her daughter came out to her. "She said she knew because I cut my hair off and listened to k. d. lang all the time. She said she just wanted to know I was okay. And she asked a lot of questions. 'If you've never been with a woman, how do you *know* you're gay?' 'How do you know you're straight, Mom? Before you had sex with a man, did you know that's what you wanted?' She said that clicked for her. She got it. She's great. My stepfather's pretty cool too. Like when they came back from vacation one time, he brought my stepbrother a poster with women on it, and he said, 'I told your mom to get one for you, but she wouldn't!'

"My mom and I talk about my relationships all the time. She's like,

'Why aren't you going with her anymore? I thought she was cute!' The really important thing, though, is we broke the barrier. Before, I was judgmental, I was rude, I stayed in my room, I wouldn't talk to her. I couldn't. I was horrible to her, and in response she was horrible to me. Now, I don't have to hide anything anymore. We haven't had a fight since April 19, 1993."

But some lesbians also wondered What It All Meant: Why, after years of being ignored, were we suddenly media darlings? Jubilation was shot through with a certain amount of suspicion. At the 1993 Michigan Womyn's Music Festival, an all-women's event with a strong radical separatist presence, we sat in on a workshop in the woods where gloomy dykes who had long ago written off mainstream culture were predicting that the festival was *over*, soon to be overrun by curiosity seekers and/or deserted by women who could now get their lesbo fix going to see k.d. or Melissa in concert at a straight club. "I'm afraid that visibility is going to take the fire out of what we do," mourned a woman from Montana.

Olivia Records president Judy Dlugacz fielded some flak for appearing on *Geraldo* to discuss lesbian chic. "There's a minority in the lesbian community, just a minority but a very loudmouth minority, that resents visibility," she said. "They *still* want their little women's music culture underground."

San Francisco Bay Area therapist and author JoAnn Loulan came away from the *Geraldo* experience with misgivings. "What I got was that they've discovered that there are some lesbians who look like straight girls. So we're acceptable, and they'll put us on TV because aren't we pretty, and don't men come on to us—which was all Geraldo was interested in discussing." If being a lesbian means anything, she added, it means that women should be able to "look how we want, dress how we want. It was so frustrating to be categorized as, 'Oh, you look like real girls.' I *love* lesbians who don't look like us. I *like* being different than 'normal' people are."

Longtime political activists were especially perplexed, since the attention being paid to us seemed to have come out of nowhere, or at least nowhere that lesbians had been lobbying. Often it seemed to be fallout from heterosexuals who, burned out on AIDS, date rape, sexual harassment, and the rest of it, were sniffing around for new takes on sex and romance. "I don't trust this trendy crap," Lea De-Laria declared when we ran into her at the 1994 Dinah Shore festivities, where she was headlining. It was exactly a year since her *Arsenio* debut. "If all this exposure is happening because I'm flavor of the month, fine. But I don't even think it's *lesbian* chic. I mean, lesbian chic was started by Madonna. Could we have a lesbian start lesbian chic? Hello?"

Beyond Madonna (who has shamelessly milked porno-lez imagery in her work, meanwhile insisting to the press that she has never actually done the dirty deed herself), lesbian chic owed an undeniable debt to gay men. Even the spectacularly influential coming out of lang and Etheridge followed in a straight line from the "outing" controversies circa 1991. Most of outing's architects were gay men, like the journalist Michelangelo Signorile, who felt that AIDS had created a crisis in which it was the moral duty of famous queers to stand up and be counted. A huge chunk of media interest also apparently arose from straight journalists' perception that lesbians were an "angle" on gay men, who were already newsworthy for the most tragic of reasons. Lynn Sherr, who reported the *20/20* segment, explained, "I had been wanting to do a lesbian piece for a long time. Largely because of AIDS, the gay community had become vocal, and then it occurs to you, 'Wait a minute, it's not just guys.' I had never seen a piece on lesbians as people, and I felt it was time."

At a fund-raiser in Miami in the fall of 1993, Liz Hendrickson, the attorney who then headed the National Center for Lesbian Rights (the largest national lesbian organization), wondered if lesbian visibility even had anything to do with political progress. "I don't know what to make of it," she said. "Maybe it just has something to do with sex. Straight men's porno has had that lesbian component always. For all I know it could be part of a phenomenon that's happening all over mass culture: bringing all the private, fringe stuff into mainstream TV and breaking down boundaries." Hendrickson was in Miami to raise money for Sharon Bottoms, a

Virginia woman who had recently lost custody of her two-year-old son in large part because she was a lesbian. Apparently the judge hadn't been impressed with how chic she was. "We're at the White House, we're in *Vogue,* but this is what happens to us on a day-to-day basis," Hendrickson lamented. "The problem with visibility is that it's kind of . . ." She groped for le mot juste. "Kind of *shallow.*"

We briefly met Sharon Bottoms and her lover, April Wade, at a garden party in their honor a few months later in Oakland. They had vaguely Appalachian accents. Sharon was a high school dropout who had worked part-time as a supermarket cashier and dreamed of being a beautician. April was a short-order cook. Except for their twin tattoos, they were a classic opposites-attract butch/femme couple in appearance; at their commitment ceremony, petite blond Sharon wore a gown, while muscular April (who looks not at all like a guy, but definitely like someone you want on your flag football team) sported a tux. It may be that a lot of their trouble comes from trying to get simple justice in a straight society that confuses butch/femme with imitation male/female. Although Sharon was allowed limited visitation with her son, April had been forbidden all contact with him, because Sharon's mother, who was seeking custody, insisted that April was giving him confused ideas about masculinity and femininity. The proof, Grandma revealed in court, was that she'd heard baby Tyler call April Dada.

"The kid's two years old?" snickered a garden party guest, the mother of two sons, deftly removing the eight-year-old's toy truck from the giggling three-year-old's sticky clutches. "He's probably calling the toaster Dada." When the two guests of honor were introduced, April looked around at the sea of lesbian mothers with children in the crowd. "It's good for me to have the opportunity to be around kids," April began, "because I don't get that at, um . . ." And then she burst into tears.

In April 1995 the Virginia Supreme Court upheld the original ruling that Sharon Bottoms was an unfit mother, because, among other reasons, she engaged in oral sex, a felony in her state, and because her sexual orientation would subject her child to "social condemnation." The day of the ruling, our copy of *W* arrived in the mail. It described how, at the ready-to-wear collections in Paris, Claudia Schiffer and other supermodels had vamped down the runway in man-tailored Chanel suits. Much fuss was made over the gender-bender factor. "Nothing is forbidden anymore," designer Karl Lagerfeld exuberantly announced to a reporter. But as for the fashion, he added, "It's not really lesbian. It's more bisexual."

There is nothing wrong with being a bisexual, or a lipstick lesbian. It's just that part of what we love about being lesbians is how easy it is *not* to worry about what men think. Lesbians often have a habit of falling in love with each other even when we're old, fat, "unfeminine," or too smart for our own good. The lesbian social world is shaped by the fact that we're all *women*, the gender that's stereotyped, not altogether without basis, for nurturing, bonding, and wanting to talk endlessly about how we feel. Even when our personal lives are the pits, it isn't because one of us is from Mars and the other from Venus.

As the nineties lurch toward the millennium, lesbian chic seems to the two of us to be causing a midlife crisis in our community. We wonder whether the world can learn to appreciate the range of qualities that lesbians value in each other—or whether "acceptance" is only going to mean a bigger comfort zone for those cute young luppies who identify with, or at least don't run away screaming from, the possibility of bisexuality. In other words, pretty much the same kind of girls whom the porno kings have happily accommodated for years.

Identity

The Way We Were:
The Michigan
Womyn's
Music Festival

For years, just the word "Michigan" was a code for those in the know—the kind of thing that gay men used to call "dropping hairpins" to see who picked up a reference. In the seventies and eighties, lesbians could kerplop an entire Midwestern state into the conversation. You might innocently ask some interesting-looking woman if by any chance she was planning to go to Michigan in August. If she looked at you blankly and said that actually, she was going to the South of France, you could assume that she had never heard of the Michigan Womyn's Music Festival, and that therefore she was very likely not a lesbian. There was even a classic bumper sticker that simply said "See You in August." Honk, honk, honk, and thumbs-up from every other dyke on the interstate.

Not that every lesbian actually *went* to the festival, or to any of the dozens of offshoot retreats where lesbians can still escape for a weekend or a week to listen to lesbian-oriented music and commune with nature and one another. The two of us didn't set foot on the Michigan festival land until 1993, when we were researching this book. We are admittedly more your South of France kind of lesbian, but we also had been scared off by reports of almost paramilitary political correctness.

Expectations at Michigan and events like it run high, probably because women who feel put down the other fifty-one weeks of the year want the festival to be a utopia. Indeed, the festivals pioneered much of what's progressive in lesbian culture: sliding-scale ticket prices, free child care, signing for the hearing-impaired. But there are also rules that, to an outsider, are the stuff of parody—like no "male music" allowed on tape decks and radios. There have also been major schisms over the presence of persons who are demonstrably male (boy children), possibly male (male-to-female transsexuals), or allegedly "male-identified" (sadomasochistic women), among other issues.

We had heard rumors of the lesbiunatic fringe that flocked to these events—for example, the Michigan workshop leader who insisted on "a moment of silence for all the lesbian lab dogs." Or the "chem-free" contingent—not only recovering alcohol and/or drug abusers, as in the real world, but women who claimed to be oppressed by other women's soap and deodorant. A decade earlier, we had briefly braved the New England Women's Music Festival, where Pamela's former band had been invited to play a reunion performance. We should have gotten our first hint from the ban on studded black leather clothes (which supposedly might upset women who had been victims of sexual abuse). Then there were the official program's biographies of organizers and performers, each more victim-wannabe than the last, and capped by someone who, suffering from no more compelling oppression, felt the need to list her propensity for yeast infections. But our moment of truth came when a grim sentry from the festival's security forces accosted Pamela and reproachfully thrust a crumpled-up beer can into her hands. While on a walk deep in the woods hours earlier, according to this human bloodhound, we had committed the cardinal sin of tossing it into a "chem-free trashbasket."

We got into our car and never looked back.

• • •

Until now. It's two A.M., and here deep in the northern Michigan wilderness just outside the tiny town of Hart, more than ninety miles from the nearest city and more than four miles from the nearest paved road, the sounds of midsummer night waft through the nylon walls of our tent.

Crackkk! "Aaargh!" *Crackkk!* "Ow! Oh! Oooh!" *Crackkk!* "Aaaaaah . . . Aaaaah . . . AaaaaaAAAAAHHH!"

Early-bird hunters with hideous hangovers, shooting their own feet? Hearty but klutzy Midwestern lumberjacks working the night shift, without enough flashlights? Nah. Just the dozen or so s/m dykes camped in the clearing next to us, winding up their "Stations of the Cross" party, wherein participants draw penance cards directing them to Number 4, the whip-equipped "Flail and the Wail," Number 9, the tit-piercing needles of "The Thorns," and other numbered soft-torture theme posts stationed around the wooded glade.

It had seemed like a good idea at the time to pitch our tent in the "Twilight Zone" area, described in the festival's promotional literature as the "loud and rowdy" sector. Here, we reasoned, we would avoid incorrect-trashbasket-type confrontations that would get us kicked out of the festival and thereby compromise our journalistic operation. Possibly we envisioned a festival enclave of like-minded rule-haters.

The Zone turned out to be adjacent to the unofficial s/m area, whose denizens don't always feel welcome in the main camp area. Their gripe clearly isn't with rules per se. They're merely into their *own* rules.

The Twilight Zone is also the cruising ground for everyone from every other part of the 650 acres of field and forest who wants to party before heading back to her own quiet tent space. Our sleep is punctuated not only by the sounds of consenting adults getting off on the "Whip in the Willows," but by worse, far worse. For instance, we are also victims, consenting or not, of all-night jam sessions by a bevy of enthusiastic, yet profoundly arrhythmic, Canadian drummers. The beat is the old classic that accompanied *The*

46

Lone Ranger, Hopalong Cassidy, and every other 1950s TV western from our childhoods, just as the smoke signals arose from them thar hills: *DUM-dum-dum-dum, DUM-dum-dum-dum.* When they aren't drumming, the Canadians sing favorite folk songs by famous female musicians most of the outside world has never heard of.

This is all very hard to explain to anyone who hasn't been there—or who hasn't been a lesbian for a long, long time.

Every year the festival transforms woodland into womynland—an entire, if temporary, city of women, with water (including hot showers), electricity, phone lines, public transportation, a commissary, its own health and security facilities, a one-hundred-and-fifty-booth crafts marketplace featuring everything from drums to dildo harnesses; a sports/workout area; three stages, including a basketball-court-sized, canvas-roofed main night stage, with full professional sound and lighting systems; and a population of at least seven or eight thousand. In June, the festival organization's year-round staff of ten grows to six hundred volunteers, among them nearly a dozen and a half full-time interpreters for the deaf, seven full-time street performers, and two full-time sweat lodge operators. A fair share have spiritual-sapphic names like Dreamwalker, Wolfsong, Flame, Flowing, and Pyramid VanCrowbar (on the plumbing crew).

Although the festival's billed as for "women," "women" means, mostly, lesbians. Except that the name actually says "womyn"—a variation that had a fair amount of currency in the seventies, along with "womon," "wimmin," and even "womb-moon." What this spelling conveys is that "we mean something slightly different than wo-'men,' " explains Barbara "Boo" Price, an Oakland attorney who coproduced the festival for ten years, through 1994. "In fact, it makes men uncomfortable. Male printers doing our program over the years have changed it for us, because they think it's a mistake. It also makes some women uncomfortable—like, 'Why do you have to be so alien and weirdo?' Our feeling is, if it makes you somewhat uncomfortable, fine, because we're getting together to do this very woman-identified thing. The spelling is just a prod that says, Think about it a little."

For twenty years, most of the straight world was clueless. Then in 1994, *Esquire* magazine squinted off into the horizon and realized there were thousands of women carrying on in the Michigan woods. A male reporter was dispatched to the scene, but the closest he could get was "Camp Trans," the tiny tent city transsexual protesters and their supporters had set up across the road from the festival's main gate. That gate is closed to all except "womyn-born womyn." (The sole exceptions are a few unobtrusive, suitably wary local garbage-men who, escorted by female security chaperones, clean out the festival's Dumpsters and "Porta-Janes" in the middle of the night.)

Banishment from the festival, however, didn't stop the *Esquire* man from nattering on about "the wonders of seeing thousands of bared breasts in all their blue-veined, nipple-dancing glory" and a "dazzling profusion of pubic bushes . . . on brazen display." The festival, he claimed, bears "striking resemblances to the ecstatic rites performed by the ancient Thracian cult of Dionysus," at which orgiastic women gathered to exalt "the swampy, reeking, blood-dimmed mysteriousness" of female fertility.

Well, he got the swampy part right. The Land (often pronounced by festies with a reverent capital "Ah" in the middle) features two major marshes which gay men would have had dredged, bombed with DDT, surrounded by imported Caribbean white sand, and supplied with a nice floating grass-roofed tiki hut bar, pronto, had this been the Michigan Myn's Music Festival. The environmentally minded womyn festival producers, however, have preserved the swamps as "animal sanctuaries," right down to flourishing creepy-crawly hives labeled with helpful signs ("Insect Nest").

As for the rest of Mr. Journalist's description . . . well, it *is* true that thousands of women run around shirtless at Michigan. So do thousands of men on Miami Beach, Jones Beach, Malibu, Waikiki, and the Bradford Pool and Tennis Club in Upper Montclair, New Jersey. At Michigan unclothed women are just as routine—although for some "festie virgins," as newcomers are known, the sight takes some getting used to. "I have an old friend I grew up with, very straight, who came to the festival in 1993," recalls Boo Price. The friend sought Price out for a reality check, telling her, "A woman came to breakfast this morning, and she didn't have any clothes on except hiking boots and a down vest. Would that shock you?"

Price replied that she probably wouldn't even notice.

"I always thought I was fat, and when I came here for the first time and saw naked women in all shapes and sizes, feeling comfortable, it was very empowering," said Beth Ackerman, a therapist from Ohio. She remembers going bicycling on a blistering hot day with her then-husband. He was shirtless. She began thinking about how nice it must be to feel the wind on one's chest. "I said to him that I wished I could go naked. His response was, 'Guess who's horny?' "

Not too long afterward, Beth had her first lesbian affair—at Michigan—and dumped the husband.

For all the women we spoke to at the two festivals we attended, the freedom to go without clothes oneself was a far bigger draw than the freedom to ogle some other babe's blue-veined, nipple-dancing glories. "Where else could I walk stark naked in the moonlight and not have to *worry?*" a blissed-out woman who was doing just that asked us one night as we were strolling on Lois Lane. The word we constantly heard to describe the topless option was "safety." (The second most used word was "sunburned." According to staffers at the festival's medical headquarters, a tent called the Womb, burns on areas where the sun don't shine in the real world are the festival's major danger.)

Mary Sims, a fifty-year-old florist and longtime feminist activist from Miami, has been coming to Michigan off and on since the seventies. In fact, she thinks she may have been the first black festie on the land. "That first year my lover and I drove up in our funny little Honda with the tents on the back, and we started unpacking. And in the middle of the field there, there were women with absolutely no clothes on," she recalled. The fact that there were no other folks with black skin on didn't, at that moment, even seem to register. "I said, 'We have *arrived!* Freedom!' It was like the greatest high you could ever have. I never was in a place before with no men. Like right now the three of us are here, but if a man walks in he wants all the attention. Everybody's conversation goes to him. There was none of that, there. So Judy starts stripping. I said, 'Not yet for me, girl.' " Sims reflects: "I finally did let my saggy tits hang out. But her pubic hairs were the only thing covering her.

"After Michigan that first year, my lover and I went up to Canada and camped," she added. "Because I couldn't live with *life* coming out of Michigan the first year, you know?" Postfestival trauma is a common complaint, probably second only to toasted tits in terms of festival medical problems. We ourselves will understand when our first tour of duty ends and we suffer reentry into the real world. Men will look a little strange, halfway between human and gorilla, and heterosexual couples will seem bizarrely mismatched.

Arriving at Michigan is far more amusing. Festival festivity starts miles before the Land, in front of the Hart general grocery, with a "Welcome Womyn" sign almost as big as the store. And it's no wonder. "The whole summer economy of the surrounding region is based on the festival now, truly," claims current festival producer Lisa Vogel, "everything from hardware and gravel for the roads to the people we hire to grade the roads, the well-drilling companies, and the local police we hire to patrol the bordering roads for weirdos. We buy ten thousand dollars' worth of ice locally; that's that guy's summer. For the month of August we're the largest customer of a Grand Rapids mega-company that's the largest single food distributor under one roof in the U.S.A. Even with small stuff, our volume is just very high. Can you feature the economic impact of seven thousand women stopping at the general store for a hoagie?"

At the festival's front gate, each arriving car is hailed with wild waves and whoops of welcome from official festie greeters. Our naked-lady license plate holder elicits enthusiastic cheers, but not nearly as many as the two sixtyish women two cars ahead, who drive in with their bras hanging from the rearview mirror. Off to one side, some other women are gathered around a fire pit, singing. Michigan really is like Girl Scout summer camp—only this time you *can* kiss that riding counselor . . . or even use that riding crop on her, if you're in the Twilight Zone.

Before setting up camp, festies have to undergo Orientation. "Is this your first time?" a woman with long dreadlocks asks us. "You'll *never* be the same." Mostly, Orientation consists of watching a video about the festival (replete with scenes of naked garbage stompers on compost duty), and then, the real crux, "volunteering" to do chores, which producers say enables ticket prices to be held down to around $250 for the full six days. "We suggest that each womon who is attending the festival for four to seven days sign up for two four-hour work shifts," reads the Orientation tent's sign. This means, Sign up for the shifts or you don't get a festival program, which is the only complete schedule of the festival's hundreds of concerts, films, workshops, and classes. You do want it. You do your shifts.

After signing up and setting up your tent (in campgrounds with names like Amazon Acres, Crone Heights, and Bush Gardens), you hop a tractor-pull shuttle for the several-mile journey "Downtown." Surrounding the concert stage area is a veritable village of canvas, including the Womb, the Oasis ("a safe space for us to attend to the emotional experiences that come up during . . . these days of womon-centered celebration"), and resource areas for Twelve-Steppers, disabled women, deaf women, older women, foreign women, and women of color. The Land also has optional day camps for girls and another for babies and toddlers of both genders, as well as Brother Sun, the secluded boys' camp several miles away for three- to ten-year-old male children. Boys are banned from the festival proper.

What to do all day in this womyn-centered space? Well, for starters, you can get a haircut, learn to line-dance, join a quilting bee, take up stilts ("Womyn Walking Tall"), or network with everyone from lesbian AT&T employees to lesbians with beards. Then there's always the traditional girl activity: shopping. Since the real world is mostly quite unaware of the lesbian subculture, it's fairly astonishing to realize that many silversmiths, potters, and other craftswomen make their livings mostly from the summer women's music festival circuit that has, for twenty years, simmered away beneath the straight Beach Blanket Bingo scene. "As I've gotten a reputation in the art world, the straight world has sought me out a bit. Which is fine," said Vicki Leon of San Diego, a glass worker whose neo-Egyptian geometric and stylized goddess-imagery designs would be at home in the toniest Art Deco condo. "But I don't seek them. I haven't needed to. Eighty percent of my sales are in the women's festival circuit. I'm just going, going, all summer. And Michigan is the climax, my lesbian New Year. It begins and ends for me here."

Your festival ticket entitles you to three free meals a day from the Ringling Brothers–sized food tent. The festival kitchen has progressed beyond its early experimental stages, when everything was cooked in old oil drums. But this is not Club Med. Festiefood, while filling, tends to focus on simple stick-to-yer-ribs "Cook 30,000 lbs. brown rice"–type fare, like carrot salad, bean burritos, "marinated vegetable delight," corn on the cob (the week's culinary highlight), and scrambled tofu, which, at six-thirty A.M., is a real eye-opener— a good thing, too, since coffee isn't served at any meals. Also not served: any meat substances whatsoever. In fact, it has become something of a Michigan tradition—or standing joke—that on the Monday morning after the festival ends, redneck greaserias for sixty miles around Hart are packed with politically-correct-vegetarian-for-a-week lesbians scarfing down giant, dripping, vampire-rare steaks and burgers. Still, despite the jokes, festiefare is indisputably healthy. (Well, except for a massive shigella outbreak in the mid-1980s, anyway.) Alcohol is allowed only at your tent site, BYOB. The festival's famed backstage beer bathtub disappeared in the mid-1980s, when Lisa Vogel stopped toking and tippling, along with a lot of the rest of the hard-partying lesbian community.

Michigan also offers food for the spirit. Workshops called "Goddess Moving Meditation Practice," "Menstrual Magick and Empowerment," "Healing with Crystals," "Rebirthing," "Astrology: Symbolism of Planets," and "Fairy Training" are but a small sampling. There's "Dare to Drum," "an exploration of the meditative, soothing, reverent aspects of drumming as well as the high energy and enlivening 'great heartbeat of life,' " and "Tambourines of Power," for women who can't get enough getting down. In the crafts area, you can buy flowing "Goddess Gowns," not to mention a "spirit sack," in which, according to the accompanying literature, you can "collect the spirit of the festival. Hold the bag open while your favorite artists perform and fill it with their music. Preserve the energy from those moments for a lifetime."

The dark dome of sky over the flat Midwestern field is shot through with starlight, a cosmic version of those speckled enamelware bowls beloved of backpackers. On the enormous stage, a tall woman in a black suit is alone at a white grand piano. Her manner is girlish, although she has sprizzles of gray in her wildly curly hair. In 1977, when the feminist revolution looked like it was about to happen, Margie Adam headlined the closing session of the Carter administration–sponsored National Women's Conference in Houston. National network cameras whirred as she led ten thousand delegates in a rousing three-part harmony version of her original composition "We Shall Go Forth." The song was later put in the archives of the Smithsonian.

At the time, Margie (pronounced with a hard "g") was one of the bright lights of the genre known as women's music. A lot has happened between 1977 and 1993—for years she dropped out of performing altogether—but now she's on the night stage at Michigan in her first festival appearance in eons. She seems a little nervous at first. But most of the middle-aged women spread out on blankets and sitting in camp chairs know the words to her old songs, and they sing along, especially when she starts playing her biggest hit, "Best Friend (The Unicorn Song)":

> *When I was growing up my best friend was a unicorn*
> *The others smiled at me and called me crazy*
> *But I was not upset by knowing I did not conform*
> *I always thought their thinking might be hazy. . . .*

As Margie hits the second verse—"When I was seventeen my best friend was the northern star"—the sky starts a slide show.

Shooting stars slam-dunk across the heavens. In unison, the audience gasps, "Oooooooh! Ahhhhhhh!" Margie can't see over the lip of the stage roof, but she keeps singing:

The northern star and I would share our dreams together
Laughing smiling sometimes crying in all kinds of weather
And we'd sing, Seeing is believing in the things you see
Loving is believing in the ones you love.

The dazzling special effects on high continue, as do the mass cries of pleasure. It's like old times—women, nature, and music as one. We are in the realm of the Goddess.

Michigan has often been called the "Lesbian Woodstock." The comparison is apt, even though at least two other long-standing women's festivals had been founded before Michigan got off the ground in 1975. More than any other single event, it symbolizes a whole generation: that of the lesbians who came of age after feminism and before lesbian chic. "The music is just the excuse," according to coproducer Boo Price. "The festivals are a whole lesbian culture kind of crucible." Today Michigan and events like it are the largest remnant of an idea that now seems almost embarrassingly innocent: that, as lesbians, we could create an alternative culture based on female values.

The most visible representation of lesbian culture in the early to middle 1970s was the "women's music" network. There are lesbian writers and artists, but their audiences don't gather in the woods for a tribal experience. Women's music incorporated the lesbian passions of the time, personal and political. It revolved around a variety of women-owned businesses—record companies, distribution companies, sound/performance production companies—and a concert circuit that were mostly collectively run and, at best, marginally profitable. The main idea was *not* commercial, in contrast to gay male bars and other businesses of the time. The very noncommercial—at first, in fact, deliberately anticommercial—idea was to create an independent women's culture. Gay men's 1970s disco music moved asses; 1970s women's music was intended to move mountains.

The world of women's music was our signature social rallying point, the milieu where 1970s lesbian feminists met one another, our first real alternative to gay bars. It was also a significant political fund-raising tool and a cultural wonder: an odd underdog that ruled its own pond and almost, through sheer charisma (and perfect timing), crossed over to the mainstream. *Almost.* Although some of the nineties' most successful lesbian musicians, like Melissa Etheridge and the Indigo Girls, have played on the female festival circuit and have acknowledged (belatedly, along with their coming out) a debt to their seventies predecessors, big-time success never happened for women's music. It was, and still is, a subterranean world.

What *is* "women's music"? Pamela asked herself this twenty years ago when the term first began circulating. It seemed certain, to her band members at least, that The Deadly Nightshade played it. The group was all women, played music, and was even pretty successful in both commercial and political terms: It was a frequent opening act for both Peter Frampton and Gloria Steinem, and issued two albums and a national Top 100 single on a major mainstream label, but had an unprecedented contract clause enabling the band to reject any advertising that was "exploitive or offensive to feminist sensibilities." And in an era when politics and rock and roll were considered incompatible, The Nightshade not only did benefits ranging from the New York City Gay Pride rally to National Secretaries Day, but played some actual "message" songs (admittedly at such volume that the messages were received mainly through the seats of listeners' pants). But it soon became apparent that in fact, The Deadly Nightshade was not in the women's music club. Neither, for that matter, were Bonnie Raitt, Sister Sledge, Mary Travers, or any number of other major-label women musicians of the era.

In theory, what made something women's music was a matter of consciousness. "It has to be written or performed from the point of view of women breaking away from traditional roles and rules about what a woman has to be," said Holly Near in 1980. In practice, women's music developed as a separate, independent entity with its own stars—the "Big Four": singer/songwriters Adam, Near, Meg Christian, and Cris Williamson—plus hundreds of regional artists who were even less well known, all working the same circuit.

In theory, women's music could have embraced all musical styles, although classically trained avant-garde performer/composer Kay Gardner, who *was* in the club, early on suggested that the "natural" form of women's music was an arch, in contrast to the form of male-composed music, which was—surprise!—linear, with a final peak. Certain less schooled musicians, like Casse Culver, a hard-core cowdyke whom Janis Joplin's ex-manager, Albert Grossman, had briefly attempted to groom as the new (i.e., nondead) Janis, went so far as to insist there was such a thing as a "female chord change"—which, in one 1977 demonstration Pam heard, sounded virtually identical to the chorus of a then-popular antiabortion song by Seals and Crofts. (Perhaps coincidentally, in the 1980s Culver became a born-again Christian.) In practice, the best-selling women's music has, overwhelmingly, been rather sweet pop/folk-tinged one-artist singer/songwriter stuff, with a major bias against loud, electrified music, a.k.a. "cock rock."

The radical lesbianism of the nineties takes its cues from out-of-the-closet, in-your-face gay men. Twenty years ago, radical lesbians were *women* first. The values that mattered most were the feminine virtues, like gentleness and spirituality, and the feminist ones, like independence from men. Women's music had its own record and distribution companies. It had all-women concerts for, usually, all-women audiences. Concert production was by all-women production companies. Sound and lights were by all-female techies. And these records and concerts were advertised not in *Billboard* or on WKOK Power Hit Radio, but in women's publications and bars and via that old stand-by in tight communities, word of mouth. Completing the insularity was an Underground Railroad–like accommodations plan for performers, who stayed in women's homes rather than motels. As Pam discovered while briefly playing bass in Culver's band in 1978, it was possible to tour nationwide for six weeks without encountering a man, except at toll booths.

If you haven't guessed yet, the term "women's music" almost always means lesbian music. Just try singing a feminist but hetero-sexual love song at an all-women's concert. Reactions range from gooselike hisses to (in the interests of sisterhood) awkward silence. Then try the song again, using the magic word "dyke." Wild enthu-siasm. To a performer trying to negotiate the mid-1970s women's music circuit, it was puzzling: On the one hand, political astuteness had developed to the point where innovations like sliding-scale tickets were standard practice; on the other hand, there was the con-cept that substituting "she" for "he" transformed "Take It Easy" from a cruising song to a feminist anthem. It was unsettling to real-ize that some unknown, but probably large, percentage of the audi-ence was responding not to what you were saying or how skillfully, but to your presumed sexual orientation. And it was disconcerting that something called women's music did not actively support and address itself to all women trying to define themselves—that it barely tolerated straight and bi women.

Why the term "women's music," when it was really lesbian mu-sic? "It wasn't really to begin with," insists Margie Adam. "It *be-came* lesbian music because lesbians were the strongest organizers, the most articulate leaders. At first, it was just about being a woman and being independent." Lesbian domination of women's music de-veloped organically, "because there was this tribe of women who'd never had anything that looked like them: actual public lesbians, or women who they thought were lesbians, or about whom 'everyone knew.' The hunger was fed for the first time. Lesbians simply needed this more than straight women."

"I've had to explain over and over: Women's music is not about cutting-edge musical style. It's about other things. Music was just a by-product," says Judy Dlugacz, the sole remaining member of the mother-of-all-labels Olivia Records collective. Olivia produced women's music's first record (a single, Meg Christian's "Lady") and its biggest hit, Cris Williamson's 1975 album, *The Changer and the Changed,* which has sold more than 300,000 copies. "Our theory was all about changing the consciousness of women, about women finding out that feminism and lesbianism were an option—and then they'd all come out! It was just a matter of any woman getting the information. And the music was the most amazing way for that to happen, because it hit your heart before your intellect. I was a fan of Meg's and Cris's music because it nurtured me. It gave me what I needed beyond the political stuff. The music was gentle. I saw the possibility of the music's impact on society because I saw its impact on myself."

But thanks to the priorities of artists and audiences, the music never had a chance at an "impact on society." After the first single came out, the prestigious independent label Rounder wanted to distribute Olivia, but, according to Judy, "We said, 'No, you're guys.' "

In 1975, Olivia Records organized an event called "Building Women" with Meg, Cris, Holly, "and, originally, Lily Tomlin, though Lily dropped out soon after because it was too scary for her. Women in audiences were screaming, 'Say you're a dyke!' " Soon Margie Adam replaced her in the fearsome foursome. "They kind of fell in love, all four of them. Any combination, it was like"—Judy makes a noise like a bottle rocket—*"whooosh!"*

Actually, according to Margie, the most important group lovefest happened a year earlier, at the premier National Women's Music Festival on the campus of the University of Illinois. "By the end of that first festival, Cris and I were lovers. We'd completely flipped for each other because of the most important thing to both of us, which was our music." Having just met, they found a piano in a dorm lounge. "We began to trade songs. I'd sing a song; she'd sing a couple of songs. We'd talk about the music and ask each other advice—no sense of competition or defensiveness or vulnerability, completely exposed to each other. I just never expected to hear my music out of the mouth of anyone else; I never expected to hear someone reflect my experience. It was very powerful. We sang until five A.M. We sang each other into bed."

And, Margie added, "had not Meg been with [Olivia collective member] Ginny Berson at the time of that festival, it could have been Meg! Or Meg and Cris! Really, we all fell in love, and I think it was through the music. The sexualizing of that passion and that central connection, it was just like submerging ourselves. Well, I'm now forty-seven, and I don't think it's always necessary to sexualize that kind of energy today. But at the time . . . !" Eventually, she ticks off on her fingers, "Meg was with Holly. And Ginny was with Boo. And I was with Boo. But there were some major 'withs,' and some that were passing. Like Meg and I had a little moment, in around 1981." Additionally, there were Cris and bass player Jackie Robbins, who was then the girlfriend of another women's music performer, June Millington, who'd come to visit her friend Cris. Next came Cris and guitarist Tret Fure, who at the time was once-again-visiting-June's next girlfriend. (June! Stay home!) And then there were Boo and Lisa Vogel; Boo and premier women's music sound technician Margot McFedries; Boo and comic Robin Tyler, who produces both the West Coast and Southern Women's Music and Comedy festivals . . .

With all this musical and sexual energy buzzing around, there were those who were certain that women's music was about to cross over and change the world. Margie, Meg, Holly, Cris, and most of the above cast all played on *Changer.* According to Judy Dlugacz, "We were getting it into major record stores. It was even being aired on *Billboard* commercial stations. They didn't catch on yet, but we were told it almost charted."

Then came the joint "Women on Wheels" tour of nine California cities, tied in to the women's prison activist movement. The tour drew high-powered feminist political organizers into the women's music arena for the first time, and ABC-TV was hot to film it. Before the tour, concert sizes for all of the Big Four had already zoomed from fifty or one hundred tickets per gig to five hundred or six hundred. "Well, that tour took it to two thousand tickets, all sold way in advance," said Judy. "There was an explosion of interest, excitement in women's music. We were so close to making something even more incredible happen."

But crucial decisions were being made to determine whether women's music would really open itself up to mainstream attention or remain a cult force. Key issues were whether the concerts would be recorded, and whether the concert series poster would say "Everyone Welcome"—meaning men, who in those volatile times would most likely have been assumed unwelcome at women's music concerts, unless otherwise specified. Separatism may seem like a quaintly P.C. doctrine today, but in the mid-seventies—when women had only recently won the right to wear pants to work and were fired as a matter of course if they got pregnant—it had currency, even among straight feminists. Proving that women could do a good job or have a good time without men made sense, and the argument within the feminist movement was generally not over whether to exclude men, but when, and how often. Hard-liners wanted to exclude all of them, all of the time, and the hard-line policy did work on a small scale. Inherently, though, it was impossible to mainstream.

"By this time I'd already had a mixed-gender-audience concert picketed, in Chicago," Margie Adam recalled. "It was leafleted, and men were also aggressively blocked from entering the concert hall. The flyer said, 'Rape is defined as an act of forced penetration. Any man who walks into this concert hall is a rapist.' Many years later I ran into the woman who'd been doing the leafleting again. And this arch–dyke separatist comes up to me, and says she's now married. To a man. And I realized, the most rabid dyke separatists I ever dealt with ended up going back to men. Which led me to believe it was *always* about men, for these most angry extremists, never about loving women; and once they had worked through their stuff about men, they went back where they belonged."

In the end, separatists, spearheaded by Meg Christian and the Olivia women, squelched the "Everyone Welcome" poster line. And Holly quashed the recording, arguing, Margie enunciates carefully, "that four white women with privilege should not get still more validation for our work, when there were so many equally talented women disadvantaged by race and class who still had not had the opportunity to record at all."

At least, those were the political issues as they appeared on the surface. In retrospect, Margie feels that many women's music network "political" policies were really based on ego and business. "We were doing basic competitive bullshit, just like every human. I don't think any of us would have said then that any of our decisions had to do with moving our own agendas forward businesswise,"

60

Margie reflected; and indeed, it's hard for any impartial observer to imagine whose business would have been moved forward by not moving into the mainstream. "But it was true. Absolutely. We had different definitions of 'business' at the time. It had to do with selling out, being impure. I think the separatists had a position they had staked out that they really needed to honor. They had constituencies; those audiences bought records and tickets; those audiences had strong opinions; and boycotts really had impact on record and ticket sales. That's business."

Meanwhile, Olivia Records was also trashed by the larger lesbian separatist community for hiring a transsexual engineer. "By that point, a certain number of our community disapproved of us, anyway," said Judy Dlugacz. "We had what they perceived as an unacceptable level of power, because, for example, we said yes or no to people who sent us tapes; we were arrogant. We looked too successful, so envy took over. We got hate mail. We got hate press. And it continued." At one point Judy, who is Jewish, was accused of being anti-Semitic because Cris Williamson put out a Christmas album. "It was a shock, something we hadn't anticipated: destruction from within."

By the mid-1980s, three of the emotionally devastated Big Four had made a break with women's music: Meg to become a disciple of Gurumayi Chidvilasananda; Margie to get sober and then to become a substance abuse counselor (she dropped out of music for more than seven years); Holly to diversify musically into political priorities other than women, and personally into lovers other than women.

Olivia survived, although it's telling that less than half the company's income today comes from music sales. The music component is largely subsidized by profits from the company's wildly successful lesbian cruise-vacation sideline, an accidental by-product of a shipboard concert that had been expected to be Olivia's last. Olivia has also branched out into lesbian comedy, an art that has far more mainstream appeal than women's music ever did—and far more bite.

Another reason for the decline of women's music is the music itself, which, as the 1980s progressed, sounded even more mellow—

and dated—than John Denver. Further contributing to the perception of women's music as wimpness music, especially among the last decade's younger, queer activist lesbians, was that some of its main lesbian stars were . . . in the closet. Meg Christian and even the bisexual Holly Near were out as lesbians, but most others (including the members of The Deadly Nightshade) simply didn't mention lesbianism. Of course, everyone *knew,* but in interviews, the L-word tended not to surface. As recently as 1989, when the women's music journal *Hot Wire* questioned Cris Williamson about her fifteen-year career as a lesbian performing for lesbians, Williamson's response was "No one knows if I am or not." When the obviously astonished reporter persisted, Williamson went on to explain that lesbianism "has nothing to do with my music," that her music was merely "talking about my life."

"But it was not just Cris," said Judy Dlugacz. "Olivia, the company known as the Lesbian Record Company, was full of semicloseted artists."

"At the time I called myself a 'conscious woman artist,' " said Margie Adam. "I did not identify myself as a lesbian singer, or a lesbian feminist, in public, at all. When I think back on my decision I see myself in the context of a lot of other lesbian feminists in the leadership of the women's movement at that time who made a deal, either tacitly or out loud: As a political strategy, we would stay in the closet so as not to discredit the feminist work we were trying to do. I think that collusion was realistic. And in fact, many *lesbians* wouldn't have come to the concerts if we'd been more out."

When women's music artists were criticized, as they were in the seventies and eighties, for not producing overt message music, the industry response was always: Love songs *are* revolutionary, when you're a lesbian. And so they were—when people knew. But all the evasions and waffling about sexual identity made lesbian musicians seem weak and dishonest.

In the end, the dream of a genuine alternative women's culture fell between the cracks: The work wasn't mainstream enough to welcome heterosexuals, but it wasn't lesbian enough to speak to the emerging lesbian chic or queer sensibilities. "The audiences stopped coming, and the producers stopped producing," acknowledged Margie. "Why go through all that work and hassle to produce something where you're not going to hear your own life expressed? Who wants to hear about whales, and wolves, and the Middle East, and Nicaragua? It's like, 'What about *me?*' She paused, blinking. "But you know, none of us at the heart of that women's music explosion ever talked about not talking about it."

We were sitting in Margie's living room high up in the Berkeley hills. Sprinkled here and there were unicorns, in fabric, ceramic, and crystal. We were all of the generation whose lives had been shaped by the larger promise of feminism. Each of us had believed that women could change the world. How had it all dribbled down into political correctness at worst, a once-a-year celebration in the woods at best?

By now Margie was crying softly. "I think the experience we went through is absolutely emblematic of every other organized gang of women," she said. "We were completely in the grip of forces like low self-esteem, anxiety, envy, competition. And alcoholism, drug abuse, codependency, and all this other stuff we now understand so well and many of us have moved into recovery about. But then it was all way beyond us. And it was absolutely *not* okay to talk about. So we talked about it at the level of politics. We tortured each other and broke each other's hearts in the name of feminist politics, and in the name of women's music."

The many ironies of women's music and the Michigan festival do not escape founding producer Lisa Vogel. "Years ago we were labeled man-hating, too radical. Now we're labeled sex police, too establishment." Given Michigan's current gay-community rep as Power P.C.—no "substances," no public s/m, no transsexuals, no music not sweet enough to make your fillings hurt—it's odd to consider that when the festival first started, its driving force was a nineteen-year-old college dropout who'd grown up in the Michigan auto industry's "fan belt" (with a factory worker dad and housewife mom) to become a self-described "hippie acidhead" who dug the

Jefferson Airplane. There is still a bit of the mellow Midwestern rural hippie punkette about Lisa, although she now lives in San Francisco's East Bay. She has a broad Germanic face, an impish smile, and an asymmetrical haircut. The long bits constantly flop into her laser-clear eyes.

The original idea for the Michigan festival arose during a stoned all-night road trip. After being inspired by a regional outdoor women's camping festival, without music but with "women walking around with no clothes on, which was, um, very liberating," Lisa and several of her friends had driven from Michigan to Boston for an indoor women's festival with women's music but no camping. On the way back to Michigan in the van that night, "loaded, basically, and thinking what a bummer it was that everyone'd had to leave when the music was over, and drive fifteen hundred miles home," they began musing about how great a combo of the two festivals—sort of a backyard women's musical pajama party—would be. The Michigan Womyn's Music Collective was born.

"We'd never produced a concert," said Lisa. "We'd thrown good parties. We were seriously into doing a festival. But we were also seriously hippies." At the time Lisa worked, when she worked at all, as a housepainter and as the manager of a women's rock band. "Women's music didn't really turn me on musically, and that hasn't changed that much. I just loved the idea of it, the women's space, the politics."

The collective's first problem was getting taken seriously. When women from the fledgling women's music network asked Lisa what her credentials were, she would have to reply, "Well, nothing. I'm a teenager." Eventually Boo Price, who was then manager (and lover) of Margie Adam, "decided we were persistent enough in calling that just maybe we might get it together." Commitments from Holly Near and others followed. Next problem: paying the performers. The collective managed to cobble together their whole $22,000 budget from garage sales, keg parties, car washes, and the like. "But we didn't pay ourselves, of course." The current festival performer budget is around $100,000, and producers do draw a salary, but remnants of 1975 remain. "Because of that hippie egalitarian thing, we decided that the only way we could deal with pay was to have a standardized performance fee, one for everybody. We still do that, though we could book more people from the mainstream if we'd pay famous people a lot more. If you send in your own homemade demo and we hire you, you get paid the same as Holly."

Since 1982, Michigan has been held on the land the festival corporation owns, about an hour east of Lake Michigan in Hart. The first festival's Land was a bargain-basement hometown rental: $400. "We looked in the paper, and found a hundred-and-twenty-acre site that this guy wanted to sell to urban Detroiters in 10- to 20-acre tracts. I called him and said, 'We don't want to buy. But we want to hold an event where there'll be a lot of them city people, and if you'll let us rent it for a week I bet we'll get you some interested buyers.' We got a piano the same way, by telling this dude from a music store that we couldn't buy, but a lot of pianists would be at our event. The dude brought a concert grand piano from a hundred miles away, to the middle of the woods, for fifty dollars."

Water was courtesy of Uncle Sam. "There was no plumbing in this big bare field, so we thought we'd truck water in. But we had no money. So who subsidized part of the festival—for years, actually—was the U.S. Army. We were hippie, drug-dealer cons. I'd call up the Army and say I was a reserve person calling from some other post, and I was involved in a women's musical 'retreat'— which sounds respectable; it implies religion—and I'd bullshit. And I got a big water truck. The festival's opening, and this guy pulls up in this giant, like, fatigue truck . . . and freaks. I hadn't realized quite what the festival would look like on opening morning. We never had the Army *deliver* again. But I got a bunch of free cots and tents from them, too, the big tents. We didn't rent tents for a couple years. I worked my way around maybe six big reserve offices before they finally caught up with me."

When it came to building a stage, "we priced boards and plywood, and didn't have enough money. So we went to the sawmill. 'We need wood, and we're only gonna put two nails in each side.

Could we rent it from you?' We didn't understand for years that nobody rented wood." Stage stairs were ripped off by a collective
member from a construction site. "We stole a *lot* of stuff." Lisa
grinned.

Oddly enough, the Michigan Womyn's Music Festival originally
was not going to be women only. "The truth is, like everything else
about the festival, we hadn't really thought about it. It was, 'Oh—
now we need brochures.' 'Oh—it's time to build a stage.' 'Oh—do
we need to have a policy about men?' But when Boo first got involved, through booking Margie, she said, 'If it's a camping festival you really can't have men.' And it made sense to me. It was like,
'We want to create a safe overnight space, and a safe space for nudity. Hmmm . . . I might want to party with my good friend Keith,
but it *would* be kinda hard to wake up next to him, much less nude
men I didn't even know, wouldn't it?' " Unfortunately, "it turned
out to be a big issue in our local lesbian community when we made
it women only. Several women left." Michigan's first fight.

But not the last. The second was also about men, and nearly finished the festival for good. "We hadn't even thought about security,
so we organized it at the last minute, by state. 'Ohio and Illinois, if
there's an emergency, you're at the front gate.' We laugh about it
now, but there was a lot of potential for trouble." In the festival's
one near-disastrous incident, the producers found themselves in the
middle of the Land's border road, between "men saying 'I always
wanted to give a dyke seven inches' and a woman pawing a ma-
chete and saying, 'You wanna leave with those seven inches?' "

The men eventually huffed off. But the following year, when the
collective found different land and Lisa and her sister went to pay a
courtesy call on the local sheriff, he interrupted them as they were
introducing themselves, threw down the local paper, and said, "I
know who you are, where you're from, everything about you." On
the front page was the headline "2000 Lesbians to Converge on
Oceana County," with the sheriff, according to Lisa, "quoted all
over the place saying what we were about was parading around
without our clothes on to lure men into the camp so we could beat
them up, and he'd heard we'd even used knives on a few of them.

He hadn't been able to get an ordinance to stop us from gathering. So he'd gotten an ordinance for outdoor gatherings from the health department, with regulations no camp on the face of the planet could meet." It took many negotiations (and legal arguments that the government couldn't require the festival to meet standards that weren't mandatory for state campgrounds) to smooth the waters.

These days, on the new Land, Lisa has "a first-name rapport with the sheriff. And the police are very respectful. We hire them, we pay their fee, and they'd be there if we needed them. The worst incidents involving outsider males have been just creepy stuff, like guys blowing off guns in the road, or, one year, turning our 'Road Closed' back gate sign around and writing, 'Lesbian AIDS Factory.' "

The sheriff is also theoretically on call in case of a problem inside the festival. But there's never been one that the organizers couldn't handle. Maybe that's because lesbians tend to submit problems—lovers' quarrels, freak-outs, or ideological schisms—to the peristalsis of processing.

For better or worse, Michigan is the place where political and sexual controversies often get thrashed out first. There have been ongoing debates, for instance, about how to make the festival truly accessible to disabled women, and truly inclusive of women of color. The latter has even spawned a subdebate, about, believe it or not, drums—specifically, about whether it was respectful or a rip-off of Native American culture to allow non–Native American craftswomen to sell drums and similar spiritual paraphernalia in the crafts area. (An almost epidemic number of white lesbians seem to identify spiritually as, somehow, Native American. One sign outside the Womyn of Color tent in 1994 actually had to clarify: "10:30 A.M., Meeting of Native American Womyn: THIS LIFE ONLY.") Several years ago the festival imploded when a white performer did a monologue about the black "mammy" who raised her. But such consciousness-raising confrontations have resulted in innovations like the Womyn of Color tent and the hiring of a Mexican-American activist who runs cultural diversity workshops.

Lisa Vogel feels these and other festival solutions all have a common-consciousness root. "I personally think more lesbians are vegetarian because as a group we're more politically conscious, globally. The politics of diversity are really important in our community, probably because whoever we are," she suggests, "we're really marginalized in the culture. So even as mainstream as we've become, we tend to stay a half-step ahead about issues like not wanting lives to be dictated by the industrialization of food. Society at large goes for the lowest common denominator: 'Hey, eighty-five percent of us eat like this, so you fifteen percent can go fuck yourselves.' That doesn't fly in the lesbian community, because at least half of the eighty-five percent will speak for the fifteen percent. The festival provides an opportunity to experiment how a planet would run if we could decide, so we're going to devote more time and thinking to the fifteen percent."

The "most gut-wrenching controversy we've had here," in Lisa's opinion, was the banning of boy children, "because when we said no male children, we appeared to be over the top on the man-hater thing: 'Not only do they hate men, they hate little boys.' But excluding our sons," she explains earnestly, "including Boo's son, by the way, was something we had to do, most especially for our daughters." The crux of the problem: a number of bitter arguments, in the festival's early years, over where to draw the line. At what exact ages do babies become boys and boys become men?

"We said six was maximum"—Lisa sighed—"and mothers brought nine-year-olds. Who were going around at night with flashlights, flashing them on women's breasts." And more disturbingly, she adds, picking on girls in their peer group. "These boys might be cool kids at home, but at the festival the power play is in place differently—they're out of it for a change—so what they do is pick on eight-year-old girls. Girls who came to the festival were not only not getting taken care of, they were faced with guys their age who're more defensive than usual and acting out. I'll never forget getting this one bitter letter from a ten-year-old girl after the second festival, when the age limit was twelve—and moms brought fourteen-year-olds—saying, 'Good for you that *you* have women-only space.' "

Though the gay community grapevine reduced the controversy to a simplistic "festie fascists strike again," real life, as always, was more complex; festivalgoing mothers of sons themselves were divided. Mary Sims used to bring her daughter to the festival, but she wasn't upset at having to leave her two sons home. "The truth is, I really didn't want boys over five in the showers, myself," she admitted. "When I first went, one thing I found is Michigan is a very open-feeling space, because there are things you don't have to deal with there. And, even as the mother of two sons, I appreciated that one of the things you didn't have to deal with is boys, and their . . . stuff. And they *do* have stuff! I don't care if they have mothers who are lesbians, and how much we try to raise them as feminists and integrate them into women's things. Because society trains them different than we do at home."

Another notorious conflict, raging for several years in the eighties, pitted women who wanted the freedom to strap their sweeties to any tree that felt good against women seething at encountering masochists tied to maples every time they strolled over to the Porta-Janes. The festival producers reluctantly refereed, as usual. Public group sex was ultimately banned (the idea being that it was nonconsensual, since other women hadn't consented to watch), a policy that effectively restricted loud anytime-and-anything-goes scenes to the Twilight Zone. Some s/m women instantly retaliated with a group orgy in the workshop area. The producers pulled the workshop tent down. The following year, the s/m women hired a plane and bombed the festival with leaflets blasting Michigan's leadership as antisex fascists.

Nowadays the Whip Wars seem to have cooled down, and some s/m women apparently never leave their sector in the deepest thickets of the Twilight Zone. But other s/m women are now on the festival staff, and the hard core seem to be into outreach, not outrage. We briefly attended an open-house workshop in the woods, where the Headmistress was teaching curious novices how to pierce their skin with fishing line and then decorate it with dangling Christmas ornaments, fruit, and jingle bells—a sort of leatherdyke version of *Martha Stewart Living*.

So ancient are the worst of the tensions at this point that Lisa Vogel can laugh about the time back in 1984 when a group of women from a Chicago-based porn magazine put up flyers recruiting festies as models. The centerfold wannabes were asked to meet the porn editors just before dinner at Triangle, the festival's hub. "Certain women who did a lot of antipornography organizing saw these leaflets and went, 'This can't happen here. Not here.' So Boo and I drove down to Triangle, trying to find the pornographers before the protesters did." But how to identify them? "Like, all these leatherdykes were showing up in collars and whips, because they were auditioning to model. You couldn't tell who was who. So Boo and I were just waiting, and watching the jocks having a predinner volleyball game.

"Suddenly, there's this roar coming down road: the protesters. So you have the jocks playing volleyball, the leatherdykes waiting to be models, and the antiporn dykes marching toward Triangle with the signs and the chants. And what they're chanting is, 'No more porn!' But what the jocks hear is, 'No more *corn.*' It's almost dinnertime. The game stops. '*What?* They're already out of corn?' So they're beside themselves, too. It was a perfect festival moment."

In 1994, the crisis du jour is actually about music: the appearance of the punk band Tribe 8. In a way, though, it is also a reprise of the s/m fights of the previous decade. Tribe 8 (as in Tribade . . . get it?) is the first truly loud, kickass group ever to be hired by the festival, and their biggest following on the Land is in the Twilight Zone. Their material includes howls of fury about topics that are about as far from unicorns and waterfalls as one can get—a girl's rape by her father, for example. As the festival bio they wrote for themselves puts it, they are "San Francisco's own all-dyke, all-out, in-your-face, blade-brandishing, gang-castrating, dildo-swinging, bullshit-detecting, aurally pornographic, Neanderthal-pervert band of patriarchy-smashing snatchlickers." For some of the sweetness-and-light separatists, those are fighting words.

"I just hope this doesn't drive older and younger lesbians further apart," sighs Emilie Elisabeth Miller, a twenty-year-old Tribe 8 fan we meet at a special preconcert workshop to process the band's set in advance. She describes herself as an "aspiring Amish/Hispanic punk rocker" (as a domestic violence counselor, she has worked in Amish and Latina communities and admired both), but she looks more like the all-American girl from Indianapolis she is. "What I think a lot of the older women here don't understand is that things like really loud music and in-your-face words and slam dancing isn't just something that violent misogynist boys do. It's part of younger people's culture in general. Tribe 8 isn't scary. It's scary to be *alive* these days."

This is Emilie's first time on the Land, and apart from the Tribe 8 tribulations, "I love it here! I've been going to lots of workshops— stuff about goddesses; 'Dark Phases of the Moon,' which dealt with astrology . . ." She sees no contradiction in being into Tribe 8 and tarot. "Oh, not at all. Being here makes me feel as though I'm connected with many groups of lesbian women: the spirituality women, the old-time feminist politicos, the granola hippies, the Tribe 8 punk baby dykes. It's an intriguing position to be in. Way cool!"

As women arrive for the evening concert, about a dozen grimfaced protesters stand on the side of the road with signs reading, "Stop Woman-Hating" and "If you are a survivor of any form of sexual abuse you may not want to attend the Tribe 8 performance at 8 as it contains explicit sexual violence." At one point, a Tribe 8 guitarist stops to take in a sign that reads, "Tribe 8 Promotes Sexual Violence Against Children," shakes her head in dismayed disbelief, and introduces herself as an incest survivor to the banner-holder, who refuses to shake her hand. (We later learn that fifteen women were disturbed enough to check into the Oasis during the group's set, some of them women who hadn't even heard the band.)

On stage, Tribe 8 lead singer Lynn Breedlove walks out arm-in-arm with 1970s dykon folksinger Alix Dobkin. Without doubt early women's music's most inflexibly P.C. hard-core lesbian separatist, Dobkin these days is probably its most enthusiastic builder of bridges with P.I. punkettes. Topless, in black knee-length jeans with boxer shorts bulging over the top and a belt that clanks like a Sherman tank, Breedlove announces, "I brought Alix Dobkin to hold my hand because we're here to recognize a common enemy. We're not here to promote violence against women." The band itself, she continues, includes survivors of a variety of assaults, but "women who are worried Tribe 8's music might trigger them can leave now." Alternatively, she points out a spot in front of the adjacent crafts area "where abuse survivors can watch but get support, if you'd like to stay."

Announcements over, Alix joins the band for a stereotypically sweet intro to the first song, with all warbling a cappella, in celestial-choir voices, about women's love being like herbal tea. Then . . . *rrragh rrragh rrragh!* The instruments kick in and Breedlove breaks into her real voice, which approximates industrial-grade sandpaper, for what is probably the band's most problematic song, "Manipulate."

> *I just wanna slap around my girlfriend, I just wanna make her scream and yell,*
> *I just wanna tie her to the bedpost, and call her nasty names like "You evil bitch from hell."*
> *It's such a sin, it's so wrong, I don't give a fuck what you think.*
> *She loves me so when I do it, it gets me high so I don't have to drink.*
> *It's such a sin, it's so wrong, so what? So I'm a social defect.*
> *If it's a sin, if it's so wrong, it sure is fun bein' a social reject.*

"That is about consensual sex," Breedlove tells the audience. "My girlfriend at the time was an incest survivor, and that is how she worked out her pain. Even though my lyrics don't always spell out consent—or condoms, latex, blah blah blah—I take that as a given." She pauses, searching for the right words. Obviously, the band does not have to discuss triggering, and so on, onstage at the Putrid Punk Pit, et cetera, where its customary audiences are 90 percent male. "Truthfully, when I wrote that song three and a half years ago, I wasn't really looking at having all this responsibility. I didn't know it was going to cauliflower into this. We knew they would never, ever, *ever* invite us to Michigan." She looks out over the sixty-five hundred women sitting in the grass and grins. "And here we are!" The crowd roars.

Meanwhile, down in the mosh pit—Michigan's first ever—women packed sardine-tight bob like pogo sticks, while other women tear down the ramp from the stage, take running dives into the oscillating throng, and are caught and gently lowered to meld seamlessly into the sardine school. In the pit are a number of hooky-playing kitchen workers, shirtless but wearing aprons.

Finally Breedlove, who has by this time stripped down to boxers, strapped on a leather harness, and inserted a huge dildo so that it sticks straight out of the fly of her underpants, strolls up to the mike. "Our solution to gang rape is somewhat similar. It's called 'Gang Castrate.' " This is a song for which Tribe 8 has become notorious. During the long instrumental lead, Breedlove walks out on the stage runway holding the dildo in one hand and a knife in the other—and saws it off. She then sticks it on the knife and holds it triumphantly aloft while she sings on.

"That wasn't threatening, was it?" she demands at the song's end. "It was empowering! This"—she shakes the dildo—"was once a tool of the patriarchy. Now it's just a dead sex toy." She tosses the stump to the crowd in the mosh pit, which by now includes quite a few oldsters along with the younger punkettes. They begin to play catch with it.

The next day, just like the festival's oldest vets, the scary band holds a workshop. About one hundred women show up for "So You Got a Problem with Tribe 8," most of them apparently in the hopes of finding some common ground.

"Frankly I didn't expect to like Tribe 8," a gray-haired woman confesses. "In fact, between the program bio and the demonstrators out front, I'd thought probably I'd leave before the set. But I'm so glad I stayed! Where else would I have the chance to be exposed to that, to what this generation of lesbians we brought along is doing? And what I realized is, I'm not supposed to like that kind of music. But I did!"

"Even the leatherwomen," adds another convert. "They all came in pierced and dressed like they do, looking so threatening. But in the mosh pit they were just all smiles, jumping up and down. I jumped in. It was like . . . like being in the womb!"

"It was a great trust experience," says Alix.

There is no parallel sense of healing about the other great debate of the nineties: how to treat transsexual women. This controversy started in 1991, when a postoperative male-to-female transsexual named Nancy Burkholder was ejected from the festival. A gentle giant whose visible Adam's apple is at odds with her bare breasts, the forty-year-old electrical engineer had the surgery in 1983 and came out as a lesbian two years later. She wasn't the first transsexual lesbian we'd met and she wouldn't be the last. Like most of them, she said sexual orientation and gender identity were separate issues. She was married to a woman when s/he was a man, and she still prefers women; her ex-wife, alas, "really couldn't handle it. Basically she's heterosexual."

Nancy came to the Land without incident in 1990. "I just felt so welcome here. . . . Some people would say, 'Oh, your voice is really low, you're broad-shouldered, you have such big hands and feet.' So I came out to a few people." At a festival that makes a point of welcoming women who choose not to tweeze their chin hairs, a transsexual woman almost *has* to flaunt it to be recognized.

The following year, Nancy came out to more people—and got 86ed by a security guard, even after showing her driver's license (which says she's female) and offering "to drop my drawers." In 1993, she returned with a crew of other transsexuals and set up an information booth, with flyers and free "Friend of Nancy" buttons. "I've learned to kind of accept that issues have to be worked out and the Goddess has chosen me to participate," she tells us. In 1993 it took the festival powers several days to get around to booting the transsexuals, which was really what they'd been waiting for: They had already arranged to set up an alternative "Camp Trans" in the forest across from the main festival gates.

At the nub of the ongoing dispute is Michigan's policy of welcoming only "womyn-born womyn," by which Boo Price and Lisa Vogel mean a woman born with female genitalia. Nancy Burkholder insists that she *was* born a woman, inside, and that her surgery just made the externals match her essential reality. Most of the Camp Trans contingent supports a standard called "the dick in the drawer": If you can put your penis in a dresser drawer, slam the drawer, and walk away, you should be allowed into the festival. Dildos *sí*, pre-ops *no*. (Several of them admit that the definition is "classist," since it excludes men who don't have the money for surgery. But you have to draw the line, as it were, somewhere.)

Meanwhile, in the various workshops, we ponder and process. Many of the women from the Twilight Zone, as well as many of the younger women, take the civil libertarian line that the oppression of any sexual minority is wrong, period, and that if we do it, we're no better than the right wing. (In fact, the festival's policy—allowing Nancy to clomp around on her big feet as long as she keeps her big mouth shut—is an ironic variation on the military's antigay "Don't ask, don't tell.") Plenty of women just can't stand the way the festival regularly breaks down into these squabbles. One unofficial but traditional festival event is the redhead parade, wherein women with red hair march through Downtown singing a song that celebrates the superiority of this hair color and recruiting any woman they spy with red hair—or fake red hair, or hair that isn't actually red, but spiritually feels red, or girlfriends of women who meet any of the above criteria. "You don't have to be a 'redhead born redhead,' " yell several of the paraders after Nancy's ouster. "Join us! No panty check!"

Other lesbians insist that Nancy and her friends are men and always will be. "If you cut off their heads, they could come to Michigan. It's the dick in their heads I don't want here," says a woman in the "Radical Lesbian Politics" workshop who is trying, the day before the official heave-ho, to organize an "action" to steal all the flyers from Nancy's booth. Alix Dobkin has already gone on record as saying that at the very least, the transsexuals aren't "real" women. "Look, you can take an orange and paint it red and shoot it up with apple juice, but it ain't an apple. It may not be an orange anymore, but it's still not an apple." She thinks the transgendered women should have their *own* festival.

We meet a black woman from Denver on the lunch line who says that she of all people doesn't want to be a bigot, but what, really, is the difference between the transsexuals and all the ditzy white girls who think that deep inside they're really Lakota Sioux medicine women? Others point out that the *only* reason that the transgenderists are making a stand is that they're not allowed. At some of the other festivals they would be welcome, but it's almost a badge of womanhood to crack Michigan. There is a suspicion that Nancy and her three friends are spoilers who care less about expanding the definition of "woman" than about expanding the domain of men. That point of view will be somewhat vindicated the following year, with the return of a much larger Camp Trans protest group that includes several pre-ops (i.e., with their original-equipment penises still attached) who briefly penetrate the festival in a triumphal march, singing "This Land Is Your Land, This Land Is My Land."

We ourselves disagree on the issue—Lindsy takes the civil libertarian view, and Pamela is more in the skeptical middle—and we are already pretty processed out by the time we hit a workshop called "More Than a Woman: On Being a Male Alter at an All-Woman Event."

"So Marcy was trying to pack," a woman is saying. "She wanted to bring, like, three giant suitcases, in this little car." Apparently there are multiple personalities packed in her body, and Marcy is one of the female alters. Marcy explains in a high, femmy voice: "Well, I have to have these blouses in case we go somewhere nice. And rain gear, in case it gets all muddy."

Suddenly, her voice drops two octaves. "And then Jack's there, going, 'Hey, I'd better throw this jack and lug wrench in the trunk, too. What if we pass a pretty woman on the road who's got a flat tire?' "

There are empathetic nods. Love is a many-gendered thing. And although the workshop appears to have roughly a dozen participants by body count, there are evidently more like forty of us here, at least twenty of whom will probably be joining Jack later tonight (after Marcy and the facilitator's other female alters get back from the concert) for a man-to-man discussion of next year's Super Bowl.

"Um, I'm not sure I'm comfortable with male identities," one hesitant woman finally volunteers. "In a way, male-identified women are more troubling to me than male-to-female transsexuals; I think they're possibly more dangerous to us here, in practice. I don't know quite how I feel about transsexuals, either. Though I also have mixed feelings about the festival policies. It's *all* like, 'Here we are in your face, with issues you didn't want to deal with.' But, in a weird way, that may be for the best. This is certainly the best place I can think of to start dealing with it." She shrugs helplessly.

Actually, it is hard to hear any but the shrillest femme and boomingest male alters. In the wooded clearing next door, a loud spirituality workshop is circling up and getting down. "We all come from the Goddess, and to her we shall return like the drops of rain flowing to the ocean!" the facilitator/guru chants, accompanied by whooping, arm waving, much loud drumming, and Salvation Army–style tambourine banging.

"But I *need* all these high heels!" shrieks Marcy.

Months later, when we interviewed Lisa Vogel in California, she told us that the transsexuals would be welcome on the Land only over her dead womyn-born body. On the other hand, "We will not become gender police, possibly harassing gender-ambiguous women while trying to find the three transsexuals or male cross-dressers attending a women's event. But those of us on the organizing end have a political and personal feeling of spirit that femaleness is not something that's particularly ambiguous—or created. We don't work this hard, come this far, leave our jobs to create this space to wake up next to this maybe-guy, even if I feel for his experience."

Lisa was especially appalled at the notion that womanhood might be defined by the absence of a penis. In fact, even though it had never come up, *she* would theoretically support the right of a female-to-male transsexual to come on the Land, assuming that s/he were repentant about having had the surgery. "I'd say a post-operative female-to-male would be okay, if she identifies as a woman. I've met women who've had a lesbian relationship, couldn't hang with it, had a sexual operation as a way to make her life legitimate so she could be a man with her woman lover. And then the woman lover left her. If a woman went all through that and then said, 'Oh, God, this was all about societal pressure; I'm a woman, and now I'm stuck in a man's body,' I'd say, 'Yeah, you're welcome here.' " In the showers, too.

She sighed. "It's a complex issue, really hard. Everyone's exhausted around it. We could chase a cat's tail around gender questions forever. But I don't want to be curator of that. Transsexuals are not going to be our focus. We are pretty *over* spending a lot of our time and energy having an event of seven thousand women be focused on three or four guys—and that's what these three or four guys are asking us to do, and that is such a guy energy thing! Men get to feel like they get to be whatever they want, even if it's a lesbian."

The group that we are most shocked to find at Michigan is one of the sexual minorities: the heterosexuals.

"I come because I just like being around women, and I'm not intimidated by them, straight or lesbian, like I am by a lot of men," explains Californian Nancy Griggs, whom we've met riding one of the flatbed shuttle trucks that commutes between the front gate and Downtown. This is Griggs's second Michigan festival, the first being three years previous, just before she got married—to a man.

"It's very odd to think about coming out as a straight person," reflects Nancy, whose toddler daughter, Lolly, is asleep in the crook of her arm. "That first year I was totally paranoid. I was here with a straight woman friend, and we were not even wanting to talk about our male friends. We just had this Big Brother feeling, like the crowd would hear us and suddenly go silent! So we had code names. Like my husband's name is Michael, so I called him Michelle."

This year, she confides, "I do feel different, a lot better. I went to a bisexual workshop and came out, and got a lot of support." Nancy comes mostly for the music and the feeling that the Land "is one of the few safe places in the world for me as a woman, and for Lolly."

Sometimes, the festival "still feels like a party I'm not invited to. But it's an educational experience for me, as a straight white woman, to be in the minority. When people here say something like, 'All us lesbians . . . ,' and that's the assumption rather than the exception, it's like I'm feeling what a lot of lesbians feel every other week of the year."

The festival organizers estimate that as many as fifteen to twenty percent of those in attendance are bisexual or straight. Some lesbians bring their straight mothers. A fair number of straight mothers bring their girl children. One of the Michigan festival's most inspiring experiences, even childless festies will tell you, is watching girls arrive on the Land grafted to Mom's leg and, within hours, metamorphose into self-confident, free-flying little beings, strutting around like they own the place, hitching rides all night on the shuttle, and holding spitting contests with their official festie water bottles. This is one place where their mothers don't have to worry about them ending up on a milk carton.

We meet Denise sitting on a bale of hay outside the Womyn of Color tent. A forty-three-year-old knockout (think Bessie Smith physique and presence, improved by much better cheekbones and a thirty-thousand-watt smile), Denise was raised as a U.S. military brat, and now lives in Detroit, where she's a realtor—although Michigan has inspired her to think about career options.

"I came to my first festival in 1990. I heard about it from women in a therapy group I was in, and just wanted to see what it was about. I'd never ever even heard of a women's festival, or women's music before! Isn't that terrible? But you know, I spoke to another woman of color my age last night who said the same thing. And we were saying to each other we figured if we'd known about this in our twenties, how different our lives might've been. Because of the positive influence of being with so many different aspects of what it's like to be women. In our experience of growing up, you just had one way of looking at how to be a woman, coming from your mother or your aunts or something else family and familiar like that.

"How it is here to have this much input, to be able to sit and talk with someone you hardly know, and say, 'Yeah, I thought about that too,' and find that all kinds of women who are very different from you in many ways have felt the same thing. . . . Well, I think it would've changed my life. Maybe I'd have been more focused. I still don't really know what I'm about, even career-wise—and at my age, that's pretty scary. So what I'm trying to do here is to think about change in a positive way; even if it's to, say, stay in real estate, to look at it from a positive angle rather than working from fear, as has been a major motive in my life. What was so appealing about the first festival for me was not being afraid, at all. I'd never known that feeling before. I can't believe I let four years go by before coming back!"

The catalyst was Denise's nineteen-year-old daughter, who has dated boys, but "I've just had a feeling women has been something she has been considering. She has already brought one girlfriend home. And I bet she's confused what's happening with herself. You know, in the black community particularly, with this whole lesbian/gay issue, we're majorly into denial. At least part of the denial, I think, is when you are not the group who has power, you feel you don't want to put yourself in double jeopardy. So she doesn't talk about it. But I know she's experimenting trying to see where she wants to go. And to be as happy as she can be on this planet, I feel she has to do that. I didn't, and I wish I had."

So far, the trip to Michigan seems to be working out, though it's hard to tell: Denise hasn't actually seen all that much of her daughter. "Yesterday she met a group of women, women of color, and she's in heaven! She loves the whole experience. She's really got the lay of the land here, no pun intended," Denise chortles.

We figure Denise could very easily get the lay of the land here herself—if she weren't straight and likely to remain so. (Her super-supportive second husband drove Denise and her daughter to the festival, in fact, knowing exactly why they were coming.)

Nevertheless, Michigan has inspired Denise to do a little thinking about her own sexuality, if only in theory. "Even that first festival, which was tremendous but at the same time overwhelming because it was my first exposure being around so many women who were gay, the intensity of love and passion women feel for each other really struck me. I'd never seen people be so affectionate with each other. I even felt kind of like a pervert, because I'd stare, I'd really get involved! It wasn't like disgust. It was more curiosity, and things I was lacking at the time."

Since then, Denise explains, "I've had four years to work a lot of stuff out in my own life. I have more self-esteem myself, more confidence that I have something to bring to the table. I don't feel like I have to stare at people no matter what they're doing, no matter how they're dressed . . . or undressed. I feel very comfortable here."

Do we sense crossover possibilities? Denise breaks up. "Well, I can't believe you mentioned that! You know, before I came here the first time, I wouldn't in any way have been open to it. I was walking around with blinders on. See, I think it is true I carry, and so do many other women—which is maybe why they won't leave their bad relationships with men—the idea that gay people are all born that way; that's who they're attracted to and it couldn't be any other way. For the longest time, to justify my acceptance of gayness, I've said, 'Well, they don't have a choice. Why can't people accept that? I can't change that I'm black.' "

After almost a week at Michigan, Denise admits, "I'm still not sure the whys of gayness all compute for me. Tell you the truth, you're kind of an experiment, because this is stuff I haven't said to anyone yet; I've just started thinking about it myself, and I suspect it's gonna take a lot longer than this festival to sort it out completely. But after being here, I can see how easy it would be to be with a woman. I *certainly* can! Even just the intensity of watching one woman touch another woman . . . It's overwhelming, just something else."

She leans forward. "And I can't say I'm not attracted to women. In fact, last night on my work shift I met a friend who was coming on to me—and I did think about giving this woman my number!"

After rethinking and rebalancing the possibilities of curiosity and attraction against the probability of screwing up a good marriage, Denise didn't make the date. "I thought, Why? What am I doing?

Where *am* I coming from? I'll tell you, though"—she laughs—"I think that attention was very appealing."

But Denise is quite aware that not everyone is so open to Michigan's transformative magic. "I can tell you, within the black community, verbal gay-bashing is all over. I haven't experienced that there's so much of a problem with the physical gay-bashing as with teenagers in the white community, but there's a *lot* of putdown of lesbians. When my daughter's girlfriend comes over, if my stepson happens to be there, he always has a whole lot to say about it to his father. 'Why's she here?' 'What's she all about?' I think some of, especially, the younger black men like him are so afraid their masculinity is threatened or something by a woman who wants to be with a woman. And I always think about my first husband, how he used it as a weapon. If I didn't want to have sex with him, it was always, 'You don't want to have sex with me? You'd rather have sex with a woman?' When something is accepted as dirty, as the lesbian/gay issue is in the black community, these men who are homophobic can use it as a horrible mentally destructive weapon.

"I know there are some women in my life, too—my mother, my sister, my niece—who would just not be open to this festival at all. They just would not get it. I felt my daughter would. And even if being gay turns out to be not my daughter's choice, to see women being loving to each other, it's a great thing. I would love to share this with every woman in our lives."

To our surprise, in the end we got into the Michigan spirit, too. Despite the schisms, the humidity, the caffeine withdrawal, the seventies time warp . . . despite everything about Michigan that seems too weird to experience (much less put in a book and beam out to the general public), it's in a social laboratory that works. No crime. No litter. Not even any mess in any of the Porta-Janes we use (and no seats left up). You get a little bit high, stimulated by the feeling of infinite possibility that seeps into your bones after a few days on the Land. It's a strange combination of emotional overload and total physical security. The only other experience we can think of offhand that delivers that particular payload is meeting the right person and falling passionately in love.

Everybody Out of the Gene Pool: Sexual Fluidity

In the summer of 1995, research scientists at the National Institutes of Health announced that by transplanting a particular gene into the bodies of male fruit flies, they could turn the insects gay. Their report described conga lines of boy bugs, humping hornily away. The genetically altered girl bugs, meanwhile, lurked on the edges of the petri dish, showing no signs of wanting to pursue a lesbian flystyle. Around our house, the joke was that maybe the unromantic lighting was to blame . . . or perhaps the scientists had failed to charter sufficient numbers of miniature U-Hauls.

The search for a genetic explanation of homosexuality has gone into high gear in recent years, although almost all the research has been done on males. Scientists have measured the hypothalamus and the anterior commissure of the brain, analyzed DNA markers on the X chromosome, examined serotonin levels and prenatal hormones, explored homosexual behavior in the animal kingdom, compared gay and straight fingerprint ridges and hearing patterns, examined the possible role of birth order, and investigated the incidence of homosexuality in families. The scientific consensus du jour is that there's strong evidence of a genetic link to at least some homosexuality.

Still, no one in scientific circles is claiming that people are as sexually programmable as male fruit flies. For instance, while identical twins are more likely to have the same sexual orientation than fraternal twins are, there are enough mixed sets of gay-straight identical twins to indicate that genetics isn't the only factor at work. And there's also strong speculation among the leading researchers in the field that to the extent that sexual orientation *is* inherited, the genetic path may be different in men and women. A 1995 National Cancer Institute study found, for example, a statistically significant link between male homosexuality and the Xq28 chromosome region—but no such correlation with lesbianism. Maybe they'll find a parallel marker for women someday, but right now lesbian genetic research is at the 101 stage.

The gay community has largely welcomed the clues that we might be attracted to our own gender through no "fault" of our own. In 1993, when the National Cancer Institute reported that gay men were more likely to have gay brothers (but not lesbian sisters) than was statistically probable, Gregory King, a spokesman for the largest gay rights group in the country, the Human Rights Campaign Fund, said: "We find the study very relevant, and what's most relevant is that it's one more piece of evidence that sexual orientation is not chosen."

The genetic theory certainly jibes with the personal experience of significant numbers of gay people, especially gay men, who almost invariably tend to recognize same-sex attraction at a very early age. But it's also true that the "born that way" argument happens to be convenient public relations. If we're gay from birth, we could make a persuasive claim that we're irrevocably as nature intended us to be. The gay rights movement would fit neatly onto a grid that the average moderate American understands, piggybacking the claims of the civil rights and women's movements. Our parents wouldn't have to feel guilty about the way they raised us. Nice, feminist gay men who genuinely like women could feel justified about not being sexually turned on by them. The "born that way" argument also has the potential to make the far right look mean-spirited and irrational, because if our sexuality is set in utero, what difference would it make if Heather has two mommies? Biologically straight children would presumably stay straight no matter how many positive gay role models were dangled in front of them.

It's much easier for any group to assimilate into the fabric of American life if its members can claim that their values are the same as everyone else's. An innate gay sexual orientation is no more a critique of mainstream values than left-handedness is. The trump card of the essentialist argument—"We must have been born this way, because who would *choose* to have a sexual identity so despised?"—is even a form of flattery to the heterosexual world: "We would be exactly like you, if only we could."

The problem is that huge numbers of lesbians, possibly even the majority, don't fit the paradigm. Although plenty of women insist that their lesbianism was a given, plenty of others say it felt more like an option—one they may well have pursued because they *do* challenge the prevailing arrangements between men and women.

Whether or not there turns out to be a genetic predisposition to female same-sex attraction, it's still impossible to talk about lesbianism for very long without talking about bisexuality. Our own interviews, a look at what's talked about in lesbian publications and on online bulletin boards, and what academic research exists on the subject all indicate that a great many women in the gay community appear to be Kinsey middles and Kinsey rovers who, for various reasons, label themselves lesbians. We're not referring here simply to lesbians who have had heterosexual sex; study after study has found that most of us have done the deed, including those who realized they were gay from a young age. The pressure to test out heterosexuality is intense, especially from anxious parents and well-meaning peers (although "How will you know until you've tried both?" is advice that's rarely given to straight kids). Then there's the Woolf-in-sheep's-clothing tradition of marrying a man, fooling the world and subconsciously semifooling oneself.

But if there's a single word that describes much of female sexuality, gay *or* straight, it's "fluidity." One index is that there appear to be a fair number of women who have the capacity to feel sexually and/or romantically for both genders. Obviously no one wakes up in the morning and makes a list of the relative merits of the various points on the Kinsey scale. But ultimately it makes no difference whether people are born bisexual or not: They do have the option to "choose."

"I feel I don't have a choice as to my color," Mary Sims told us in Michigan. "I do have a choice as to my sexual lifestyle. I had satisfaction in both fields. My husband was great. I'd get my nuts off with him. He gave great head. And he was very sensitive and helpful. He'd change diapers, and he was very special about me."

She thinks she "probably always was attracted to women. But everyone preaches this fairy-tale lifestyle to you where you get married and live happily ever after, and when you come from a family that was split that dream gets even more intense. I was born and raised in Pennsylvania—in Beaver Falls, near Pittsburgh, in the sticks. Before my parents divorced, my home was very traditional. My mother never worked; she stayed at home and cooked and made sure we had the right clothes. Three pairs of white shoes, and all of them always had to be clean, you know? You lay down to take a nap, and while you were asleep, she'd clean 'em. She came from a very religious background, so you went to church on Sunday. I was raised Pentecostal.

"My mother and father separated when I was five, and she moved to Florida. But they decided between them they wanted their children educated in the North. I started coming to Florida in 1953, when I was nine. We'd fly down for the summer. Eventually I moved down to live with my mom. My father was a veteran, and worked at Armstrong Corporation for like thirty years. He was a very mellow man, but my father always told me, 'Men are no good. And I should know, because I'm a man!' He was always very much a 'You're okay, you're dynamite, and you can get it on your own' kind of man. Because he made sure we were provided for, so we didn't have to depend on nobody. By the time I was thirteen, I had a home. He bought homes for me and my sister and my brother when we were young, so we'd never have to starve or struggle.

"I hung out with gay people down in Florida from when I was thirteen. They came down from Fire Island. They took me under their arm, like I was their kid. I'd go to all the parties, with Martha Raye and all of those—big time, the upper echelon of the gay community. The woman from *Our Gang,* Darla, she had a penthouse here where she kept women. She approached me and gave me a ten-dollar gold piece. I said to myself, I don't wanna be kept, and I gave it back to her. But even if I wasn't doing anything with women then, probably the reason I didn't stay in Pennsylvania was that somehow I knew there was no way for a gay lifestyle there, if that's what I ended up choosing."

In fact, Mary got married. "My husband was my second lover. I was nineteen when I had my first. You just weren't sexually interested much in boys before then; they were ignorant, and you didn't want to get pregnant for *anything.* That was it for girls back then, you left school, you were finished. We met when I was working as a waitress in Overtown [the Harlem of Miami]. I'd lied about my age. He used to come in and flash his money around, 'cause he worked for the Mob in the garment district. He chauffeured the big guys who came down from New York to the bars. My husband was like my father. He was sixteen years older than me, because those older ones were the ones who weren't so threatened, and I could be who I was. I was always a tomboy, always handy around the house because my father always encouraged that, and so did my husband. He was good to me and the kids. I was with him for seven years, and left not really because of anything he did. I just sort of like outgrew him."

Sex, at least, was not a problem. "We had sex *all* the time. Especially before we had TV! We used to work together, and we'd come home for lunch together and have sex. I liked it fine. If I wasn't satisfied, he'd let me get on top and rub and do whatever until I was gratified. We lived right across from the factory, in the garment area, so we did that at lunchtime for two years. Then we get a television, and the sex slows down, and I get pregnant. He told me he was sterile! But anyway, the sex was fine. At least until the TV."

Although Mary had been a faithful wife, one night she found her-self comforting an old friend whose boyfriend had dumped her. "One thing led to another, and we ended up in bed. And the sex was great! She went all out with the vibrator and everything. I said, 'Oooh, baby, what have I been missin'!' Well, when I get home my husband smells something. I didn't even get through the door. We had this huge argument. He walks out. And I pack up the three kids, put 'em in her car, and go back to her place—all before the sun comes up. She hasn't even woke up from the sex yet! And I'm naïve enough to think she's in love, because I am."

That relationship lasted only a few months, foundering on the rocks of the other woman's insistence on staying closeted, even dat-ing men as a cover. But Mary never looked back. "What happened when Betty and I broke up is I said to myself, I'm gonna find a woman who *knows* she's a lesbian. I said, Men aren't it. Men are okay, but even before my consciousness was raised I wasn't gonna take all that shit they lay on you. And after I got in the feminist movement my men friends dropped to, like, zero."

What was it about women that made her dump one of the good guys and change her life forever? "The gentleness, I guess. The softness. And, you know, a penis is . . . it's so *dirty* after being with a woman. Even if you're soaking down and dripping wet with a woman, there's something clean about it, something refreshing, something sensual about it. A man is hard. Even if he's gentle—my husband was gentle—it's not the same. Listen, when you have good sex, you can hurt along with the pleasure, whoever you're with. But if you *choose* to hurt with a woman, that's your choice. I just know I had six months' supply of birth control when I first slept with a woman, and I gave 'em right away!"

For other women, it's not necessarily the sex that turns out to be the tie-breaker. Jorie Richards had several serious long-term relation-ships before she came out at twenty-seven. Now thirty, she was working as a carpenter in Seattle when we met her (her credits in-clude helping construct the sets for *Northern Exposure*) and was also an aspiring acoustic guitar player and songwriter. Although there was nothing "masculine" about her, she had short hair, wore no makeup, and was sometimes mistaken for a lesbian before she actually was one—a mistake she did not find threatening so much as irrelevant. During the six years that she lived with a man, "I kind of had a vague feeling of, I'm not really satisfied, but it wasn't sexual. It felt like he couldn't connect, in a way. I've found it a lot easier to connect on that profound level, where I don't have to explain myself so hard, in the women's community; we think alike. I don't mean intellectually so much as there's more understanding of where you're coming from, less having to apologize for what you fear or for the things you like.

"Like just recently I finished a song about childhood experience—playing with tools and building things, and how boys didn't want to play with me after a certain age because girls weren't supposed to do that, but girls didn't really want to play with me, for the same reason," Jorie explained. "The straight men I've shared that song with don't understand that, except to say something like, 'That's a neat story,' " she added. "The women who've heard it have been *moved.*

"There were so many things of myself I gave up to be in that relationship with Brian. I felt like I became this dead person. I stopped reading a lot. I stopped writing. I stopped playing any music. He wasn't interested in it, or he'd put it down, so it just became easier not to do it, and do whatever he wanted to do, even though I'd never dreamed I'd be that kind of person. It just got too hard to fight all the time."

Meanwhile, Jorie had lesbian friends and was comfortable with gay relationships, even though she didn't see possibilities in them for her own life. Then, when she and her boyfriend finally broke up, "I was out on a date with this guy at a bar, and totally bored. He went off to talk to a friend, and this other guy sat down and started talking and asked me out. And I thought, I don't really like either one of these guys. . . . I don't think I want to be with guys, at least not any of the ones I've been dating. They weren't blatantly offensive. Just boring."

Given Jorie's social life, it wasn't hard to find women once she'd made a conscious decision to try them. The woman she eventually got involved with "was just a very complex, interesting person, and yet was interested in me. I didn't feel *either* she or I had to be the interesting one. There was a balance." Their sex life "was certainly different than with a man. I felt she was more present, she didn't go somewhere else. We weren't speaking a different language. It was easier to talk about what I wanted her to do, what I liked and didn't like. . . . With guys I was in control; I could choose how involved I wanted to get, even in sex. It was a lot easier to be distant if I wanted to be distant. They wouldn't notice. So in some ways, sex with a woman was scarier, because you couldn't hide."

Still, although she's happy with her girlfriend, Jorie acknowledged that "in terms of attraction, I think I'm not entirely lesbian. I met a young guy—twenty-three—recently who made me think, If more young guys are like this they're doing something okay. He was not just New Age sensitive; he was genuinely interested in women, and different. I realized I could be attracted to a guy like that. I think if I'd met more lesbian role models when I was younger, I would have been a lesbian first and then bisexual, instead of straight and then with women. I'm *more* lesbian, because I've found I have more profound relationships with women, and I'd rather be in that community. But I'm still able to be attracted to men—almost against my will."

That women who love other women don't necessarily run screaming from the heterosexual experience is one of those truths that we almost hate to have out on the airwaves; it plays so easily into the fantasy that your average lesbian couple is just dying to bring a guy home to bed. But lately the more complex fluidity of lesbian sexuality has begun to come out of the closet. *Go Fish,* the surprise hit lesbian-themed film of 1994, featured a subplot in which a woman is scorned by her friends for having sex with a man. In a June 1995 cover story in the gay newsmagazine *The Advocate,* Janis Ian told interviewer Melissa Etheridge that when she was married, "we had a wonderful physical relationship. Sex was great. Lesbians are going to hate reading that, but it's true. I don't know if that makes me a bisexual. I don't think so. I knew when I was nine that I was gay."

Several months earlier, Etheridge herself had been quoted in *Vanity Fair* as joking that Brad Pitt was such a hunk that he "could change a woman's mind."

In fact, a report by Celia Kitzinger and Sue Wilkinson on the available academic literature, published in 1995 in the American Psychological Association's *Journal of Developmental Psychology,* concluded that "whether a woman has had or enjoyed sex with men was not a reliable guide to whether she became a lesbian."

It's considerably easier to say what's *not* a reliable guide than what is. For example, lesbians have not, as a rule, turned to women because of a terrible experience with a man. "If that's all it took," goes one of stand-up comic Suzanne Westenhoefer's classic lines, "there wouldn't be any straight women left in America." A 1990 Chapman College study published in the *Journal of Homosexuality* showed that gay and straight women reported equal numbers of traumatic experiences at the hands of men, including rape, incest, molestation, and physical abuse. The only difference was that heterosexual women were twice as likely to report traumatic experiences in multiple categories.

Then there's the popular myth that what differentiates lesbians from straight women is that we are man-haters. Since we have removed ourselves from the necessity of dealing with guys in what their wives and girlfriends say are their prime problem areas—emotional openness, deep communication, commitment, intimacy, sex that lasts longer than the flavor in a Chiclet—we would argue that we're generally able to appreciate men's pluses far better than many straight women can. (During a recent hurricane scare in our hometown of Miami, the straight male guest of a lesbian couple we know sprang instantly into action, boarding up their entire house with huge sheets of plywood. As the eight visiting lesbians in the house sat around taking a more classic lez approach to crises—processing the hurricane over gallons of white wine—one of them said, beaming, "I never thought I'd say this, but it's *soooo* nice to have a man around the house!")

Nor do women necessarily become lesbians because they feel more emotionally connected to women than to men, or find their company more interesting, or trust women more, or feel better understood by them. Or rather, most lesbians probably do feel all those things—but so do a great many straight women. In a landmark 1980 essay called "Compulsory Heterosexuality and Lesbian Existence," the poet Adrienne Rich pointed out that many women who don't have sex with other women still live on what she called a "lesbian continuum . . . of primary intensity between and among women, including the sharing of a rich, inner life, the bonding against male tyranny, the giving and receiving of practical and political support."

Even many of the early experiences that some lesbians trot out when they talk about what destined them for dykedom—"I was a tomboy"; "I had a crush on another girl when I was in seventh grade"—are familiar to plenty of heterosexual women. According to one researcher's estimate, more than half of boys who exhibit "feminine" behavior grow up to be gay, whereas only six percent of girls who exhibit "masculine" behavior (such as a liking for rough play and sports) grow up to be lesbians.

It's hard to know whether gay and straight women's early experiences are truly different, or whether the difference appears retrospectively, in the light of adult sexuality. It's human nature to want to look back on our experiences and see our lives proceeding according to some orderly pattern. A gay woman might well put an intense, nonsexual adolescent relationship with another girl in the category of "the first time I fell in love." For a straight woman who felt the same, no such category could possibly encompass a same-sex experience, and she'll probably trivialize the relationship in hindsight, if she thinks about it at all. In much the same way, we found that some of the lesbians we interviewed put fairly compelling past relationships with boys or men into a kind of psychological limbo.

The conventions of the coming-out story have been honed over the last twenty years or so; it's standard to dismiss heterosexual feelings as produced by societal pressure, before a person accepted his or her "true" gay self. In some cases, this is certainly accurate; in others, it denies a messy reality—which may be one reason why "lesbians who sleep with men" has burbled up as a controversy in the nineties. In our experience, this fluidity is rare in the gay male community. Gay boys typically seem to feel a sexual pull toward other boys or men, struggle to come to terms with that reality, accept it, come out, and never look back. There aren't scads of articles in the gay male press about "gay men who sleep with women" or about the experience of living with a lover for years, only to be dumped for a member of the opposite sex. These things surely happen, but they're not common. The lesbian community also appears to have many more middle-aged and older women who lead untortured, sexually conventional heterosexual lives for half a lifetime before making a switch to women.

The logical explanation is that male sexuality is relatively hardwired and female sexuality relatively elastic, and several sexuality studies have indeed indicated that there are more bisexual women than men. For instance, the twins studies done by J. Michael Bailey, of Northwestern, and Richard C. Pillard, of the Boston University School of Medicine, found twice as many bisexual women as men. We're personally a little skeptical of almost all sexual research, even when it buttresses things that we believe to be true—and we do believe from our own experience that most bisexuals are female . . . maybe even that most females are potentially bisexual. Another possible explanation, however, is that there are bisexual men out there who are invisible because they didn't choose to be gay. There are compelling pushes toward heterosexuality for men, including social acceptance, a family life with children, a lower risk of AIDS, the perception that women are more emotionally supportive than men, and the desire to live with someone who is socially programmed to pick up your socks. Except for social acceptance, none of those factors would propel bisexual women toward men.

Whatever the explanation, bisexuality is part of lesbian life, even when it's not labeled as such. In a study by sociologist Paula C. Rust of Hamilton College, only a third of more than three hundred self-identified lesbians surveyed stated that they were 100 percent attracted to other women; the remainder were predominantly attracted to women, but rated themselves as from 50 to 95 percent attracted to women over men. Some 43 percent of Rust's lesbian sample had had heterosexual relationships since coming out as lesbians (although they were likely to have had them less recently than women who called themselves bisexual).

"Based on this study's findings," Rust writes, "lesbians collectively define lesbianism as the dominance of homosexual feelings and behavior over heterosexual feelings and behavior. This definition is capable of subsuming considerable heterosexual experience. Lesbian identity is claimed by women who report that up to 50 percent of their sexual feelings are heterosexual, by women who have had heterosexual relationships they describe as 'serious,' and by women who are likely to have heterosexual relationships in the future."

There are powerful economic and social reasons not to leave the institution of heterosexuality and join a despised minority group; that's why people who call themselves "bi" rather than "gay" are often presumed to be screwing up the courage to finish coming out of the closet. But women, including some lesbians, are also obviously attracted to men for sexual and personal reasons. In another study of hundreds of women, Rust found that one in three lesbians has wondered *after* coming out as gay whether she may really be bisexual. One in five lesbians has had a period of identifying as bisexual after coming out as gay. And most women who now labeled themselves bisexual had labeled themselves lesbian at some point in the past. Indeed, 58 percent of the self-identified bisexual women and 14 percent of the self-identified lesbians reported fluctuating between the two sexual identities two or more times.

One can look at this sexual turnstile as a mass of confusion, although we don't. It seems to us that some women may be firmly gay or straight, but others end up in one camp or the other because of circumstances having much more to do with opportunity, personality, political values, or falling in love with a particular person than with genetics. In an ideal world, the gender of one's partner wouldn't have to remain consistent any more than ordering chocolate today would commit you to swearing off strawberry forever.

Of course, we *don't* live in an ideal world, and because of that, some of us care very much about being in one camp or the other.

But that decision isn't necessarily sexual. The two of us sometimes play that loaded lovers' game of "Well, if you were single, would you . . . ?" Well, if we were single, both of us admit that we would probably still be sexually attracted to men, at least once in a while, but neither of us would do anything about it. We're too attached to queer culture and queer identity. And we'd hate for anyone to have the satisfaction of thinking that our lesbianism was Just a Phase.

Sexual fluidity gets downright dribbly when it comes to labels. The trickiest part is that no one in our community knows precisely what anyone else means when she describes herself as a lesbian, a bisexual, or a heterosexual. Sometimes women's choice of label is based on their current partner. Once, when Lindsy wrote an article for *Ms.* magazine in which she acknowledged her heterosexual past, she got angry letters from lesbians who didn't feel that she deserved the gay honorific, even though she had by then been sleeping with Pamela, and only Pamela, for well over a decade.

Among those we interviewed for this book were two women whose stories were remarkably similar, on the surface. They were approximately the same age, thirty and twenty-eight. Both had had disappointing sex with men when they were young and had settled comfortably into lesbianism in college. Now each was, to her surprise, in a primary relationship with a man. The relationships were serious, although neither woman was willing to predict what the future would hold. One of the women said that if she had to choose among calling herself heterosexual, bisexual, or lesbian, she would pick lesbian. "I have this great aversion to calling myself bisexual. I think it's because of my political past. Bisexuality is generic, it's milky, it's nothing. You've caught me in the flow of not wanting any label." She had moved to San Francisco specifically to be an activist on the lesbian cutting edge. She'd grazed at every sexual fad of the past decade: separatism, monogamy, open relationships, butch/femme, sex toys, androgyny, one-night stands, lipstick. Nothing had really clicked (with a woman or a man). But her security blanket through it all was her identity as a sexually adventurous lesbian.

The other woman, who lived in Seattle, admitted she didn't like "dealing with that rejection from some lesbians—you know: 'You're bi? I don't want you touching me, contaminated by male cooties.' " But she still felt "bisexual" was an accurate self-identification, at least for now.

The main difference *we* could see between the two women had to do not with their sexual behavior or feelings but, quite frankly, with how much they needed to be in with the in crowd. The Seattle woman was a black graduate student who had gone to a mostly white high school and college. "I think I'm definitely more comfortable with feeling estranged from the lesbian community than many women who really want to belong," she told us. "I'm adamantly not a belonger; I've felt difference of various kinds my whole life. I mean, to me, 'coming out' meant . . . Well, I still haul out pictures of my debut, senior year in high school. Long white dress and everything. It was one of those cotillions put on by a black women's organization that are traditions for Southern black women, very different from white society balls—and very different from the general African-American lesbian experience."

Conversely, we interviewed a woman who by our standards was every inch a lesbian. But she had had sex a few times with a very dear gay male friend, and thought that if she didn't call herself bisexual, she would dishonor that relationship. (Some bisexual/lesbian women consider sex with gay/bisexual men to be deliciously queer sex; it's not the male body they object to, but the expectations that straight men have about their place in the world.) We encountered women who called themselves lesbian, even though they were celibate. We met two women from Boston who were committed enough to the idea of a lifelong lesbian relationship that they were about to have an elaborate synagogue wedding; they had met, however, in a group for bisexuals. We encountered a woman who had always known she was a lesbian, had never slept with a man and didn't want to—but enjoyed fantasizing about them.

Then there was Jane Neven, the co-owner of the lesbian guest house near Northampton, who told us she and her ex of many years had broken up because the ex "wasn't a lesbian" and had left her to marry a man. However, after the breakup, Jane herself "told people I was looking for a new partner and I didn't care which gender it was. I just wanted someone who would love me, someone for whom I'd be really important." As it happened, she ended up with another woman. We were stymied: What made Jane a lesbian and the ex not? To Jane, the answer had nothing to do with the parameters of desire, and everything to do with a sense of self. "It was the social pressure she couldn't handle, not the sex. She came from a large Syrian family, lots of aunts and uncles always saying, 'When are you getting married, where's the boyfriend?' I don't think she knows who she is yet. She got a job at a local department store chain, and had to take on the corporate image and give up the lesbian image. That was very hard on her." And so she stopped being a lesbian.

We've heard other lesbians use the same rating scale: A lesbian is someone who, regardless of the range of her sexual appetites or even the depth of her closet, is prepared to give up some of the privileges of heterosexuality. It's about guts, not pussy. As Gretchen Phillips, formerly of the rock band Two Nice Girls, puts it: "Lesbianism is not for the frail."

The women we interviewed for this book were such a mixed bag that we concocted our own lesbian Kinsey scale. Behold:

A perfect 6L would be a woman who does not now, has never, has never really wanted to, and would not voluntarily have sex with men.

A 5L does not now have sex with men, nor has she ever. But she has been, and possibly even occasionally still is, to some degree—and/or in some typically lesbian overly complex or offbeat way—sexually attracted to guys (though not anywhere near as intensely as to women).

A 4L does not now have sex with men, but has done so in the past, more for societal than for genuinely personal/sexual reasons.

A 3L does not have sex with men now, but has in the past, at least in part for genuinely personal/sexual reasons, although she can't imagine ever doing it again.

A 2L is a 3L who mostly can't imagine ever sleeping with men again, but doesn't rule it out.

A 1L is a lesbian but accident-prone, meaning she basically does not sleep with men and does not want to, but occasionally has, or is vulnerable to slipping in understandable circumstances. Like: She's single, and out with a great gay male friend, and they're both horny—and drunk as skunks. Or her girlfriend has done something totally gross, such as leaving her for her own personal best friend (who's probably, knowing the lezzie community, also her own personal ex), so she naturally reflects, "What's the worst revenge I could have on that bitch?" You know.

A 0L is someone who "feels like a lesbian" *but* who regularly has sex with men and/or whose primary partner is a man, especially if she feels "a fascination with male energy" (this quote from Holly Near's autobiography, *Fire in the Rain*). A 0L ought to think about defining herself as a 6B bisexual (as Holly now does).

The pure 6L lesbian archetype is a rarity, although we found a few. We met Sarrah Kelly, an electrician from Charlotte, North Carolina, at the Key West Women's Week festival. She had long brown hair, a "Death Before Dishonor" tattoo on her forearm, and possibly the best bikini body we'd seen on anyone besides a fashion model in years. She was undoubtedly the only woman in Key West with a pickup truck that had a pro–Desert Storm bumper sticker. "I remember in kindergarten having crushes on some of the little girls," Sarrah drawls. "I could never figure it out until I was, like, eighteen. Danny and I had been together for four years, we were real close and like best friends. I was around sixteen; he was maybe twenty-six, twenty-seven, twenty-eight. We were gonna get married when I got out of high school; you get raised in a Methodist Christian home, you get out of school, you get married, that's what you're supposed to *do*. We hadn't done anything sexual, and I decided, Okay, I wanna know what this is gonna be like *before* I get married, check it out here. So fine, we had a real romantic evening, I was laying in the bed, and everything was fine. Until he took off his pants . . . and I threw up on his feet. I just went, 'Death by impalement, uhnnnn-uhhnnn!' But we were just such good friends that he put his pants on and got back in the bed."

More often we have encountered women who said that sex with

men was okay, but sex with women more complex. Or they felt that men were satisfying sexually, but not in other crucial ways. "I was almost married once, and came pretty close two other times," said Dr. Dee Mosbacher, whose father engineered George Bush's presidential campaign at the height of the "family values" era. She's now been with her female partner for more than seventeen years. "But once I switched [from heterosexuality], I can't see myself switching back. I feel the sex wasn't the problem, and the intellectual level was fine, but then there was the emotion. That's the biggie. Like a sandwich with the middle missing."

"I mostly used men for sex," admitted a woman from Louisville. "I felt they could never reach the places I was emotionally. There was inevitably some bit of mutual hostility, mistrust, foreignness. Sex was often like an out-of-body experience: detaching and watching these two people doing stuff, and kinda getting off on that, and enjoying the physical pleasure of it—but it wasn't really *me* that was involved. Whereas sex with a woman for me is a totally *in*-body experience. I'm in mine, in hers; there's no difference; we're equal; we merge."

We've heard this a zillion times: "With a man I was giving, but never getting back. . . ." "There was always something missing, and I couldn't put my finger on it until ten years later when I was with a woman, and it all fell into place. It was an emotional thing, a connection, where the other person understands what you feel, most of the time, anyway. . . ." "No matter how sensitive a guy may be, there's always been a wall beyond which it's impossible to go. With a woman I don't have to be anyone other than who I am. . . ." "I felt a certain peace. I really didn't have to prove myself so much; I could just be."

On the other hand, we have a straight friend who insists that one of the major advantages of being heterosexual is that one can have a close sexual relationship and still have a zone of emotional privacy. Different strokes for folks with blokes, we guess; more often, though, we hear straight women being angry at husbands and boyfriends for not, well, being more like their female friends. Chronicling the dissatisfaction of women in relationships with men is by now a growth industry. According to *Good Housekeeping,* most married couples spend a total of four minutes a day in meaningful conversation. (Part of that is him trying to get her to have sex, and her trying to get him to talk.) *The New York Times* has reported that men's sexual fantasies are typically about "physical gratification, devoid of encumbering relationships, emotional elaboration, [or] courtship," whereas women daydream about the opposite. One study after another shows that in working couples, the woman still does most of the housework. When *Redbook* asked its readers to rate various activities and decide which was the most pleasurable, only 9 percent voted for having sex with their husband or boyfriend. (Twenty-nine percent wanted to relax on a beautiful tropical beach. Eight percent went for a piece of chocolate cake with whipped cream and hot fudge.) More ominously, the Justice Department estimates that current and former spouses and boyfriends are responsible for a third of all violent attacks on women.

The list goes on. And yes, we know, not all heterosexual couples are dissatisfied, emotionally distant, unfair in their division of labor, sexually mismatched, or violent. But the fact is that a significant number of lesbians are women who have left those particular problems in the dust. Lesbians who *do* feel their sexuality is genetic also often say the same thing: They're grateful for not having to deal with the issues that feed an entire best-seller genre about men who hate women and the women who put up with them. Some people might call what we feel man-hating, but, born that way or born again, the point is not to have to bother. In Kate Clinton's great line, "Man-hating? Like we have time."

Even women whose genetic backgrounds are virtually awash in homo chromosomes sometimes perceive themselves as having made a choice. Pamela, for one, has a fine gay pedigree: a grandfather, possibly a great-cousin, and *both* brothers (a perfect three-out-of-three gay kid record for the Brandt parents; just imagine their delight). Many consider this proof positive of the genetic theory. Pam feels that, *au contraire*, it's proof of proper upbringing.

We have another friend, a lesbian with a lesbian identical twin, who also doesn't think she was born gay—although she does think that the physical intimacy of growing up as half of a female unit was a factor.

The genetic predestination theory is of particular interest to Jorie Richards, who came out around the same time as her father. "He was a Presbyterian minister in Topeka, Kansas, and he was caught making a pass at an undercover cop in an adult movie theater, and arrested—photos in the newspaper, the whole thing," she said. At one level, she found her father's outing liberating, since "he was a real asshole while I was growing up, always angry all the time, and particularly hard on me. My two brothers he pretty much left alone, even though they got in trouble, which was hard for me. I was a straight-A student, I did everything to please my father, but I wasn't trusted. I thought it was something wrong with me. I think now maybe it was because he was in this life he didn't want to be in, because I was female, and because I was different. He wasn't comfortable with me, and was constantly pulling me in. My mother was, I think, acting pretty typically for the times—going through a depression—so the doctor was giving her a lot of drugs. She was out of it. And my dad wasn't very nice to her, either, so she was busy shutting down. He finally came out and apologized to me."

We wondered if having a gay father made her think that her own lesbianism was genetic after all. "I think my dad feels he didn't have much of a choice." Most of the gay men she knows feel the same. "Though I'd be curious to know how much of that has to do with growing up in a society that doesn't generally like women," she said. "I personally think most people are bisexual, somewhere along the Kinsey scale, and that it's more a matter of socialization that we have either/or. If there's any coincidence in my family, it's that my dad's coming out made it easier for me to acknowledge that, more than any genetic thing. And I think that's been true of other people I've talked to who have siblings who are lesbian or gay. It was like the other person broke the ice and said it's okay to challenge the way things are."

• • •

"I don't necessarily know if I was *born* a lesbian," said comedian Suzanne Westenhoefer. "But I definitely feel that I was born to *be* a lesbian. If I never had sex with another woman, I'd still be a lesbian. My personality and the things I felt I was supposed to do in this world meant I was going to be a lesbian. It would be the only way I would get anything done and have any happiness. Had I not had ambitions, I could have been straight, had a beautiful home. . . ."

Then she shook her head. "Nah. I can't see it. I'm too independent to be with men. They're actually attracted to that, but they don't like it that they are. As soon as they have you they go, 'Do you have to be so loud at parties? Why are you working all the time?' Women just aren't that way."

Westenhoefer is a blond Midwesterner who looks like the high school sex kitten cheerleader most likely to have landed the football captain. Which she was. "I can wear a DYKE T-shirt at the grocery, and people *refuse* to see me as lesbian. They don't want that, because I look too normal: their next-door neighbor, the girl they took to the prom. It's like, 'If *she's* a lesbian, ohmygawd *anyone* could be! Aaaaaah!!!' A lesbian who looks like someone who *can't* get a guy, they're comfortable with that."

Getting guys, Suzanne reports, was never a problem. "My mother was really surprised when I came out, because I'd been such a heterosexual. I never didn't get a guy I went after, I never didn't have a boyfriend. And I had sex with men from early on, because I was really pretty as a kid; at twelve, I had the body of an adult twenty-year-old. I got an incredible amount of attention from men, and very quickly learned there's a lot of power that goes with that. When I was fourteen, I seduced the man who lived across the street, who was forty-one years old and married. I look back on it now and I realize I had a huge crush on his wife and this was how I got attention from her. His wife left him, he got kicked out of church, they tried to arrest him: It was horrible. Then when I was sixteen, I got pregnant, and my mom went through an abortion with me. My mother was *not* proabortion in any way, but she was pro-me.

"A handful of guys I had sex with I cared about a great deal. I enjoyed men. I liked them. I thought I was in love with them. But I would never have an orgasm with a guy even if they did everything right. I was the Glenn Close of orgasm faking. I would never be that relaxed with a guy; I'd never trust him." One night when she was twenty, Westenhoefer "got drunk with a girlfriend and she made love to me—though she is not a lesbian, to this day—and I had an orgasm with a person for the first time. And I knew why." These days, Suzanne's answer to the classic hetero query about what lesbians do in bed is "It's just like heterosexual sex, only we don't have to fake the orgasm." Straight audiences roar.

She has another line when she's asked whether she's a lesbian by nature or by choice. "*Yes!* . . . Whatever it takes, I'm there."

Heart
of Dykeness:
Coming Out

The first time you really kiss another woman, the most startling impression is of *softness*. Lips, cheeks, back of the neck—all meltingly soft. Even on a woman with muscle, body contours seem lush, especially if your previous sexual experience was with men. Where he was scratchy, she is downy. Where he was governed by rhythms that seemed to have a beginning, a middle, and an end, she flows. Her throat smells different. The bones of her rib cage under your fingertips feel different. Then there's the light bulb realization: "I feel like this, too." Most of all, there's the flash of emotional connection. Your lover is of the gender that mothered you, that best-friended you, whose skin you've lived inside all your life. There's no abyss to reach across. When you look in her eyes, it's like diving into the depths of a clear, reflective lake.

Being with another woman, for a few hours in bed or for a lifetime, is always a matter of pumping up the femaleness. There's a female dynamic, even between two butch lesbians, that's just not the same as what happens between two men, or a man and a woman. Whatever it is in our nature or upbringing that makes us women, two of us bring an undiluted dose of it to any relationship. For better and for worse, our lives have a quality of woman[2]. (Which is why we communicate so well, and then talk everything to death.) We can easily put ourselves in another woman's place. (Which is why even the most obnoxious, horny lesbian is unlikely to act like a male construction worker when a babe walks by.) With all this femaleness in overdrive, it's disconcerting, and Orwellian, to realize that to a lot of the rest of the world, our identity has mostly to do with men, or their palpable absence.

To speak about lesbian identity is also, inevitably, to get bogged down in the common perception that the defining reality of our lives is either the lack of a penis or the presence of a vulva. There's a myth that lesbianism doesn't involve any sweaty, butt-grabbing desire, being essentially an ethereal escape from the rigors of heterosexuality. Consider Colette's description of "two weak creatures who have perhaps found shelter in each other's arms, there to sleep and weep, safe from man who is often cruel." The converse myth, mostly perpetrated by straight male pornographers and religious fundamentalists, is that lesbianism is *only* about sex.

The development of a lesbian identity virtually always has a sexual component, but *identity* goes far beyond that; after all, women who prefer men can and do have sex with each other. Identity is a matter of who we are and where we belong, not just what we do in bed. To stand up, even in front of your own bathroom mirror, and say, "I am a lesbian," is to have been through a process whose end point is the understanding that *femaleness* is home, sexually and across the board.

Still, the most basic question about lesbians—What *is* one?—has plagued us throughout the writing of this book. Is someone a lesbian if she says so? Is someone a lesbian if she doesn't say so?

Lisa Limm is twenty-six and works in a Federal Express office in Torrance, California. She thinks she "probably knew always" that she was gay. There have been men, and "I loved them, but I wouldn't say I was *in* love with any of them. I think I was gay all along but in a society where I felt almost coerced into a heterosexual lifestyle."

When we met Lisa, she was in the process of telling all her friends that she was a lesbian, and trying to figure out how to drop the bomb on her traditional Chinese family. "I think it's much more emotionally daunting to come out in a family like mine than even a Catholic family," she said. "Catholics are betraying a God, Jesus Christ, who is all-knowing, all-powerful, but who, when you get down to it, is a construct, not a real flesh-and-blood person. With Asians, family is the most important thing, and individuality is not something you should strive for: 'If the nail sticks up, you hammer it down.' So when you come out, you're betraying all your ancestors, as well as all your immediate family, who are real people you're seeing every day." Why come out, then? Because Lisa wanted her family to understand, however painfully, who she really is.

Oh: small detail. When we interviewed her, Lisa hadn't yet slept with a woman.

At the other extreme from her are women who "just happen" to fall madly in love or lust with only women, or those who don't even recognize that what they're feeling *is* love or lust. Not to mention those who, in Kate Clinton's great line, "wouldn't say the word 'lesbian' if they had one in their mouth."

The circuitous route to a lesbian identity is complicated by female sexual fluidity; girls and women who are attracted to both genders may genuinely not feel like "lesbians." But we've met hardly *any* gay woman who had an easy time putting a label on the constellation of sexual, emotional, and political feelings that add up to a lesbian identity. Gay males appear to be more resourceful at recognizing same-sex attraction at a young age—probably because an erection is a pretty unmistakable clue that what's going on is sexual. Female sexual response is more subtle, more diffuse, and more open to interpretation. Girls are also more programmed than boys to think about their worth in terms of the opposite gender and to imagine their futures in terms of marriage and children. When they begin to grapple with lesbian feelings, there's an extra layer of previously formed identity to strip off.

Coming out as a lesbian isn't a single event. Until recently, it rarely involved going public (that is, coming out of the closet), and it's still primarily a personal journey. It usually involves acknowledging in your own heart that you're a lesbian, having a sexual and/or romantic attachment to another woman, and identifying with at least some part of the larger lesbian community. But those things can happen in any order.

"I knew I could love a woman emotionally," said Jess Rhyn, a crinkly-eyed, round-faced forty-six-year-old visiting nurse from rural Kentucky. Before Jess came out (she was then a young married woman), "I knew I was mentally much more in sync with women. I knew I wanted to spend most of my time with women. All that. I just didn't know about the sex. And once I did know about the sex, I definitely knew I was gay."

Before her first affair, Jess had had crushes on girls, but no way to categorize them. She had crushes on boys, too, and craved validation from them to the point of putting herself in situations that became sexually exploitative. "I lost my virginity at nine, to a fourteen-year-old neighbor boy. I was feeling in a bad place about myself, because my mom had rejected me. I was a little pudgy, and she'd rather be dead than fat. So I needed a lot of attention and affection, and that's how I interpreted what this boy did to me. When we were done, I asked, 'Are we blood brother and blood sister now?' I never really call it rape. Insofar as a nine-year-old can consent, I did, and I considered what he did to me okay, because I would have done anything for attention and love."

Over the next five years, she had sex with all the boys in the neighborhood, including a male relative, who heard about her reputation and wanted to get in on the action. "No one talked about feeling attraction to your own sex—not then, or at least not there. But I would break dates with guys to go out with my girlfriends. And then I'd be over at my girlfriend's spending the night, holding hands . . . and praying. I *did* wonder, when I went to the bathroom, why I was really wet—why I was wet with her like I was wet with him, the same response. But it was just like, 'Hmm, that's odd.' And that was all."

After she was married and in nursing school, while her husband was overseas in the Navy, she fell madly in love with a classmate.

Still, even after having lesbian sex and realizing that she was gay, she was briefly drawn back into the marriage. "One night when I got home to our trailer, the whole thing was a wreck, he'd broken all my records and things. And there was a note on the bedroom sliding doors: 'When you can decide to stop running around all over down and being a slut you can come in here and sleep with me again.' I packed all my clothes and left. Of course, next day the car broke down. So my escape was not very effective, because I had to call *him* to come help me with the car stuff! So I did go home for a little bit before we finally separated. And somewhere in there he went to the store and got a bottle of wine—though he did not approve of my drinking—and I thought, Wow, he's really trying to be nice. So we had a real nice relaxing time. And sure enough if I didn't get pregnant that one night. I still could have a passably good sex life with him, even then."

The stop-and-start trajectory of so many lesbian comings-out is a direct consequence not only of the fluidity factor but also of lack of visibility. We don't know what we have in common with other lesbians until we can see who they are, which is one reason why large-scale events like the Michigan festival are so popular. Lesbian girls without role models are like the Ugly Duckling without the Swans. "I personally cannot imagine being fifteen and coming out," said Pittsburgh therapist Claudette Kulkarni, who herself came out as an adult. "What I see about many people who struggled at an early age with being gay is that when they should have been discovering who they were, they were working on pulling in the real self and putting out a false self." A fair amount of Claudette's practice involves undoing the damage.

Alison Bechdel remembers having had crushes on girls from the time she was two or three, and identifiably sexual feelings at a young age as well. "There was this girl in my class I was enamored of. One day, she slipped with her armload of books and fell on the floor. As she got up, she was laughing, and—big joke—she leaned against my leg. And I got this surge of electricity that just shot through my body and right out the top of my head! I knew, in that instant. Like, my God, this is *not* the right thing to be feeling. From that moment on . . . Well, there was this dictionary I used at home. One of the guide words was 'lesbian.' And it would flip me out so much to even see that word, I would skip the 'L's whenever I had to look anything up. That's why I think this visibility stuff is so great. Having the option presented to me, that you could be a lesbian if you were a little girl, it sure would've saved me a lot of wear and tear—the pain you go through figuring it all out for yourself."

Alison sometimes fantasizes about reliving her childhood, this time with other future lesbians. As it was, "I wanted to be like a boy. And I was a real misogynist. I didn't like girls. I hated all that girly stuff. It was all humiliating to me." Today the thirty-three-year-old Vermonter is a successful cartoonist whose strip about lesbian life, *Dykes to Watch Out For,* is syndicated in numerous gay and alternative papers. But "even the drawings I did as a child were always boys. When I tried to draw girls, they'd always look like guys. I never drew women until after I came out. Finally the only way I could draw a woman was if I drew a lesbian! I mean, the picture I was drawing when I first had an orgasm was this skeevy guy who worked at a gas station. But it wasn't like I was turned on by this guy. I wanted to have that kind of power, and authority, and toughness in the world. And it totally got me off! It was the thrill of *identification.*"

Sometimes even when there are other lesbians around, they can be impossible to identify with. "I didn't learn the word 'dyke' until many years into my life. But I knew I wasn't a wife and mother, and I wasn't a man, so I didn't know what I was," said Jean Grossholtz, who is now a professor of political science at Mount Holyoke College. After growing up "confused and marginalized" in a small town during the Depression, she joined the Army. "And of course, I met a lot of women who had sex with other women, but they didn't want to talk about it. What they did was drink a lot, and beat each other up. I thought, This is not me."

Jean did what plenty of other lesbians did: She tried to find herself by "reading everything I could get my hands on." (Libraries were to pre–Gay Nineties lesbians what the backseats of Chevys were to straight kids.) But, she admits, "I could never figure it out, and I felt like shit and so did everyone else. It was something you did that you felt was wrong, and disgusting and unacceptable, and you were constantly under pressure that 'they' might find out about it. And then one day I decided I was going to talk about it to a lieutenant. She got furious with me and said I was a troublemaker, and I was ostracized."

Jean didn't feel comfortable until years later, after she got involved with the civil rights movement and met lesbians who were kindred souls. In the early seventies, she came out at a faculty meeting, in defense of two lesbian students who were being shunned. "The next day, when I walked down the street, people cut me dead—including women [on the faculty] who owned houses together. Even one who wore men's suits and a tie!"

It would be nice to report that things are easier today. And in many ways they are. For what it's worth, however, early on in the research for this book, we made a decision to stop interviewing deeply closeted lesbians. We were looking for insights and connections; closeted women, however bright and decent, have an investment in walling off their lesbianism from everything else in life. It isn't that they don't toe some party line so much as that they don't even look at their toes.

When lesbians talk about coming out *publicly*, they're usually describing a process of empowerment, of learning to rely on their own instincts instead of the opinions of the world. "Once that happens, you never turn around, and you're never willing to put up with any bullshit," said Jean Grossholtz. The almost ethnic feeling that surrounds Gay Pride events always sets off tedious nattering from the 'phobes about why we have to proclaim "pride" in our genital activities blah blah blah. What we're celebrating, of course, isn't whether we like innies or outies, but our pride in surviving a hostile environment—and our way of guaranteeing that the next generation of gay children feels less alone.

For many women, coming out feels like coming home. Former Seattle councilwoman Sherry Harris, who was the first openly lesbian black woman elected to public office, recalled having "had a sense I was gay from the beginning of when a child begins to have sexuality. For example, I remember—What ages do you play house? Seven, eight, nine?—I always wanted a girl to be my husband. From the beginning there was this affinity that if I was going to be romantic it would have preferably been another little girl. But you don't have *anyone* to discuss this with or explain it to you or say it's all right. It never went away, that feeling. When I finally got to college and pledged a sorority house it was the first time I ever talked about it with anyone else, and this one woman I became really good friends with, she was the first one I ever slept with. So it wasn't a revelation to me. It was more like this natural thing I could have been doing all along but there were no role models to say it was okay."

Sherry nearly married twice and had several male lovers who were "very good in bed, but I couldn't form a *relationship* around that. When I think back on relationships with men, I feel like we didn't really relate to each other that well emotionally. Things had to be explained. They definitely were steeped in roles—or not even roles so much as expectations of roles. Suppose you really didn't want to be cooking dinner, for example: You had to have this whole conversation around it, whereas the nice thing about being with a woman is that there are *no* expectations about who's going to do what. It's all open to negotiation, and you just kind of have to work it out, and what you end up doing in terms of relating to each other and living with one another is, whoever has an affinity for whatever job around the house is probably who gets it. To me it's easier, it seems natural, less problematic. [Lesbianism] seems *normal* to me. When I made that transition from being a straight person to acknowledging the fact that I was gay . . . well, for me it was a more normal kind of thing."

When we asked Seattle carpenter Jorie Richards what was great about being a lesbian, she instantly replied, "The community. As a straight woman carpenter, it was very lonely. In the straight community, it was not okay to be different. One thing that's wonderful about the lesbian community is that it's able to embrace a lot of differences straight people run from." The program where Jorie learned carpentry was full of lesbians, "and I sometimes wonder: Are so many lesbians into this kind of stuff because we like it better? Or are straight women's options just more narrow, in terms of what they can do and having interesting lives? For me, the most liberating thing about coming out as a lesbian was that I could do anything I wanted, and didn't have to think about whether people would think I was weird. Because they probably *already* were going to think I was weird."

The embrace of weirdness is actually a pretty good predictor of which women are going to find lesbianism an easy fit. The two of us like to say that we were queer years before we were gay. To be a lesbian is, by definition, to flout social conventions. Bookworm? Tomboy? Rule-breaker? Felt like a changeling in your family? Women who answer yes to any of the above may feel instantly comfortable with the outsider status that more readily comes with the lesbian territory.

Outsiderhood was certainly part of the appeal for Kim Osborne, who is assistant to the chair of the Public Safety Commission of the city of Seattle. "With the straight men/women thing, there are so many stereotypes built in that it puts up barriers to having deep relationships," she explained. "It's like after X number of years you probably should get married; and X time after that you should buy a house; and X after that you should have children. And even though I knew I didn't want that 'normalcy,' everything's just channeling you and pressuring you into thinking according to those expectations. With women, so far, that's not there for me. You start at ground zero; it's just two people, and you find out for yourself the strengths and weaknesses and roles in the relationship—who can hammer a nail, who can do dishes. So you can more clearly see how much time and commitment you *really* want to devote to a person."

When we met Kim, the picture of conventional femininity with her flowered minidress and well-cut blond hair, she was twenty-seven and had been out for less than a year. She hadn't ruled out men for all time, although she wanted to work on one identity at a time. "What I say is that I'm dating women right now. And I'm *not* dating men." Just prior to hooking up with women, she had dated several bisexual and gay men; it was her gay male friends who had helped walk her through some of her early forays into picking up women. One of the things she immediately adored about dating women was the unprogrammed spontaneity of being queer, in all senses of the word. At first, "the difference was more mental than physical. Like, you'd take that mental right out the next day; you'd just be walking along and go, '*Whooooah!* Different today! Look at all these people! Wonder what they did last night?' It was like, the candy store is *open*."

Alison Bechdel agreed. "If you're a little heterosexual kid you have this paradigm shoved down your throat, that boys are like *this* and girls are like *this*. And you're pushed to be attracted to each other from when you're, like, two-year-olds, in a Life Savers commercial! It's sick! So I feel in a way, it's really a blessing for me to have always felt queer, because I didn't have my sexuality corrupted, you know? For most straight people, it's commodified. There's no choice about it. You never have that moment, that purity of just feeling an attraction to someone and not having any conceptual framework around it whatsoever, or even, like when I was growing up in this little conservative farm town, having the vocabulary for it—just feeling that feeling."

Although Alison doesn't feel her lesbianism was in any way a deliberate choice, as it was for Kim Osborne, she nevertheless experienced a similar process of deliberation and growth, the result of not being "born" with a sexual identity acceptable enough to take for granted. "I still learned a lot from the coming-out process. Before, I was totally oblivious. I thought capitalism was great. I went to church. I didn't question the world as I saw it at all. It was suddenly realizing I was a lesbian that lifted this veil and enabled me to see things as they really work. If I'd been heterosexual, I think I'd probably be working in advertising."

Being in a despised minority group can make you stronger, smarter, and sassier—if it doesn't break you. But there's a horrible paradox here, since what formed us was the very homophobia we're working to destroy. To the extent to which we succeed, future generations of lesbians will have the freedom to fit into the system and be just like everybody else. *Normal.*

We ourselves take a leaf from Christopher Isherwood, who, in discussing his own homosexuality and all it brought into his life, said that if boys had not existed, he would have had to invent them.

We're now at an age when a lot of our straight peers are statistically more likely to be hijacked by terrorists than snag a good man. So when they start in with us—"You're so lucky to be in a relationship with a woman! Men are such shits! I wish I could be a lesbian"— we naturally reply, "You can."

But in real life, it never seems to be that simple, even for many straight women who share a lot with gay women: feminist-based empathy and respect for womankind, deep emotional attachments to female friends, an understanding that a life partnership with a woman makes sense in terms of everything from housework to co-parenting. What really differentiates these straight women from gay women, or at least from lesbians-by-some-degree-of-choice, is crossing that last barrier on the path from close, and often quite flirtatious, friendships with other women to full primary-partner relationships.

When it comes to negotiating that last mile and its accompanying changes—including social acceptance (most likely way less), relationship intensity (most likely way more), but, especially, S-E-X— some women manage to cross the line from purely emotional "straight" relationships with other females to "lesbian" relationships incorporating the physical. For others, signs continue to flash "Does NOT compute." It's hard to determine exactly what does compute for some that doesn't for others, and why . . . and how to make it all compute, if that's what someone sincerely wants.

If forty-seven-year-old Pittsburgh computer systems analyst Brenda Graham was writing the how-to manual, page one of the instructions would read: "(1) Meet a woman so right that, were she a man, you'd be in bed within hours. (2) Then, three years later . . ."

Brenda was married for eighteen years and had two children. At the time of our interview, she had been involved in a lesbian relationship for seven months with therapist and professional astrologer Claudette Kulkarni. "I do think my life had for a long while been becoming increasingly woman-centered, but in a strictly heterosexual context," said Brenda. "I had begun to take vacations with groups of female friends, and I always had a social circle of good friends who had that emotionally intense thing women have with each other. But we were all straight."

Claudette, fifty-two, had also been married, although she had already been lesbian for more than a decade when she and Brenda met. "I don't *know* that we're not born with certain predispositions, tendencies, leanings," she reflects. "But personally, I buy the idea of a continuum: that some people are really basically heterosexual, some are really basically homosexual, and most of us are somewhere in the middle. That's certainly where I think I am. The advantage to coming out when you're older is that as an adult who grew up feeling straight, I'd already learned how to feel okay about myself and the way I am in the general culture, so this idea that I might be lesbian didn't seem to threaten my whole world; the more solid a sense of self one has, the easier it is to make hard decisions. People who are at the totally gay/lesbian end of the continuum maybe don't get to do what I did."

The two women met at Al-Anon meetings. First came a rapidly increasing emotional intensity, something that might have scared off some heterosexual women. But for Brenda, emotional separation had never been a plus. "A conversation we had way before we started having our relationship was that people in both our lives had told us they found each of us too intense. We'd both even lost straight friends because of it," Claudette explained. "I think one thing women can count on from men is that men will walk away from intense embroilment. That was my experience with men, anyway. I think there are built-in boundaries in most straight relationships . . ."

". . . which makes those relationships very safe, in a way," Brenda continued Claudette's thought. "That was certainly the contract in my marriage: 'Don't bring up my stuff, I won't bring up yours. We won't touch each other in any emotionally meaningful way.' So if that's the experience straight women have with lesbianism, having less control over what comes up, then they might choose to walk away from it."

"Because many lesbians do this other thing, where we have enmeshed relationships where there are *no* boundaries," Claudette said, picking up the ball. "I don't think it has to be that way. But it happens a lot."

"It's hard for me to imagine what it would be like to not want that intensity," Brenda insisted.

At the time they met, however, Brenda was recently divorced and dating men. "Claudette and I were spending a lot of time together, and I remember thinking, This is a hell of a way for me to get a relationship going. I'm spending all my weekend evenings that I don't have my kids with a lesbian! I'm supposed to be out beating the bushes for Prince Charming. So what am I doing? The answer was, Claudette was who I did want to spend Saturday night with."

Claudette was fresh from the breakup of a six-year relationship and hardly cruising. "And I'd determined never again to get involved with a straight woman. There's this sort of folklore in the lesbian community that when you bring somebody out, you can sort of assume she is going to want to do a lot of taste-testing—she's going to go off and be with other women—or else she's eventually going to go back to men, so bringing a woman out is a death knell. I don't know how often it's true. But it was certainly true of the woman I moved to Pittsburgh to be with. There was another woman who got married to a man after we broke up. And it became true with my last relationship, too. She's gotten involved with an extreme orthodox religious sect and trying very hard to be properly heterosexual."

Some of her "straight" exes did stay in the lesbian life, Claudette added. "But then there's another large group where the trade-off is too great. It isn't particularly that they love men. It's that they love the lifestyle that comes with men: the white picket fence, the two-car garage. That's what the appeal is, to look 'normal.' " And since that's not a fight even the most self-deludingly "normal" mistress-of-disguise closet case can win, Claudette definitely didn't want to chance it.

For Brenda, Mrs. Suburban Housewife conventionality had never been anything but a turnoff. But "when I was starting to cross the line, there was this fear, though a very amorphous fear. I mean, when I would think about some generic middle-aged woman making this choice, what would I think about her? Well, I think she would be really neat. So why for *me* would it be scary? Becoming a pariah may certainly have been a part of it."

One night at dinner Brenda "consciously took a deep breath and told Claudette that at the first program meeting I had been attracted to her hair."

"And I said I found her very attractive," Claudette said. "And then . . ."

. . . they had sex?

"We did . . . nothing!" Claudette laughed. "We didn't talk about it. I don't even remember what we said for the whole rest of dinner. But she was going away for a month, and I knew I didn't want to just sit on it for that long. So I called her up a few days later and said, 'You know that conversation? I'd like to understand what it was and what it meant.' And she said, literally, 'I don't want to think about it.' "

"And that it was something I didn't choose to act on," recalled Brenda. "And that I had too much going on in my life already."

"But then she came back," said Claudette, "and every other Saturday, which is when she doesn't have her kids, we did something together. And I remember saying to my therapist, 'Every time she's free, we're going out. *I* think this is, like, dating—except we're not saying it!' " Obviously, Claudette's resolve to remain uninvolved was also not working. "She was the closest person in the world to me. But she was straight. I got really depressed, thinking here I was again wanting something from this straight person that I wasn't going to get. We had both been invited to this Thanksgiving dinner, and I really didn't want to go and see her. Though then I did go, because I wanted to see her."

"And push me away. She was being really standoffish." Brenda's recollection of the holiday dinner was as another small step away from straightness. "There was this unmarried straight man there, about thirty, who had an interesting background, hippie-ish, but he'd also been an engineer. And I certainly found him attractive. But the whole dance that went on seemed . . . futile. Like, 'I don't know this guy from Adam. He's a stranger. But he's available. So okay, Brenda, here's this single guy who's about as good as they get—*go!*' It was really kind of a decisive realization for me, about this kind of straight-culture push I was submitting to, really, even though the push was coming from inside of me."

Meanwhile, on the un-dates with Claudette there had been "a progression in physical touch. Some had to do with just therapy issues we were both working out, inner child things. But other times . . . I remember once, when I was very upset and I cried and Claudette held me, at the end of that, I remember my leg was leaning on her. And I knew I didn't want to move that leg. Then one Saturday evening, we were just sitting side by side. And I had Claudette's hand and remember starting to touch it, brain gone, in a way that wasn't anything but sensual. And her responding. And us just doing this hand dance for a long time. And me realizing that I was having major big feelings of sexual attraction."

At this point, Claudette glances sideways at Brenda, one eyebrow raised. Brenda shrugs. "Claudette claims that my elbow was in her crotch the whole time. I don't remember that part. When my brain would occasionally engage, I'd say to myself, It's okay. It's just hands."

"We did this until, like, three o'clock in the morning," Claudette reminisced. "And then . . ."

. . . then they had sex?

"Then she sent me home," said Claudette. "She said she didn't trust herself. If I didn't go, she didn't know what would happen."

"Did I?" Brenda sighed. "Well, I knew I wasn't ready. I knew I'd have to reengage my brain and catch it up, sort of integrate."

"So I left," Claudette explained. "It looked like there was hope, anyway, which was a step up. But I was also scared of scaring her, that if I pushed, or acted too soon, or did anything overt she'd just, *pffft,* go away."

Uh-huh, we nodded. Three years into an almost unbearably intense relationship, and still afraid of acting too soon? "Yup," Claudette cheerfully agreed. "Only lesbians! We must be real ones."

After the weekend both women now refer to as "the Hands," however, Brenda called the following Monday night, and "I basically said to her, 'I don't think I can do this, good-bye.' What was happening for me," she added slowly, trying to get it exactly right, "was . . . I knew something real was happening, a real sexual response, and was trying to own it. On the other hand, there was this feeling of 'I cannot imagine this because I can't visualize this. There's none of the framework I'm used to. If this is really happening, why don't I undress Claudette with my eyes, like I would a man? Why don't I visualize us in bed?' Or, any image I *could* call up wasn't necessarily something I could feel a positive response to. It was scary. I remember finally getting into bed thinking, Will it feel right to touch a breast?—not yet having the positive physical response connected to the visualization that I'd been used to from a lifetime of experience with male bodies. So what had happened didn't make sense. It contradicted my life experience.

"But after basically saying good-bye to Claudette on Monday night, I then called her more than daily. I knew I didn't have much to say, I knew she didn't want to hear from me, and I knew we were in a terrible place. So there were a lot of phone calls that went, 'Are you okay?' 'No.' 'Well, okay.' 'Well, I've gotta go.' "

"Then after a few days," Claudette added, looking intently at Brenda, "I finally said to her, 'I don't think we would be having this conversation if I were male.' Because I was really mad about that. I mean, here I was all these things that supposedly mattered to her, and what was mattering was that I wasn't male, not anything else. And I said, 'Either you're not being honest with me, or you're not being honest with yourself.' "

Brenda's response was to say "I can't talk now" and hang up. "I was reeling. It took her getting that mad and saying it that forcefully for it to get through to me that it was a true statement, and that with all my efforts to be honest I was lying to myself in so many ways."

Crying, Brenda left a message on Claudette's answering machine asking her to call. "She did. We agreed to see each other to talk. By then I was feeling relief, thinking I wanted to go ahead with this. So I came over, on Saturday night. And she was sitting in that chair, and I was sitting here, and I asked her to come closer. And she said, 'I haven't held you yet as an adult. Would you let me do that?' "

"And the rest is history," Claudette smiled. "That moment changed a lot. That was it."

So that's when they finally had sex?

"Well, um, no. Actually, we only had a couple hours that night because Brenda had gotten a baby-sitter. So we sat around some more and . . . Well, we didn't have sex till a few days later."

Yup. Real lesbians.

But the sex—or rather, what it added to an almost full relationship—was also decisive. "I'd had all this fear but when I finally pulled it all apart, it wasn't there. Literally three or four days after kissing and sleeping with Claudette, I was saying, 'What was I afraid of? Where did it go?' " Brenda marveled.

So she immediately came out to virtually everyone in her life. "Yeah. Busy week. And it was all happening at one restaurant. I've always thought the waiters must have been, like, 'My God. *She's* back *again*.' Same table. New person. And midway through lunch the person goes, *'Ohhhhhh!'* "

The reason Brenda came out so quickly to her friends, she explained, is that "these are people I'm very close to, people who care about me a lot. I wouldn't hesitate to share my ugly problems with them, so the idea of not sharing something I was happy about was inconceivable. But mainly, I just think for me, the whole idea of living with hiding something from anyone is not okay."

"Anyone" included Brenda's kids, though telling them was, she admitted, the most painful coming-out experience. "I didn't do it for four or five months, which was very hard. But I had to get to a point where I could visualize them surviving the experience. And I knew it was all about my own head being calm."

The Big Event was Mother's Day, 1994. "All day long, I'd finally get both kids in the room, and then—the phone would ring. Or the kids would get too silly. Then we went to one of those movies where the screen wraps all the way around, which made both me and my older daughter totally nauseous, and I thought, This is perfect! If I tell her and she barfs, I'll blame it on the movie! It took many hours of moments that would come and go. Finally I said, 'I have something about my life I want to tell you.' Swift, huh? Both kids looked so panicked. They naturally thought I had a terminal illness. But I figured I have to have a lead-in: 'Pass the butter, I'm a dyke'? So I had their attention, and I said something like, 'I'm in a relationship with Claudette, and I'm being gay.' "

Both kids started to cry. Brenda was beside herself.

"So I just kept talking, talking, talking. About how I'm happy. About 'Everything's okay.' About 'Your lives are not going to change.' About 'Claudette will be here in our lives, but I'm not moving.' About 'You don't have to tell anyone, though I'm telling a lot of my friends and they are all okay with it.' To both of them I said, 'Are you afraid you'll be shamed if your friends know?' And they both said yes, at the time."

But the next day, "My older kid asked, 'Can So-and-So come over? She's having a hard time with her parents.' I said, 'Ahem. A harder time than *you're* having with your parent?' She laughed. And I said, 'I wish you could talk to her about it.' She said, 'I did. I made her guess.'

"Later, when I was walking the nine-year-old to the bus stop, I was asking her yet again, 'Are you feeling uncomfortable about this?' And she says to me, 'You want to know the truth? The real truth? *I don't care!* ' "

Brenda laughed, slightly abashed at recalling her parental processing overkill. "They really seemed to have the need for me to . . . fuck off. I think a lot of the crying was just about realizing I was not about to say I was dying of cancer. My being lesbian they handled just fine." Totally. In fact, it sounds like they adjusted to the idea approximately two years and 364 days faster than their mom did.

Actually, even when Brenda was coming out to half the population of western Pennsylvania overnight, she was not coming out as a lesbian per se, but as a woman who had fallen in love with a woman. This is a stage most lesbians will recognize, because we've done the same dance—and that next step's a biggie. "At that point, seven months ago, what I was saying is that I was having a relationship with Claudette. People would always ask, 'Does this mean you're a lesbian?' And my answer now is . . ." She paused to think.

"It's shifted. What I was saying then is, 'Lesbian' is an important term, a valuable term, that says a lot. I don't think you can sleep with a man one day and a woman the next day and say, 'I have become a lesbian.' I see it as a pretty major identity thing, and that is *earned,* in some sense. So I was not comfortable using the term, but not because I wasn't comfortable being a lesbian. I just thought I hadn't earned it.

"As time has gone by, I realize I've changed. I can now look at the world in a much more open way. It's not like I go around visually undressing women now, but now when I see an attractive woman I fully acknowledge that I have a response. Also I've come to believe there's nothing I am not getting in this relationship with a woman that I think I could get with a man. Whereas when I think of being with a man, I think there's so much I couldn't get; I can't imagine where a man would come from who would be someone I could have this kind of relationship with."

Brenda took a deep breath. "I'm now looking back at all this and saying, 'At what point *would* I earn a lesbian identity? Can I entertain the idea that I've earned it now?' And I do feel that, from a long history of being a heterosexual woman-identified woman, I've now put in enough time being in a sexual and intimate relationship with a woman, and realizing how it has affected my being in the world, that I begin to earn the right to call myself a lesbian."

Enough already. This woman is building to the point of *terminal* earnestness. Actually, we explain to Brenda, this wasn't a real interview. The official lesbian membership committee sent us to check y'all out, and when we get home we're sending you your certificate. We may even teach you the secret handshake.

Social Arrangements

Desire Under the Palms: The Dinah Shore Party Circuit

*P*alm Springs is an unlikely candidate for the title of Latter-Day Lesbos. In the desert a little over a hundred miles southeast of Los Angeles, it's tucked among wrinkled chocolate mountains that look like giant sleeping shar-peis. Pretty much everything else looks somnolent and pedigreed, too. The streets, named after the likes of Bob Hope, Gene Autry, Frank Sinatra, Ginger Rogers, and Gerald Ford, roll up soon after sundown. Hearing-aid stores and nursing homes appear to be growth industries. The only large-scale display of energy of any kind is the gauntlet of windmills guarding the approach to the town, giant pinwheels that transform desert winds into electricity. Huge numbers of the locals are what you might call preptagenarians; imagine the J. Crew catalog, flash-forwarded in a time machine. The most blatant crime against nature here is the presence of more wet, green grass than any desert oasis has a right to. Turning on the lawn sprinkler is clearly the water sport of choice here.

But all those Republican retirees and all that grass spells G-O-L-F, which in turn spells lesbian party animals. At least once a year, anyway, at the end of March, when the LPGA Nabisco Dinah Shore Golf Tournament takes place at the Mission Hills Country Club in Rancho Mirage.

Now that pre-1970s "Knock three times and ask for Josephine" secret sapphic watering holes have bloomed into 1990s Lesbian Chic luppiedom, there are glamorous annual women's weeks in Key West and Provincetown, upscale lesbian Love Boat cruises to the Caribbean and the Mediterranean, and, everywhere, one-night dance parties with ticket prices that would have covered three months' rent, utilities, and tofu at a 1975 lesbian commune. At the moment, however, "Dinah" is the caviar event of lesbian public social life: a long, lavish weekend of dances, parties, and shows. The women who come are famously sexy, rich, successful, and gorgeous: the cliterati.

The golf tournament (which has no official connection with the lesbian events that take place the same weekend) began life in 1972 as the Colgate Dinah Shore. Shore, who died of cancer in early 1994, had a fondness for golf and a weekend home in Palm Springs. Colgate was one of her television sponsors; the corporate sponsorship was taken over by Nabisco a decade later. We remember her fondly from our fifties TV childhoods, when Chevrolet was her sponsor, and she'd end every show by urging us, "See the U-S-A in your Chev-ro-lay." Then she'd blow the audience a big sticky *mmmmwyuhh* of a kiss—perfect high camp. Shore's obit in *The Lesbian News* reported that for years there had been rumors that she was a member of the sisterhood, and we met several women in Palm Springs who also claimed to have it on good authority. But this might have been wishful thinking.

The presence of lesbians on the professional golf circuit, however, isn't in dispute, or at least shouldn't be. In 1995, after a brouhaha over whether a television sportscaster did or didn't say that lesbians were giving the game a bad name, the former general chairman of the LPGA was quoted insisting that "I've been in all kinds of social situations with the gals and personally, I have never seen any evidence of lesbian activity, overtly or otherwise." We're assuming that means that the gay players weren't plunging their tongues into each other's throats at the banquet table. The truth is that lesbians appear to be overrepresented in the world of golf and of athletics in general, professional and amateur. There are closeted golf pros who are known to lesbian fans through the same combination of gaydar and reliable sources that spilled the beans on the likes of k.d. and Melissa before they officially came out. "Dinah" draws the golf groupies who follow their favorite players (including the straight ones) from hole to hole, and it also draws fans who want to play golf themselves at any of the sixty or so country clubs and resorts in the area.

The two of us are Adult Children of Suburban Golfers. When we first heard about Dinah, we had an acute and not particularly enticing vision of days spent tromping around a country club in dorky visors, sensible shoes, and shrimp-pink plaid pants. *Au contraire.* For increasing numbers of the thousands of women who descend on Palm Springs for Dinah, the irons that matter most aren't the fives or the fours, but the ones that curl hair—preferably long, blond, and permed. Golf now competes with such activities as black bra contests and go-go dancers, and plenty of women never even get near the fairway. The estimates of the number of those who come for the indoor sports ranges as high as twenty thousand. If the LPGA ever decided to move the tournament away from Palm Springs, which it's constantly rumored to be about to do, the annual lesbian girl-a-thon would probably live on.

Originally the lesbian presence was a discreet affair, limited to parties in private houses. The woman most responsible for Dinah's transformation into an open lesbian paradise is a pale, delicate Englishwoman who goes by the name of Caroline Clone. During the eighties, she was a top lesbian nightlife promoter and club owner in Los Angeles. She also produced club events in San Francisco and, most recently, owned Little Frida's, a successful lesbian coffee bar in West Hollywood. In 1993, she relocated to Miami, having fallen in love both with the South Beach scene and with a woman who lived there. We moved to South Beach from New York a few months after Caroline did, and we soon became aware of her when the local weekly *New Times* ran a lengthy story called "The Great Lesbian Club Wars." According to *New Times,* Clone's exodus from the other coast was such a blessed event to some of her club-owning rivals that one of them threw a "Ding Dong the Cappuccino

Queen Is Gone" party, complete with a "wicked witch piñata" for smacking. In Florida, Caroline and her associates had promptly taken on the premier lesbian promoter, a woman named Lisa Cox. They launched an ad campaign slyly suggesting that "Gay Girls Don't Need Cox to Have Fun." The whole mess had ended up in a public street brawl and threats of lawsuits. It was the talk of South Florida lesbians for months.

Caroline is reputed to have parted on bad financial terms with her business partners in several cities (although in at least one instance she was the partner who claims to have been stiffed), and she's notorious for her poaching, showing up at other promoters' lesbian events, which, by night's end, are covered from dance floor to rest rooms with flyers for her own parties. But even women who loathe her admit that her clubs have always been hot, and original. "Before I was a lesbian, I was a person, and I defined myself by what I liked, and by my background, which was in fashion and design," Caroline told us, relaxing in her South Beach condo with its wraparound view of the ocean.

What she didn't like was "downward mobility." When she arrived in L.A. in 1980, there was nothing at all for the BMW sort of lesbian. Straight clubs were out of the question, and the trendy gay men's discos discouraged women, often using policies against open-toed shoes to keep out heterosexual fag hags and, incidentally, glammed-up gay women. Most of the women's bars were in the thrall of feminist politicos and had a casual funkiness that in Caroline's view often verged on downright slobbery. "My girlfriend, a film makeup person who was a straight girl before she was with me, was horrified. She didn't know how she was going to be a lesbian and deal with this scene." Caroline's nose wrinkled delicately. "People coming to bars in golf shorts and flip-flops."

So Caroline, who had worked as a deejay at a punk club in London, started a regular party called Clone's. "Dress to Impress," said the first invitation, and patrons had to pass inspection at the door. "People wore makeup, because they were afraid that if they didn't, they wouldn't get in. We got some flak for the dress code." But, Caroline insisted, "this was also something women had been longing for. We had to make a statement, and if we'd relaxed our stan-

dards, we'd have been the same as the other clubs." The most favored customer was someone who looked as if she belonged in the
straight bars. (Kristy McNichol was a regular, according to Caroline.)

Clone's was rumored to prefer blondes and to be especially in-
hospitable to women who weren't Caucasian. Not true, said Caroline: Her first event was a White Party; some people misunderstood
and thought she was talking about skin color, not clothing. But she
did acknowledge that she denied entrance to women who were too
butch, too fat, too polyester. "Big truck drivers," she sniffed.

Though barring women who didn't meet its standards, Clone's
meanwhile welcomed certain high-profile men. "We started getting
people like Warren Beatty and Jack Nicholson wanting to come in,"
and if they called first to ask permission, she was happy to let them
in. (Barry Diller and Debra Winger showed up unannounced one
night, but were turned away because "we didn't know who they
were.") Did her clients mind serving as the unpaid entertainment
for male movie stars? "The girls loved it," Caroline assured us. The
men "always came with beautiful women. That was part of the deal.
They had to sit in a corner, and not approach women. Warren was
very good about that. We told Jack not to come back because he
started smoking cigars in the club, and approaching women in a
sleazy way. Actually [he and his friends] stopped coming on their
own. One night they picked up someone they thought was a girl, but
it was a transvestite."

In 1984, Caroline went to Dinah with some friends, surveyed the
private party scene, and heard opportunity pounding. The following
year she threw a public White Party in Palm Springs, bringing more
than a thousand young flashy Hollywood bar bunnies in ivory
gowns and pearl-white suits to Dinah, most for the first time. In
subsequent years, she launched ever more ambitious "pah-tees."
She brought in big name acts like Chaka Khan and Grace Jones, introduced the idea of an evening of stand-up comedy (starring Ellen
DeGeneres) in 1993, and once even threw a casino night in an airplane hangar.

Not surprisingly, she also spawned plenty of competition. When
Natalie Barney and Gertrude Stein were both dazzling Paris in the

twenties with their literary salons, they at least had the good sense to share the tiara: Natalie had Fridays, Gertrude took Saturdays. During the Dinah weekend, the jockeying to be Homo Hostess with the Mostest is a much messier affair. So many women, so little time.

At every large-scale queer event, there's a glad, giddy moment when we converge on each other and the everyday straight world falls away. At Gay Pride marches in New York, we used to stumble onto the Sunday morning subway, barely caffeinated, and realize with delight that the car was half-gay—and it got gayer with every stop as the IRT neared Columbus Circle. At the lesbian and gay March on Washington in 1993, it happened for us on the New Jersey Turnpike, where toll booths suddenly began sprouting pink triangle and rainbow stickers. We remember pulling into the aptly named Walt Whitman Rest Area between two women in a car with Massachusetts plates and a car from New York full of men, one of them carrying a ferret on his shoulder. A highlight of the march was to be a mass commitment ceremony, and as we all checked each other out in the parking lot, the women from Massachusetts suddenly burst into the old Dixie Cups song: "We're goin' to the chapel, and we're gonna get mah-ah-ah-ried." The rest of us burst out laughing, chimed in with the harmonies, and then—girls, boys, ferret—cakewalked into the rest stop.

At Dinah, the queer moment took longer to manifest itself. When we hit Palm Springs, we immediately headed for the Chamber of Commerce to get a decent map. There we overheard a straight couple asking the woman behind the desk if there was anything special going on in town. "Well," she answered, "there's the Harvest and Wildflower Festival." Was this a secret Georgia O'Keeffe code? We also hadn't seen *any* of the usual bumper stickers normally visible at events drawing Friends of Dorothy or even tolerant straight friends of Friends ("Hate Is Not a Family Value," etc.). The whole ambience was extremely GOP, and we don't mean Girls on Parade.

But when we sailed into the Glitz Moderne lobby of the sprawling Riviera Resort & Racquet Club, there were lines upon lines of guests, six and seven deep, waiting to check in. All of them were women. There were women at all the tables in the restaurant, women at all the lounge chairs around the pool. It was like stepping out of Auntie Em's house into a lesbian parallel universe, except that here, the Munchkins on the Yellow Brick Road drove convertibles.

We would later find out from Riviera manager Tim Ellis that the hotel, which hosted the same group the previous year, was delighted with our company. The three-day Dinah gathering was the second-biggest event of that year, just behind a five-day United Auto Workers–General Motors Health/Safety conference. The women, Ellis estimated, spent more than $250,000 at the Riviera alone—and, he added, "these women tip quite well. The bartenders and cocktail waitresses made a lot of money from these guests last year. So are they going to be nice? You'd better believe they are." The only problem Ellis had to field was a phone call "from a disgruntled Christian gentleman" whose first question was, "Are you running a lesbian hotel?" (Ellis replied that he wasn't in the habit of quizzing guests about their sexual orientation at check-in.)

The 480-room Riviera was only one of many hotels in town that had been completely booked by various party promoters. At the Riviera, the promoters were the reigning West Coast party princesses, Mariah Hanson, Robin Gans, and Sandy Sachs. They have been doing Dinah since 1991. Mariah, who promotes various events under the name Club Skirts, also runs a San Francisco club night known as the Girl Spot, a.k.a. the G-Spot. ("If you can't find it, you can't come," read the T-shirts.) Sandy and Robin are the women behind Hollywood's glamorous Girl Bar, the nineties successor to Clone's earlier club nights. They are also lovers. Ten years earlier in New York, when Robin had another girlfriend, she and Sandy were illicit lovers, who spent lovesick happy hours at Mortimer's on the Upper East Side and stolen moments where they could find them. Now, as Mariah put it, "these guys are lifers."

We'd first come across them several years earlier, when Lindsy was writing a piece about lipstick lesbians for the *Los Angeles Times*. Lesbian chic was in its infancy. Since then, Robin and Sandy have become, as Mariah said, "the lesbian poster children." When we caught up with them in their suite at the Riviera on the eve of the big weekend, Robin brought us up to date on their visibility blitz. "We did Jane Whitney. Maury Povich," she ticked off. "And Montel Williams. Jenny Jones in Chicago. And then the Mo Gaffney show."

Mariah, who accompanied the Girl Bar duo on several of these media forays, added that the down side of all the exposure had been an upsurge in heterosexual men wanting to crash their clubs. This is a legally tricky matter nowadays, since the gay community has, in the decade since Caroline Clone was picking and choosing her clientele, worked hard to pass laws preventing people from being kept out of public places on the basis of sexual orientation. Mariah generally tries moral suasion on the doorbusters. "We don't want to let them in. But you'll get an argument back from the straight guys," she lamented. "They see it as discrimination, that we're asking for tolerance. Meanwhile, they can go anywhere in the world, and I want to ask, 'Why are you *here?*' "

"To get off," Robin sniffed.

The straight crashers may be inconsiderate, but they're not dumb. The Girl/Skirts clientele is drawn from the ranks of what every talk-show viewer by now must know as the "lipstick lesbian." The three women themselves are babes, too. Mariah is blond, blue-eyed, and apple-pie (or maybe Scandinavian-lingonberry-pie) wholesome, with a master's degree in English from U.C. Santa Barbara. Sandy is angular and tanned, with long, straight dark hair. After graduating from Tulane, she got into law school but decided to pursue a career in television instead. ("She's Latin and Jewish, which means she can dance *and* count money," says her girlfriend.) Robin is a lush brunette with head-turning cleavage. She's beginning to think about retiring from Girl Bar and leaving the Dinah party biz to the other two. Pushing forty, she's working to get her doctorate in political psychology. "I want to do something that the older I get, the better I'll get at it. The nightclub business isn't that way." She's going to be a therapist. "Girl Couch," explained Sandy.

The three hostesses had just done a sensitivity training session with the hotel security staff. "With all the publicity about this weekend," said Sandy, "one of our biggest fears is rape. I told them I want *uniforms*. Gold badges."

There were also smaller fears afoot. Jitters, actually. After months of planning, it was countdown to party time. Robin breathlessly told us that this weekend was *huge,* that women were coming from all over (New York! England! Lanexa, Kansas!), that this was *the* global, high-class women's event. She hauled a rubber shark nose out of the special party bags of plastic golf visors, liquor samples, and other souvenirs from various corporate sponsors, most of them manufacturers of alcoholic beverages. "Enough of these girls drink this Jagermeister," she mused, "and they'll be wearing these shark items in the pool." The courtship of sponsors, whose logos are displayed at all the parties, is a relatively new development. Only a few years ago, hotels didn't want lesbian business and the corporate types didn't want to be associated with a lesbian event.

Girl/Skirts was throwing an almost nonstop affair over the course of the weekend. Friday night: "The Queens of Comedy," featuring four stand-up comics, followed by the "Mediterranean Magic" dance party. Saturday night: the big-ticket "Disciples of Desire" party, featuring a laser show and multiple go-go dancers. Sunday afternoon; the poolside "Isle of Lesbos" party. And Sunday night: the "Love Hangover Dance Party," a benefit for women's health services, with Chastity Bono's band. (Admission to all of them could be had with a $60 Party Passport, or $98 total at the door.) The previous year's Girl/Skirts Saturday night dance party, "Monte Carlo Madness" (featuring can-can girls), was the best-attended event of the entire weekend.

The problem was that there were nearly two dozen *other* parties. Country-western line-dance parties with mechanical bull rides. Female strippers. Poolside battles of the all-girl bands. Performances by Jane Olivor and Fem 2 Fem. Caroline Clone's "Funny Girlz II," a night of comedy at the Palm Springs Convention Center headlining Lea DeLaria. A local men's bar was reprising its popular annual lady-wrestling event: Kona the Barbarian and Officer Hardbody, in "the Grudge Match of the Century," the weapons being cans of whipped cream.

"We saw Kona the Kanine once, and that was enough," said Robin, curling her lip. "Her breasts literally hit the bottom of the floor." The Grudge Match of the Century was scheduled for Sunday night—at the same time as the Girl/Skirts party starring Chastity Bono—and, Robin admitted, "this whipped-cream thing is bugging me to no end, that these people are spending money on this. You know what? We have a go-go dancer who's going to do whipped cream, too, but she's going to do it with taste! They want whipped cream, we'll give them whipped cream!"

Mariah announced that earlier in the day, she had personally given Caroline the lezbum's rush (that is: no violence, just a stern escort off the Riviera premises). "She had the nerve to waltz in with her stack of flyers and was soliciting our clientele on their beach chairs! She's so full of it." In Mariah's professional opinion, Caroline doesn't even throw fabulous parties. At her airplane-hangar event a few years back, Mariah hooted, "Caroline was so cheap that she only had four Porta Potties."

For weeks, the promoters had been clawing it out in the pages of the lesbian press. The Girl/Skirts team had the support of the slick monthly *LN* (as in Lesbian News), where they were major advertisers. Los Angeles club promoter Joni Weir and Clone, who had competed with Weir in seasons past but hired Weir's girlfriend to emcee her comedy night this year, had connections at a West Hollywood gay bar paper called *Nightlife,* where indeed Weir and her co-organizer were listed in the masthead as feature writers. Weir was dissed as "the Tonya Harding of the lesbian club scene" by *LN,* whose "Five Star Guide to Dinah" gave its most stellar ratings to all the Girl/Skirts events. *Nightlife*'s "Un-Biased Five-Star All-Star Guide" did major snarking at same. (Their preview of the Isle of Lesbos pool party: "If your idea of a desert paradise is to be charged $15 to lay out by a pool and catch some rays, then get charged high drink prices, or be stared at by a handful of pretentious, clique-y lesbians with bad attitudes, well then, run out and buy that inflated tea dance ticket, then ask yourself: What with the high price of Saturday's Girl/Skirts ticket, hasn't enough money been milked out of the women's community?")

Such judgments really annoy Sandy, Robin, and Mariah. "The thing we get hit on the most is that we're successful and we're making money, and for women that's not okay," said Mariah.

Sandy added that in fact they've gone over budget this year.
"We'd rather lose money than put on a bad party. We spent thirty-
five hundred dollars just for the lasers for Saturday night. Wait until you see the production. You'll think you're at a boy party." Then
she blurted: "What drives me to this day isn't money. It's about that
feeling of throwing a party that nobody comes to."

"Oh, God," said Mariah. "I *did* have a party that no one came to
when I was little."

"I did, too!" Sandy said, amazed. "I put up all these little lights in
my den, and I really wanted to make it look like a disco. I had my
mother cooking for a week. Like, four people came. It had to be one
of the single worst experiences of my life."

"And now," said Mariah, "we make sure they *all* come."

The weekend did not begin with a bang. Friday night's Girl/Skirts
comedy debut at the Riviera was more like a bomb. The comics
themselves were great (we especially liked Marga Gomez's riff on
being at Dinah and surrounded by gorgeous women—while also
being half of a monogamous couple: "It's like going to a big banquet and bringing food from home in a paper bag.)" However, the
sound system, well, sucked. There is no other word for it. Squeals.
Honks. The comics sounded as if they were whipped-cream-
wrestling a herd of wild boars. At least a third of the audience fled.

When we ran into Caroline the next afternoon, she was trying, in
the understated British manner, not to gloat overtly . . . but failing.
She was also still miffed about getting the heave-ho out of the Riviera, which she referred to as "a *fortress.*" Since we're journalists
and part of our job description is making trouble, we repeated the
Girl/Skirts rumor about Caroline's airplane-hangar event having
been scandalously underpottied. "*Four* Porta Potties?" she echoed
in disbelief. "There were at least ten. When you've got as many
women as my event drew, it just *seems* like four." Anyway, she assured us airily, "At the Convention Center tonight I have more bath-
rooms than any facility in Palm Springs." We hope that clears the
air for good.

During the day, there is little to do at Dinah. Oh. Right. There's the golf, which we did actually attend, once. However, when we asked Lea DeLaria if she was planning to stop by the fairway at all, she looked at us as if we'd just suggested a fun afternoon of watching our hair grow. "Why would I? To see women walk? I can do that on the street." Instead, Lea had spent the day lounging poolside, first at the Riviera and then at Joni Weir's headquarters at the Racquet Club hotel, which Lea called "the cute-chick party. It's a much more laid-back atmosphere here. Over at the Riviera, I wanted to go around putting everyone's collar down. That's the gay women's place. This is the dyke place."

The most-favored Dinah daytime activity, at both the less posh Racquet Club and the more yupped-out Riviera, seemed to be recovery from the excesses of the night before. And these could be formidable, considering the prevalence, on weekend bar menus, of numerous how-many-sponsors-can-dance-on-the-head-of-a-beer concoctions. Most outrageous was the Girl/Skirts' "Isle of Lesbos," inventively blending triple sec and cream of coconut with (sponsored) Cuervo Gold, (sponsored) Kahlúa, and (sponsored) Miller Lite.

All those bikinis, all those drinks with parasols, all that free-floating estrogen . . . would it be any wonder if the weekend turned into a sapphic Tailhook? Actually, we did see one instance of sexual exploitation, at the Racquet Club hotel. We'd ambled by to catch the finish of the Battle of the All-Girl Bands. Several very young, very drunk women were collapsed in a heap on a lounge chair, and a young, balding guy with an impressively expensive assortment of professional press cameras and meters around his neck asked to take their picture. They shrugged an assent. Click, click. Could they just kind of get *closer?* Snap, snap. Could you maybe put your leg over hers, like that? And how about a little kiss? Before long, the girls had rolled into the pool and begun to fake making out, with much tongue and much giggling.

Frankly, it took all the patience we could muster not to stomp over and toss the photographer and his expensive cameras into the water on top of them. But figuring that these were young postfeminist lipstick lesbians with different values we shouldn't impose upon, we just watched and seethed silently. Finally, though, we decided that as reporters, we had to at least find out what gay male publication could possibly be interested in such sleazoid straight-guy lesbo porn shots. Flipping our notebooks open, we identified ourselves and asked him to do the same. "Uh . . ." It turned out the photos were "for my private collection. I just think lesbian women are so beautiful."

The glazed girls' jaws dropped. They looked at each other uncomfortably. Then two of them hopped out of the pool in one remarkably unglazed motion. We decided it was time for a beer break. The next time we glanced poolside, the Collector of Beautiful Things was surrounded by three angry Amazons and looking as though he'd stayed home with an old issue of *Playboy*.

When one of the women dropped by our table later, she was still kicking herself. "I just assumed he was from a gay paper. There's so much media coverage of this event. Shit. I can't believe I was dumb enough to fall for that. Shit." We assured her we'd fallen for worse in our lives from men (hell, we've fallen for worse in our lives from women), and at least there'd be no lasting damage from this incident. "That's for damned sure," she said with a smile, tossing several rolls of film on the table.

Dinah sometimes had an undeniable feeling of the bunker. We noticed it at the beginning of the weekend, when we tagged after a reporter and photographer from the *Desert Sun* as they tried to cover the jam-packed Girl/Skirts dance party at Sonny Bono's multilevel restaurant. Almost no woman they approached would agree to have her picture or her name in the paper. It was a first that the local paper was covering the event at all—treating lesbians just like everybody else, which is ostensibly what we've all been fighting for. As it turned out, Dinah parties did grace much of the society page in that Sunday's paper, lesbian chic by jowl with photos of staid local folks at black-tie dinners at the Desert Island Country Club. But most of the Dinah pictures were of professional entertainers, not partygoers.

The majority of the women we met were closeted, and there was often a good excuse: the tenure that hadn't happened yet; the ex-husband who had become a born-again Christian and might try to grab the kids; the parents who had no idea. But even apart from the constraints of the closet, you become aware at an event like Dinah how very constricted the lesbian world can become, no matter how blond and professional one might be.

"There aren't a lot of spaces I can feel comfortable in," sighed a Wellesley grad who was hoping to meet Ms. Right, or at least Ms. Good Enough for the Time Being. She was an instructor at the University of California at Riverside, and, she added, "Riverside is a closed community. Everyone is everyone else's ex, and you're always marked as someone who has been with X. That's probably why I'm here." Another year would go by before she'd have the opportunity to mingle with so many suitable women. No social equivalent in the straight world exists for events like Dinah, unless you can imagine being told that if you want to celebrate New Year's Eve this year, there are only three parties in the country you're invited to. There's a lot riding on the weekend for a lot of women. We Are Having Fun.

On the big night, Saturday, we caught Caroline's comedy show at the Convention Center, and it really *was* the most elegant lesbian theatrical soirée we've ever attended. There's something intoxicatingly seductive about being in with the in crowd, and that's who the lesbians were tonight, as we mingled in the massive, gleaming Versailles-in-the-Desert lobby. (We did feel a bit sorry, though, for the handful of male security guards. They grinned wanly when one of the comics cheerily asked them from the stage how it felt to be surrounded by a thousand women who didn't want to suck their cocks.)

Then we headed for the Sandy/Robin/Mariah "Disciples of Desire" party. It, too, really *was* the most fabulous lesbian dance party we've ever gone to. Now, we realize that, considering the downscale nature of so many lesbian events, we sound like a bag lady saying, "This is the most fab refrigerator carton I ever lived in." But "Disciples" truly did have the class of the last twenty years' most glamorous gay male parties.

The space, a Riviera auditorium that usually hosts big business-guy conventions, was huge, and the light show made it seem even bigger. Creeping Peter Max amoebas and other blow-your-mind oil emulsions swirled on the ceiling. "Grecian columns" made up of dramatic black and white balloons were illuminated by thousands of Christmas mini-flashers. On huge adjoining screens on one wall, old Doric temple ruins and marble statues of Aphrodite and Venus were projected. Directly next to the Greek goddesses, in a juxtaposition that says it all about our weirdo community, was a 1950s jiggle-show girly movie.

In a deejay booth, a computer jockey with a Mac input personal messages from partiers, and the eyepopping green lasergram instantly whizzed around the top two feet of the wall: *"Debbie, will you marry me? Dodi." "Angela loves Heather." "Lindsy loves Pamela."* High-tech 3-D glasses passed out at the door made all the above appear to jump directly on one's personal head.

In the hall's center were three raised platforms for the go-go dancers—a regular lipstick lesbian three-ring circus. Not all the dancers looked or acted like typical centerfold fantasies; there was one in what looked like a long white Mexican wedding dress, and another in baggy pants doing a kind of acrobatic break dancing. Then again, there were your standard-issue fishnet-stocking go-gos; go-gos in chaps over a thong; go-go teams copping feels, humping each other's knees, sidling down behind each other, or sticking their heads in each other's butts. And of course, there was the usual audience participation, climaxing in folded dollar-bill tips stuck in the various usual go-go cracks and cleavages.

With all of this as background, one might assume that the actual partiers would be totally eclipsed. But one would assume wrong. The single most popular look was seen on the Jodie Foster no-shirt brigade: a jacket (usually black), impeccably creased pants, and a very nice bra. There were also numerous girl versions of the Marky Mark designer-underpants-peeking-over-jeans look. There were lots of femmy-girl sexy clothes: clingy red strapless minidresses, four-inch platform shoes, and so on. Then there were the rugged individualists. One very tailored woman was attired in a business suit jacket with a little dress-for-success ladies' tie, and pantyhose—period. Her partner was wearing underwear—period. Actually, there were many women here whose concept of a formal top was a black lace corset—period. But most astonishing to any veteran of Michigan or other 1970s-type women's events was that there was a total of one work shirt, and no flannel whatsoever.

If we could freeze a moment to pack into a time capsule—just to prove to the incredulous right-wing Republican little green men from Alpha What's-Its-Face who descend in their spaceship a few million years from now that lesbian chic really did happen on Earth—this would be it.

Where
the Girls Are:
Hooking Up

Several months after we went to Dinah, we sat in on a psychology class at Florida International University in Miami, where a panel of gay people had been drafted to answer the class's questions about gay life. Once this would have been Abnormal Psychology 101; this time around, there was a palpable reluctance to say anything that might offend, or seem unsophisticated. Then a big-haired girl raised her hand and blurted out, "But why do lesbians have to *look* the way they do?" An unspoken "Euuuw" hung in the air.

One of the lesbians on the panel replied that in fact, lesbians look many different ways, that many of us are conventionally "feminine," and that the lesbian stereotype—short hair, blubber bod, comfortable clothes, no makeup—is exactly the look you see on moms schlepping their kids on carts back to the station wagon at every rural and suburban shopping center in America.

It was all true. But we also know exactly what Ms. Bighair meant.

The semiacceptance of lipstick lesbians is the flip side of a profound uneasiness about what *other* lesbians look like, or are perceived to look like. When we began writing this book, we asked a number of straight friends and acquaintances to ask *their* straight friends and acquaintances the things they were most curious to know about lesbians. We were surprised by how many of the questions related to appearance—for instance, "How can you tell, by looking, who else is a lesbian?" (Answer: We personally can't, even though we have crackerjack gaydar for men.)

The oddest question to land on our doorstep was whether a blind lesbian could be seduced by a man, and if so, whether a gay man could more successfully do the job than a straight one. That particular poser definitely stumped the panel. But we assume that the asker was assuming that what most attracts a woman to another woman is the way she looks, and that everything else can be faked.

What's truly faked, of course, is high-maintenance "femininity," with its Sisyphean plucking, shaving, coloring, creaming, curling, straightening, nipping, tucking, and starving. We would fight anybody who didn't think women should have the choice to do all of those things. We do some of them ourselves, and one of us writes for a beauty magazine. But it also seems a little Orwellian that women who choose *not* to get involved in major personal overhauls—in other words, those women among us who look most like real, natural, unadorned, unreconstructed females—are the ones who get dissed for not looking "feminine" and/or "trying to look like a man."

One of the lesbian qualities that apparently seems strangest to the rest of the world is that we don't all dress to please men. Even stranger—since the measure of women's attractiveness in our culture *is* attractiveness to men—some of us are actively drawn to women who don't bother to meet that standard of beauty. To those women who can't imagine not hating themselves if they were too fat or were hairy in the wrong places, lesbians must indeed seem like a perverted bunch.

There's one school of thought that says that all lesbians should be attracted to anyone at all with two X chromosomes, because it's politically correct—Goddess forbid we should be "looksist." San

Francisco Bay Area therapist JoAnn Loulan hoots at that one. "I think most of us have preferences. I have a preference about what bread I eat, so why wouldn't I have a preference about what woman I eat?"

143

There's another school of thought that says that men, gay or straight, care intensely about a potential mate's looks, and that women, gay or straight, are far more interested in other traits. Hence dowdy lesbians who get the girl are no different from Woody Allen, Mort Zuckerman, Jerry Seinfeld, John Derek, Ted Kennedy, Henry Kissinger . . . Such theories aren't entirely off the mark, but they don't take into account the fact that plenty of lesbians look frumpy or scary *on purpose* and seek out other lesbians who look that way.

Some of this has to do with a certain thumbing of one's unpowdered, unbobbed nose at society. During rebellious eras, there's almost always an overlap between lesbian sensibility and the prevailing fashion ethos. Both hippie-girl-in-overalls and buzz-cut-pierced-punkette are styles that shriek "lesbian," but that large numbers of straight women have also adopted. The lipstick lesbian look, too, is largely a postfeminist expression that crosses gay–straight boundaries: the babe with the B-school degree, who can be tough in the boardroom and soft in the bedroom. Except that the straight women in the blood red lipstick are rebelling against the idea that women who look like that shouldn't be in management, and the gay women are rebelling against the idea that competent lesbians shouldn't wear lipstick.

For all the talk-show hoo-ha about lipstick lesbians, the category has actually been around for a long time. What's different is that these days the LL is less likely to be primping primarily to try to pass for straight.

The look isn't universal, however. With the possible exception of Miami, where the Cuban majority tends to set the pace by dressing to the *nueves,* Los Angeles may qualify as the premier lipstick territory in the nation. "In L.A., it's like who can be the most foofoo," according to Girl Bar's Sandy Sachs. "The hair, the nails, the outfits." This large-scale glamour-lesbian scene does require a car culture; put a couple of perfumed, powdered dolls on the subway or the BART, exuding sexual vibes but without male "escorts" to claim property rights, and you'll have an unpleasant encounter faster than you can say, "Hey, baby, come sit on my face." In New York and San Francisco, the glamour-puss has cross-pollinated with the tough girl to produce a Babes on Bikes look. On any Saturday night in SoHo or South of Market, you can see pairs of confident glamazons with silver-studded black leather jackets and high-gloss, ruby-red femme fatale lips. Their personal style might be called Bartleby the Shimmerer: Women like this could break the heart (or the balls) of any man, but they prefer not to.

Some lesbian looks—for instance, the real stone butch, as opposed to the fashion model in a tux—are never going to be staples in the pages of *Vogue*. This is absolutely fine with lesbians like Janis Ian, who wrote a notorious 1994 column in the *Advocate* trashing the sartorial tastes of so many of her sisters whose public displays, over the past twenty-five years of gay liberation, have created an image problem for today's more stylish sapphists. "Why are so many women I meet seemingly hell-bent on looking their worst?" she fumed. "Not just cosmetic choices like avoiding makeup or growing Sherwood Forest in plain sight, but life-threatening choices like obesity . . . Nowadays anyone imitating a Hefty Bag wearing combat boots, a too-tight motorcycle jacket and several haircuts at once is an Instant Dyke." For lesbians whose life priority is to present an acceptable image to the straight world and counter the stereotype that some girls only go for other girls because they're too ugly to get guys, the Hefty Bagladies are an embarrassment best hidden. (Perhaps the closet Ian so recently vacated is available.)

In any case, the fact remains that such looks are no barrier to a zingy lesbian love life. Although individual women may reject anyone who doesn't look like Cindy Crawford, the automatic outs that exist in the mainstream don't have a counterpart in the lesbian world. There will always be women who *like*, or at least don't mind, precisely those qualities that make heterosexuals uncomfortable— often *because* they make heterosexuals uncomfortable. The freedom not to please men makes lesbians even bolder about pleasing themselves, which in turn attracts lesbians who eroticize women who have the gumption not to please men. Take short hair. It's easy and comfortable, which makes it "unfeminine" . . . which makes it an advertisement that the person wearing it may be a dyke who doesn't care who knows it . . . which is *sexy*.

"I've got a very soft spot for butch women," said Val Scott, of Oakland, "although *very* butch women are sort of scary to me. . . . I like looking at them from the corner of my eye, while pretending to be absorbed in something else, like lint or the weather. For me, the kick is that they feel *dangerous*. They're women, but they choose masculine trappings. They trespass on men's toys, which is daring, and they're visible gender outlaws, which is risky. They go men one better in a world that is supposed to belong to men. I keep expecting them to be hit by lightning, and I'm thrilled by them."

"When I was young, I chased women who looked like straight women, because that's what the media told me I should consider beautiful," said Julie Erwin of Pomona, California. "When I got a little more sense, I began to expand my definition of beauty. For instance, I think gray hair is beautiful, and it sure is a good indication that the woman hasn't bought into the beauty industry's image. I think some dykes reject the traditional definitions of beauty as a political statement. But I also think that most lesbians, because they have had to come to terms with being different in several ways, are more comfortable with the way their bodies naturally are. And with the way that other people's bodies naturally are."

We heard from Val and Julie on a lesbian computer bulletin board, where we posted a notice asking what women look for first when they meet a potential lover. Very few takers mentioned the all-American centerfold standbys, like blond hair or big breasts. What they did cite were such qualities as wit, intelligence, confidence, thoughtfulness, playfulness, curiosity, self-awareness, warmth, independence, "someone I can think out loud with," and "whole people who make a choice to be with me, not because I can complete the missing parts of their puzzle, but because they like the way I am."

Sexual attraction's "not purely visual for me," said Helen Gallagher of Ann Arbor. "I am a total sucker for white hair, and have other preferences, but that doesn't have anything to do with who I end up getting attracted to, even instantaneously. Up in the wilds of Michigan recently, I saw a lot of naked women. And I didn't find it erotic. There were some truly great naked bodies up there, but until someone does something like flash an incredible smile, and I get to see what goes on in her eyes and face, it's interesting but not arousing, maybe beautiful but not attracting." In the end, Helen added, "it's not her hair, eye color, or general physical descriptors. It's got something to do with her stance on how she meets her world. Usually, it has something to do with surprising me and tapping into the less conventional part of myself."

Although comic Suzanne Westenhoefer has an entire routine about the throbbing vein in Martina's forearm, if there's a lesbian erogenous zone—not only for the computer bulletin-boarders but for almost every lesbian we've ever talked to—it's the eyes. Not their color, or how gorgeously they're lined and shadowed with makeup, but their effectiveness as a delivery system for the attitude behind them—"the way she looks at me." A woman with a devilish gleam and a deep, direct, knowing, "I've got your number" stare turns most lesbian hearts to smush.

If we had to make one other generalization about lesbian taste, it would be that a lot of us are powerfully attracted to women, gay or straight, beautiful or not, who look as if they can take care of themselves. "Lesbians really are very sexy. They take responsibility for themselves in a way straight women don't seem to, and I think that's a very compelling thing to see in a woman," said cartoonist Alison Bechdel. "I heard this story from a friend about a straight woman who works under her in a warehouse, who came to work in these pumps, these girl shoes, and slipped on some spilled stuff, and got all upset—hadda go home and change, and is gonna sue the warehouse for her ruined outfit, and all this stuff. I just don't have any patience with that. I just don't see what men see in straight women," she said in amazement.

Most of us do think straight women are attractive, but often only to the extent to which we can look at them and see dyke potential.

Not *sexual* potential, per se, but a certain je-ne-sais-queer take-charge style. Get a bunch of lesbians in a room and ask them which celebrities turn them on and you'll hear the same names over and over: some of them belonging to women who are lesbians or rumored to be, some of them actresses who have believably played lesbians, some of them simply straight girls with spirit. There are Melissa, k.d., and Martina, of course, but also Jessye Norman, Gabriela Sabatini, Sharon Gless (as Cagney only), Sara Gilbert (as Roseanne's spunky daughter), Katharine Hepburn, Julie Christie, Diana Rigg, Barbara Stanwyck in *The Big Valley,* Dietrich and Garbo (especially in their dykier roles), Jodie Foster, Dominique Sanda, Miou-Miou, Candice Bergen, Sandra Bullock, Ellen Barkin, Catherine Deneuve (particularly in *The Hunger*), Tina Turner, Anne Murray, Joan Armatrading, Nona Hendryx, Selena, Albita, Madonna. (Not that tomboys and dragon ladies are the only game in town. We've also met legions of lesbians who had formative crushes on two of the most milk-and-cookie-ish icons in modern culture: Julie Andrews in *The Sound of Music* and Marcia Brady of the *Bunch.* Go figure.)

The little secret of lesbians is that in our hearts a lot of us feel exasperated pity for the tradeoffs so many straight women make. The week before the 1994 Dinah, we were in Golden Gate Park in San Francisco, watching a hardscrabble, muscle-pumping game of flag football played between two all-women, mostly gay, teams. After the game, we sprawled on the grass and asked a bunch of the players about the lesbo–jock connection. The consensus was that lesbians excel by default—that disproportionate numbers of straight tomboys succumb to social pressure. "Lesbians aren't tied into that thing with the straight culture of playing up to the male," said Liz Jensen, who works for a contracting company. "If you want to catch a boy, you don't want to be as good as they are at sports."

Jensen has known some good female athletes who are straight, she added, but too many of them see sports as a means to something else, like looking good. "That takes them out of their body. If you don't care about that stuff, you can be *present* in your body. It's feeling powerful, feeling all your muscles coordinating toward whatever goal it is—a basket, a touchdown, the moment when you dodge for that grounder going in at second base and throw it without thinking. Your body is working, and you're so present that you're not thinking about your body. You *are* your body."

"I've always thought of a lesbian as someone with fire in her guts who was willing to break all the rules and just be somebody she made up herself," said Mount Holyoke College professor Jean Grossholtz. Jean had just placed in the preliminaries in her age division in the bodybuilding competition at the 1994 Gay Games in New York. (She later went on to win the silver medal.) She was sinewy but buff, wearing what looked like a few black ribbons, a sign with the number "153," and a lot of grease. "I want you to know that what this is on me is Pam." She chortled. "You can put me in a frying pan."

And, oh: She was sixty-five years old.

Jean wasn't a lifelong weight lifter; she began training for the Games only the year before. "I got into it because in the back of my head, I've always wanted to stand up, grease myself, and flex my muscles. It's not a driving need, but I always thought that would be fun. As I worked out, I began liking what I was doing and what was happening to my body. I've never abused my body, but I've been indifferent to it. As I've gotten older, I've thought about how I want to walk to my grave, not crawl or go in a wheelchair. I want to be strong all the years I can. But this training put me in touch with myself in a way I hadn't been before. It expanded my universe.

"And"—she snorted—"I also have to say that over the years, the college has had to put up with a hell of a lot from me, and this is like the final in-your-face. I'm going to have a full-length picture of me in my posing garb with my medals and have it made very large and post it all over the campus. And make them eat it! Or maybe I'll tell them that this was an experiment in deconstructing the gendered body."

We're sure that there must be lesbians who don't find older women sexy, but we haven't met them. That may be one reason why aging just isn't the trauma for lesbians that it is for so many straight women. If anything, there are lots of women like Jean, who are up for new experiences because they long ago stopped caring about doing what was "appropriate." The paradox is that because we live in a subculture that lets us age gracefully, we get to remain big kids for a long time.

Standards of what constitutes "overweight" are also looser in our community. Pendants showing the chunky Venus of Willendorf can be found in the crafts areas of most lesbian festivals, and we know of at least one lesbian 'zine dedicated to centerfolds of nude chubbies. "When you're fat in the het world you're treated like a Fat Person; I don't care if you're the president of the United States," said Suzanne Westenhoefer. "But women who love women know what we really look like." The two of us are definitely pudgier than we were before we settled into hypernurturing, two-cooks-in-the-kitchen bliss together. (Free tip for the Christian right: If you really want to terrify your flock, instead of blathering on about hellfire and damnation, why not spread the word that lesbianism often causes weight gain? Or at the very least, contentment with the body size one already has.)

"My lover tries to keep me from constantly talking about how 'overweight' I am," said writer Jewelle Gomez. "I am thirty pounds heavier than I wish to be. I want to lose it for my own image and health. But my lover *loves* the way I look. She said, 'If you lose thirty pounds I'm still going to love the way you look. But don't talk about being "fat," okay?' And you know those things under your arm that kind of waggle? She loves them, too! And I like that she likes that about me." Jewelle's girlfriend bought her a "beautiful rayon dress, like a dress from the fifties, brown and orange, sort of earth tones, *very* sheer, with a little bow." The sleeves were long, thus covering her waggling parts. "And so," Jewelle reported with a lascivious grin, "we cut the sleeves *out* of the dress."

But as she is the first to acknowledge, she herself is "attracted to all sorts of women that straight men are not attracted to. I have to keep myself from saying this to straight friends. There are a couple of straight women I used to work with, and whom I love, wonderful women. And they will *never* find a guy because they're very smart and very articulate, and they're both black, and black men are terrified of them. One of them is heavy, too. I watch myself with them, because I don't want to be like the reverse of what we complain about straight people saying to us [about how we just haven't met the right man]. But it's always on the tip of my lips: 'If you would just hang out with us, you'd have a partner' "—Jewelle snapped her fingers—" 'like that!' In the women's community you can look like anything you want. You can decide 'I'm going to wear lipstick every day' or 'I'm never going to wear lipstick.' And there will be women out there who think you're fabulous."

All of which is not to say that lesbians are never looksist. Of course we are. Sometimes we've historically even been reverse looksists, enforcing our own rigid little dress codes. Back in the 1940s, before Del Martin met her partner (in life and lesbian-feminist political rabble-rousing) Phyllis Lyon, she was married— to a man. The straight sex she recalls as "okay." But the straight shoes are another story: *"Ugh!* I remember those pointed toes. Those sling pumps. Those blisters . . ." She shook her head with a revulsion most of the world assumes lesbians reserve for quite other body parts.

By the time Del met Phyllis, who worked at the same publishing company, she was divorced, was actively gay, and had adopted a suitable sartorial style, one that impressed the still-straight Phyllis. "The day Del arrived, she was wearing her little suit and carrying a briefcase. I'd never seen a woman with a briefcase! I was overwhelmed." Shortly thereafter, there was an office party for the new girl, Phyllis reported, at which Del "spent the whole time out in the kitchen with the boys, smoking cigars. They were trying to teach her how to tie a tie."

Not surprisingly, when Del and Phyllis got together romantically shortly thereafter, Phyllis found herself, by default, the femme of the couple, complete with required nylons and femmy footwear.

"Well, I didn't mind heels so much in those days," Phyllis sighed. "And you had to do all that when you were lesbian, it's just how it was. See, everyone was into butch/femme then, and couples had one of each. So I didn't have much choice, since Del had decided earlier on she was a butch. We'd dress the roles, and she'd light my cigarettes and that kind of thing when we went out in public."

That was how you met girls, Del explained, back when nobody was talking about lesbians. "One thing about looking more masculine, doing the butch stuff, it was like we were advertising."

"When we first got here [San Francisco] and didn't know any lesbians, it was my considered opinion that anyone who was wearing a Pendleton jacket was a lesbian," Phyllis added (a bit optimistically, we feel, as this theory would lesbianize roughly the entire female populations of Vermont, New Hampshire, Maine, Oregon, Washington, and Canada). "Well, I was doing secretarial temp work, and at one job there was a woman who ran the cafeteria, who had short hair; and she wore pants, and—a Pendleton jacket! I was convinced. But I didn't know how to bring it up. You couldn't just ask. So I'd go up to her and say, 'I sure did have a *gay* old time last night. Gay, gay, *gay!*' Not a nibble. To this day I don't know if she was a lesbian."

As for Del and Phyllis personally, Phyllis confessed, "To tell the truth, butch/femme didn't really work out too well for the two of us. Del didn't have any butch *skills*."

Like, building bookcases? Fixing flat tires? "That's right! Mowing the lawn. She couldn't do any of those things. I could at least drive a nail. She said she was really a sissy butch. So we never really did butch/femme very much inside the house."

And outside the house, they ditched the old dress code a long time ago for the almost as classic merged-lesbian-couple nonidentical-twins look: similar (though not identical) sporty slacks, crisply ironed blouses . . . and comfy shoes. No neckwear. "To this day," declared Phyllis, "she doesn't know how to tie a tie."

Today the butch look is still a lesbian classic, although the woman it attracts may be a femme, a butch, a butchy femme, a femmy butch, or none of the above. The butch also might be . . . Well, for a dramatic example that dressing butch post-1990 no longer, necessarily, has to do with acting butch in the 1940s sense, look no further than man's-suited, greaser-guy-coiffed Lea De-Laria, who we would have said was the biggest butch at the Dinah

Shore Golf Classic. Like, Southern Pacific *diesel*. To our astonishment, she confessed—blushing, yet—to being a femme. "Yes. I've been doing the femme thing for a while now. One of my exes called me My Beautiful Laundress. Because I did laundry so well. If people want to think I'm butch, that's their problem. It's *Italian!* Italian, not butch."

To hear her tell it, Lea dresses like Al Capone's little brother as a respectful salute to her lesbian foremothers/fathers. Whatever. Don't push her on this. "Like, when people come up and say, 'Why do you have to wear men's clothes?' Do they walk up to a black person and say, 'Why do you have to wear dreadlocks?' Do I say, 'Okay, white person, why do you have to barbecue on the patio?'

"It's part of my fuckin' culture, and get off my ass."

You would think that since lesbians are so good at knowing what turns us on that we'd know how to go get it. Ha, ha, ha. Pardon us while we fall down laughing, taking care not to impale ourselves on the steering column of the U-Haul.

Most lesbians not only don't know how to ask another woman out on a date; it's common for us to flounder about, after the fact, over whether a certain evening out with another woman was, in fact, a date. One woman we know pays for dinner as a way to signal to her would-be date that she isn't spending a night on the town with the girls. But anything short of a full-body tackle—dressing up, bringing flowers—can be misinterpreted as "just" being nice. The two of us are so lame that we didn't know for sure that we were dating until a couple of Pamela's friends informed her that in their opinion, we were.

Straight people obviously get it about dating, but even our gay male friends (some of whom used to go directly from unacquainted to unzipped) have now leaped ahead of lesbians on the learning curve. When we recently asked our good friend Richard how he had been sure that he was on a date, he explained, "Well, we arranged to go someplace at a particular place and time, and we didn't have sex with each other."

It sounded like exactly the situation that stumps most women.

"Well, we were sexually attracted to each other," Richard said. How, we wondered, had they both known, for sure, that they were attracted to each other, and not ... you know, just really good friends with a lot in common, and warm huggy feelings, or maybe one of them was attracted and the other suspected but didn't want to hurt her feelings, and ... ? Richard chortled in disbelief. You *know*, he said.

"With guys, it was real easy to get dates," reminisced Kim Osborne of Seattle, explaining to us the pluses and minuses of being a newbie at the lesbian dating game. "I had a whole list of them who were always calling: 'When are we going to go out?' As a woman, I'm conditioned that the phone rings." Kim's first date with a girl happened at the March on Washington in 1994. She went out dancing with an ex-boyfriend, now gay. "He said, 'I'm going to find a woman for you tonight.' I said, 'Okay, but she'd better be cute.' So he picked up this woman and told me to dance with her. She asked me out. She was a *doll*. She wasn't very interested in me, as a newly coming-out woman. She was into s/m—put needles in herself to go out at night—so I was kinda like a cute toy to her. But it was really fun.

"Then I got into a relationship with a woman who was like, 'Okay, promiscuous stage is over. You are now with me.' She's in therapy now, and she hates my guts. Then came another woman I probably shouldn't have gotten involved with. She was ... nothing against Prozac, or other antidepressants, but she was on some heavy shit and had too many *issues* to deal with for me. Especially for me being a shallow lesbian when I first started sleeping with women, and just wanting to play and explore.

"In Seattle, though I don't quite know what the rules are, it seems like you have to ask around first to find out if the person's available before you ask her out. Because if the person is involved, somebody will tell somebody who will tell somebody. Then you'd better just say it's for coffee. Or *maybe* a beer. Just not a whole evening.

"Actually I just went out for dinner with a woman I met on an airplane. We were drinking beers and talking about being lesbians. It turned out we were political rivals, but by then we'd had three beers and didn't care. So we're sitting at dinner talking, and she's bemoaning how women won't just go out and have casual sex. And I'm waiting for her to say, 'Do you want to come over to my place afterward?' But no. She picked up the tab. She said, 'In a couple of weeks when the weather turns nice, why don't you come over for margaritas on the deck?' And then she dropped me off. So even when you can talk the talk . . ."

On the other hand, we noted, Kim didn't grab *her*. "Well, I probably shouldn't have," she said ruefully, "because I'm seeing someone now. Who knows? I probably will call her some sunny day and say, 'Okay, let's do the margaritas.' I probably should try just asking people more often. But I don't know what the rules are."

There were other aspects of the single lesbian life that Kim wasn't wild about. "Women are more emotionally available. But that also can be troublesome if it gets suffocating. So it's wonderful, and a pain in the ass. And with women, it seems like they're all either 'married' or in therapy. I mean, I can go out dancing and meet women who are more fringe-y, but I'm not into sticking needles all over my body. So far I haven't seen just the equivalent of regular guys coming on to you."

When Jorie Richards met the woman who is now her girlfriend, the woman volunteered her phone number—a clue of the kind that in retrospect seems like an invitation to a date, but that wasn't totally clear-cut at the time. "I knew her three or four months before I slept with her. I know the first kiss took longer than sleeping together. Because I was terrified, like this was going to be *it*. I was physically frozen. We were sitting on my couch until two in the morning talking about *nothing*. She practically had to knock me on the floor."

What was so scary? "I don't know. I was always afraid of other girls when I was growing up. I don't know if that's related to not feeling okay about being attracted to them. Like I couldn't be myself around them. I felt vulnerable to girls. But I didn't really fit in with other tomboys, either, because I wasn't butch."

Even now. Jorie added, "How I actually feel changes all the time. Sometimes my frustration is that I want to be the 'woman,' but I get put in the 'man' role because I'm a carpenter. And I tend to be more assertive about things. But that doesn't mean I want to be a guy! So I have the struggle of, 'Please, *you* tell me where we're going to dinner tonight.' Then other times I'm, 'No, let me do it.' I'd *like* to be able to let it vary, switch back and forth." In the lesbian dating game, of course, you play without rules.

Unlike straights, lesbians can never presume that the cute single woman they meet in situation X is fair game. What most out lesbians do when they're looking for a girlfriend is to find where other lesbians hang out. Then they hang out there, too. Somehow, sooner or later, there will be a meeting of the minds. Groins follow. The milieu can be anything from a gay church group to a line-dancing class; what's available depends on where you live. Historically, a prime place to meet girls, even in a small town, was on a team. "Softball," as Alix Dobkin remarks in Yvonne Zipter's book *Diamonds Are a Dyke's Best Friend,* "is the single greatest organizing force in lesbian society."

A few hours' drinking and yakking with thirty-year-old Bree, in an Austin, Texas, gay disco goes a long way toward convincing a person that softball is very possibly also the single greatest recruitment force in lesbian society.

For a living, blond-braided Bree now operates construction equipment. (What kind? *"Heavy* equipment.") Before that, though, she played semiprofessional fast-pitch softball, up until . . . Well, it sounds like an old Kate Clinton joke: "The shortstop of my team isn't talking to the pitcher, because they're sleeping with the same woman, who is the catcher." Except Bree's team didn't know from Kate Clinton jokes, because, like the jocks they were, "we didn't talk much about relationships. We talked about ball. Except when relationships affected the team—like when I started dating the team's trainer, who'd been in a long-term relationship with the second baseman . . . which I didn't know about . . . Well, I hadda quit.

"The thing was, in professional sports, homophobia is the worst. Worse than entertainment, Hollywood, all that shit. You do *not* get caught in a gay bar. And you don't look like I do now." Which is like the classic, appealingly androgynous, adolescent good old girl/boy. "You're supposed to do, like, grape-colored shorts, a tennis shirt, the big hoop earring shit. Players who coach in the schools had an image to uphold. If I was dressed like this [baseball cap—backwards, natch—and a "Virginia Polo Club" T-shirt rolled to display the Harley tattoo on Bree's skinny but strong bicep] for a game outta town, they couldn't be seen with me for fear I looked like a queer. You have no association with homosexuality whatsoever—except for the small fact that about ninety percent was lesbians. That'd be accurate, though they might not've been when they first started on the team."

Of course, Bree herself wasn't one of these lezzie-come-lately converts, she hastened to explain. "I realized I was a lesbian in first fuckin' grade. I thought, Oh man! I like girls!" After a bit deeper probing, however—about three Heinekens' worth—Bree revealed that, "well, yeah, just in terms of *sex*, I've been with a couple of guys. Three, four. In high school. I had the hots for 'em. They were cute. So, hey, okay! But when I did it, it wadn't. I mean, there's a difference. You *give* yourself to a woman. I could *never* allow myself to give myself to a man. Like when these guys and me did it, sure we were fuckin' and all, and it was fine, as fuckin', but that was about it. It was way far from makin' love, I guarantee. I always felt I was in drag or something. Guys were my friends. And also, guys are what you're programmed to think you want. I knew it wadn't. I just had to prove it, to me and to whatever. Fuckin' was really okay with guys, but I like the intimacy with women far, far more. And the physical contact with a woman—you can't beat it with a stick."

Or a baseball bat. "I met the first love of my life—and she was one of those real girly girls, at first; I couldn't stand her—when I was fifteen, on my first serious softball team. It was a real good team, an exhibition group basically, the best fifteen- to eighteen-year-old girl athletes in town. We got sponsorships from a lot of companies."

Were there other lesbians on the team? *"Hah!* That was the real big joke. It was minority-majority. You know?"

No.

"Okay." Bree explained patiently: "Startin' out we were all real young women tryin' to figure out what the hell we were doin' with our personal lives, and we had no examples, certainly about bein' lesbian. I mean, we'd been way too scared to think about that, because we'd been browbeat for so long, from a religious or whatever standpoint, about how bad it was. So starting out, the queers were definitely the minority. Everyone was kinda straight."

Kinda. "By the end of three years we played together, it was like—'Majority! The *girls!*' Of seventeen of us on the team, the hets were, like, down to two."

Were these really straight girls who had a lesbian fling because they were going through a homosexual "phase"? "It's a good question, why it happened, what's the transition from straight to gay," Bree mused. "Of course it's natural to get close to your teammates. It's like sisters. We practiced every fuckin' day after school, a minimum of three hours. We traveled every fuckin' weekend, all weekend. You didn't spend much time away from 'em. So of course you're gonna get these bonds, and you're gonna start thinkin' things, and you're wonderin' if *she's* thinkin' things, and you're *hopin'* she's thinking things, and you're gonna experiment."

"Our coach, she was the butchest woman I'd ever seen in my life. I'll never forget her. Big old fat cig hangin' out of her mouth . . . She was married, had three kids, but when she dressed feminine, it looked like drag. Her husband looked more feminine than she did. Well, she caught me sending a note to my first lover. It was just somethin' like 'I love you and I wanna kiss you,' some goofy young-kid shit. But she lost it so bad. And the shit really hit the fan."

Bree never saw her girlfriend again. "Her family arranged for her to go to college, and for me to get a job in an oil field out of town." Way out. Like, Oklahoma. But, so estranged from her working-class family that she had no place to live (she actually got to the point where she put in some time sleeping under a bridge in downtown Austin), Bree felt that a job was about the best thing she could get out of a no-win situation. And she did keep tabs on some of her former teammates. "Some got married. Then some got divorced. Now they're queer again, just about all of 'em. Except my ex-girlfriend. She got married to some bubba in West Texas, and far as I know she still is.

"But you know, I think a lot of it is more than just the amount of time you spend together. It's the team spirit. When you're eat-drink-sleepin' softball so it's this unified, this workin' machine, it brings you a lot closer together. It's hard to separate yourself from the rest of them. It's like this really weird collective that has power over everything." Bree feels that even straight men, if they're deeply into playing team sports, can have a gut understanding of this part of the closeness that develops.

Another part, though, she feels is female-specific. "I think there's a certain emancipation that comes from bein' with all women in particular; every time you have an organized effort with a bunch of women, a collective effort, that's very seductive." And some of the seductiveness is physical: "When you're using your bodies together, pushing them to the limits, for this one purpose, it's even so much more intense." The result goes beyond shared sweat, Bree insists. "A lot of it, I think, may be just an emotional response to women's energy. I've been to women's festivals where pretty much the same thing that happened on the ball teams happens on a bigger scale. Women come who, they're bi or even pretty obviously, from how they seem and what they say, leanin' towards heterosexuality. And you get 'em in this situation where women are drummin' together or somethin'. And they're like, 'Ohmygod . . . Something's movin' on its own.' " Imitating an entranced straight-ish woman, Bree stared open-mouthed as her arm magically, irresistibly, levitated to beat the drums—then slapped her bicep. "Shit! Git that arm *down!*"

The other time-honored place for lesbians to meet and mingle is the women's bar. Glitzy Dinah-style evenings are a relatively new phenomenon. It used to be that the most compelling activity at a typical lesbian watering hole took place around the pool table. You would have your regular infusions of dyke drama—ex-lovers bumping into each other and having hissy fits about who the other one was with—but no one would have dreamed of showing up in her underwear.

Before the late seventies, most women's bars were sleazy little dives, often Mafia-owned (and looking the part, from the male gorilla at the door to interior decoration inspired by a Neapolitan ice cream cake). An experience Pam will never forget from her initial foray into lesbian nightlife, around 1971, was a simple trip to the ladies' room of one of New York City's classiest lesbian bars. Musing somewhat tipsily about how unusual it was to have red shag carpet not only on the floor of a bathroom but on the walls, she glanced up from her toilet stall to check out whether there was red carpet on the ceiling, too—and found three formidable-looking brush-cut women leering at her over the walls of the adjacent stalls. Only the best for us lesbians, from the Mob and from ourselves.

Pam played music in such joints for years, and did come to appreciate parts of their raison d'être. The bars definitely offered women a zone of safety from homophobic ridicule. (If you ask a woman in a lesbian bar to dance and she turns you down, it isn't because she thinks you're the wrong sex or sexual orientation. It's just because she thinks you're a dweeb.) And sometimes even lesbians who deal very effectively in the big world need a place to be with our own, to feel support, to gain strength—and to enjoy a few hours in a microcosm where we feel unchallenged and normal for a change.

The down side is . . . Well, let's just say that we recently listened to a spiel at Parrot Jungle, one of the tourist attractions near our Miami home, about how the birds *could* leave, because the clipped wing feathers do grow back. In real life, most parrots don't fly away when they have a safe, if limited, space of their own. Nor, for years, did most lesbians.

The gay rights and feminist movements ushered in a new breed of lesbian bar, woman-owned and far less likely to be down a dark alley. Nonetheless the women's bar was in trouble in most urban areas by the nineties. Even San Francisco has been unable to support a single full-time saloon (as opposed to a one-night-a-week glam "club") in recent years.

It's a truism that lesbians spend less and stay at home more than gay men. Happily married lesbians are especially "bad for business," according to Bryher, the owner of the Wild Rose, a neighborhood women's bar in Seattle with a jukebox, a pool table, and a poster of k. d. lang on the wall. (Bryher's nickname is a tribute to the lover of the writer H.D. [Hilda Doolittle], but when she opened the Wild Rose, people started to call her "Brier.") Most bars, she explained, are just a stop on the lesbian serial monogamy U-Haul route. A woman "comes in every night, meets a lot of women, finally meets The One, and they're gone for three or four years. . . . And then they're back, and it happens again."

With such a revolving-door clientele, the regulars who traditionally kept women's bars afloat were drinkers and/or women who wanted to socialize exclusively with other women. Both groups have been on the wane. In the eighties, alcohol, the mainstay of all bars, lost tremendous ground within the lesbian community. (According to the Provincetown Gay Business Guild's calendar, for instance, lesbians attending the annual October Women's Weekend there would have a choice of seven Twelve-Step meetings per day.) "For about a year after the clean-and-sober movement started, we had probably a stronger A.A. crowd than a drinking crowd," said Bryher. "For a while it was like I couldn't get a staff! They were all going to A.A. They'd have A.A. meetings in the back room here!" Bryher now stocks a lot of juices and nonalcoholic beers.

She also began welcoming gay men. The patrons of an earlier era had been steeped in feminism and sometimes in lesbian separatism as well. In any case, they were committed to the then-radical notion of trying to wean themselves from prioritizing men, socially as well as politically. In the nineties, though, younger women tended to have gay male friends, and they wanted to party with them.

Additionally, even if younger lesbians didn't want to go out every night, when they did go out they wanted access to the kind of parties gay men had: held in expansive spaces with great sound systems, lots of gorgeous bodies, a little flash, a little trash. Suddenly there were bars with names like the Clit Club, and a typical lesbian night out on the town sounded like the wet dream of a frat boy on spring break. Lingerie parties. Wet T-shirt competitions. "Leather 'n' Lace" nights. Kissing contests. Body painting. Drag king Halloween parties. Go-go girls. (Not, we might add, go-go women. After a generation in which feminists doggedly fought to be called women, modern lesbians, especially younger ones, have decided to be girls. In addition to Girl Bar and the Girl Spot, we have Girls in the Night, Caroline Clone's rival in Miami Beach; the magazine

Girl Jock; the Riot Grrrl movement and the lesbian rock groups Two Nice Girls, the Indigo Girls, Yer Girlfriend, and Girls in the Nose.)

It would be a mistake, however, to assume that the girls are now just like the boys. If anything, all this stuff just explicitly sexualized a dating scene that, Goddess knows, needed a little goosing.

We missed the Whipped Cream Wrestling Grudge Match of the Century at Dinah, although we hung around several hours for the preliminaries. These mainly consisted of delaying the start of the bouts until everyone in the bar was sloshed enough to believe that coating the G-stringed bodies of amenable stripper-wrestlers with several cans of nondairy spray topping in preparation for the match was the hottest experience of a lifetime . . . or hot enough to bid $35 for, anyway.

By then, we had also missed the rival whipped-cream event at the Girl/Skirts party, in which dancer Giselle Garcia apparently went beyond mere Reddi Wip—she sprayed it on her fishnet stockings and invited women in the audience to lick it off—into an entire Hot Fudge Sundae Special, featuring cherries, strawberries, honey, chocolate, and bananas.

We did catch up with Giselle and her girlfriend at the hotel pool the next morning. She was a professional dancer, small, dark, earnest, and peppery with energy. We recognized her from the Saturday night "Disciples of Desire" party go-go cage, where she spent part of the evening femmed up in a wig and fishnets and part of it in baggy harem pants. Far more than sexual come-on, her routines projected enthusiastic athleticism and a friendliness that seemed equal-opportunity to all onlookers, not just those with large bills.

In fact, Giselle said, she tries to do her very most special shimmying for the shy girls. "I don't care if someone's thin or heavy or beautiful—in fact, I pay more attention to the other side, because the beautiful girls always get all the attention. And I know, because I used to be a hundred and fifty pounds, and it's incredible how different you're treated."

Giselle works in both straight and lesbian clubs, and she seemed amazed when we asked her if there were any differences between the two. "Are you kidding? Men are horrible. Women just want to relate. The worst problem I ever had with a woman is one getting angry when I wouldn't let her up on the stage because she was too drunk. I've had men actually grab me. I kick them right in the nose with my heels. I won't put up with that from anyone, but it just doesn't seem to come up with women. Women seem to have much more tact and class. Either that or at least they have more friends who are sober enough to control them!"

Who tips better? we wondered. "Guys put out more money," she acknowledged, but pointed out, "Guys *make* more money. Women put out more appreciation, so I would dance before women preferably even if I need money. When I dance in front of men I almost feel robbed, because with women it's give-and-take; with the guys it's take and take and take. It's almost like they're buying you, so they assume they can do whatever they want, they have this power, this man thing. And they try to get me drunk. Women are, 'Can I get you something?' With guys it's, 'Can I get you screwed up?' "

Giselle's dismissive comments about the relative importance of money were not the empty bravado of privilege. She had been go-go dancing for a living for a dozen years, since she was fifteen, when her conservative Puerto Rican–born mother found out she was gay. "I never exactly came out. I was *thrown* out."

And now that we're all so terribly chic? Actually, Giselle had already been drafted to do her bit on a talk show. And the part she couldn't stand was when a middle-aged feminist was brought onstage for the usual television morality play: feminist prune versus nonfeminist go-go bimbo.

"You could tell the audience really wanted us to fight." She seethed with heartfelt horror at the memory. "I got really upset! I said, 'Look, you would really love me to argue with my sister here. We may see things differently. She also came from another era, you know? She did the footwork for me. If it hadn't been for her, I wouldn't be able to sit here and be a lipstick lesbian.' "

Pulp Friction:
Sameness
and Difference

The great drama of heterosexuality lies in the attempts of two people in love to reach across a divide of difference.

Some straight people eroticize and celebrate it. Take Michael Norman, writing in the "About Men" column of *The New York Times:* "Her maternalism—her woman's sensibility perhaps, her woman's physiology for certain—separates us and sometimes sets us at odds, but without those differences I would not want her. I love the stranger she is to me, the conundrum that makes her so inscrutable. Here in this new house we thrive on the tension that nature has given us—her estrogens sending her in one direction, my androgens in the other, often on a collision course."

Other heterosexuals put a lot of sweat (and therapy) into understanding their mates. In the preface of a cover story and special section on "the dismal state of male/female relations in America," *Utne Reader* publisher Eric Utne passed along a tip to his battle-of-the-sexes-weary readers: "When locked in yet another of those recurring arguments my wife and I have about who does what in our relationship, I had a rare flash of crazy wisdom. I found myself asking that she try not to think of me as a man. Instead, I suggested, 'Think of me as your lesbian lover.' It did wonders. Suddenly we were equals—two human beings who share a host of commitments, dreams, and logistical problems."

Frankly it's hard for us—and, we imagine, most other lesbians— to read either of those sentiments without rolling our eyes. But we also appreciate that there's some human pain involved, and that people who are working to improve their relationships deserve support, not public ridicule. We think it's about time that heterosexuals returned the favor. The ways in which some lesbians bridge the sameness/difference gap, most notably butch/femme and top/bottom sexual role-playing, are at least as time-honored and as worthy of public respect as the "Vive la différence" theme of so much butch/femme top/bottom heterosexuality—maybe even more laudable, since the lesbian version requires the courage to go against the grain. But no aspect of lesbian culture is more scorned or misunderstood by the outside world.

The two of us, to be honest, are mystified as to why anyone would *want* an assigned seat in a relationship. For both of us, part of the appeal of lesbianism was the freedom from societal expectations about who does what. We also tend to eroticize the sameness of our difference from the rest of the world: We've had pleasurable fantasies about being extraterrestrials and Siamese twins.

But when we began researching this book and talking to scores of women about their sexuality, one of the surprises for us was that a large minority identified at least somewhat with butch/femme dynamics. Occasionally, we even met lesbians who were as inflexible as Jesse Helms in their belief in the eternal verity of the proposition that opposites attract. Surely, one of us must be the butch and one the femme. (But who? Lindsy manages the money, kills the bugs, fixes the computers . . . and had the kids, and wears black lace underwear. Pam drives the car, goes fishing, usually has a set of keys hanging from her belt . . . and does all the cooking, and has long, high-maintenance fake-red hair.)

We also had a hard time getting lesbians to agree on definitions. People used the words "butch" and "femme" to describe differences in appearance, in flirting techniques, in who does what around the house, and in bed. Some women used the terms interchangeably with "top" and "bottom," and others were adamant that who orchestrates sex has nothing to do with butch/femme. About the only constant was that a fair number of lesbians program *some* kind of sex-role difference into their intimate lives.

Lesbians and straights are always swimming from opposite shores when they hit the reef of sameness/difference. We take at least a certain amount of emotional synchronicity for granted, but all that comfortable womanly understanding sometimes merges into one big, snarled, codependent hairball. "A lot of women in lesbian relationships are in this pattern where they get together and become one person. They'll become this *amoeba*," said Los Angeles nightclub promoter Joni Weir, who watches the morphogenesis start on the dance floor every weekend.

Sometimes lesbian merger is a factor leading to what's known in the community as lesbian bed death: A female couple, who may be intimate in all other ways, just stop having sex. "Lesbians are dealing with femininity squared," says writer and sex guru Susie Bright. "Femininity is about merging as fast as possible, not saying what you want, not being selfish or territorial or aggressive. Trying to be as much like each other and have everything integrated, not fighting. Those feminine characteristics, doubled, are going to be natural lint traps for sexual boredom."

Lesbian couples are also awash in a double dose of the sexual moodiness that sometimes drives straight men bonkers. Somebody always has PMS, and somebody else is sympathetic. There are always two of us who have been programmed from birth to be the one who receives the candy and the flowers, and not the one who initiates sex. Even a certain frisson of hostility (from the staircase rape in *Gone With the Wind* on down) is considered part of normal, sizzling straight sex; it isn't pretty, but it has its uses as a sparkplug. Lesbians can easily get caught between an "Euuuw" reaction to sexual aggressiveness and an inability to think up anything that works as well.

"You wouldn't believe how many lesbians come up and say, 'I

don't know why you don't talk about the *romantic* side of our relationships,' " said Bay Area therapist, writer, and lecturer JoAnn Loulan. "They want to know 'Why do you just talk about sex?' Another thing that happens, and that isn't talked about, is that there are those of us, and I would put myself in this category, who can go for long periods of time—*months*—without sex, and not even *remember*. Then the second I have a partner who gets turned on to me, whether it's my lover or I'm having an affair or whatever, I am *instantly* turned on. [At my lectures], when I ask the question of who is horny no matter what—whether your girlfriend is, how your relationship is going, whether you're in trouble financially or you're having problems with your kids—only about a fifth to a fourth of the room says yes. So if you have many more women than not who need to have someone else get the turn-on going, then that's . . . difficult."

Understandably. And one way to keep a little healthy friction and challenge in the lesbian bedroom is butch/femme. "The heart about butch/femme is not about roles or certain behaviors or beliefs," said Suzanne Pharr of Portland, Oregon. "It's about some kind of edge of difference. That edge is very much what keeps a sexual attraction alive. I love butch/femme because of that. Our intimacy is based not so much on sexual activity as on verbal stuff and affectional behavior with each other, which also makes us lose that edge."

On the other hand, butch/femme is only one way of negotiating coupledom. "There is no predictability about lesbian sexuality, which is what I think makes it exciting," said JoAnn Loulan. "I know virtual twins—women who are totally alike, merged, into this, you could say, narcissistic scene. They wear each other's clothes. They *look* like each other, without trying; they're just totally into each other. And it's totally hot. Or there are the classic androgynous, Birkenstock, T-shirt–blue jeans–flannel shirt girls. Certainly they can be together and have a hot sex life." However, the bubbly former high school prom queen stresses, "I think there are definitely those of us—I'd count myself as one—who love the difference on a gender basis. I identify totally as femme. And I love women who identify as butch. The more they identify as butch, the better.

"Then there's the idea of, what percentage of the time do you want to get done, and what percentage of the time do you want to do someone? It doesn't necessarily have to be tops and bottoms. What's amazing, as I take this idea around the country, is women coming up to me with *so* many variations on that theme. Done/do. Top/bottom. Length of time you get done/do. Does she do you first or you do her first? How you initiate: actively/passively. I think if we could get a real language for lesbian sex we could revolutionize the entire world."

There are also an infinite number of ways besides butch/femme that lesbians can work the sameness/difference terrain. We met a couple of schoolteachers who said they thought of themselves as "cheerleader and jock," and that this *wasn't* the same as butch/femme. We met another couple—one of them third-generation Chinese, the other a recent immigrant—whose relation-ship dynamics, both positive and negative, were powerfully informed by their cultural differences. "I was raised to be a good upper-middle-class girl," remarked JoAnn Loulan, "and one of the things I find very attractive is the whole working-class attitude thing—the out-loud, in-your-face, fuck-you, swaggering, leather-jacket, hands-on-hips, smoking-cigarettes, bad-girl attitude. It doesn't work out so well for a relationship," she admitted. "But in the sack, it's my favorite!"

Then for other lesbians, adoption of some aspect of butch/femme has nothing whatsoever to do with an "opposites (natural or cre-ated) attract" dynamic. Many who, to the straight eye, look stereo-typically butch or femme are only or primarily attracted to women who look like themselves.

And there are lesbians who don't look butch/femme at all, but are. We were awfully surprised, for instance, to learn that butch/femme was a dynamic for a couple we know who are both very conventionally attractive, successful professional women. They ex-plained that one of them is a "femmy butch," and the other is a "butchy femme."

Even within classic "Me Tarzan, you Jane" couples, there are subtleties that the outside world doesn't get—mostly about the

Tarzanettes, who are assumed to be second-rate male wannabes, but also about why any woman would prefer them. In fact, according to Susie Bright, "most lesbians prefer a woman who has a feminine to cutely tomboy appearance. Only a minority prefer obviously butch women. Just as well! I wanna keep 'em all for me!"

The only down side of dealing with butch sexuality, she said, is that "a lot of butches like to see you get aroused first, or you have to come first before they can come. This is one way they're not like men. They have to get you off spectacularly, and that's what lets them get over; they can't give it up until then." She sighed. "In the beginning that seems like a dream come true. But further along in the relationship, it can be hard when you always have to produce this huge orgasm."

"Butches live to serve," added JoAnn Loulan. "That's totally different from a guy. [Butches are] invested in making women happy. There's a particular kind of gentleness about butches, that's all about them wanting to care for me."

Writer Jewelle Gomez remembered being eight years old and "having very specific sexual desires for older women in uniform, like the crossing guard. Ooooh! I don't know what deep-seated reason I had for enjoying the uniforms. Maybe because I grew up in such a liberal home, the sign of authority became eroticized. I don't know. But a brass-button jacket, a little fringe on the shoulders . . . Women who dress like that are *dashing!* They're crisp! I always go for butch women. I've hardly ever been with a woman who wore makeup and dresses. I might think that person was attractive, but there's a way that, in some cases, we look for our complementary partner. Sometimes it translates into butch/femme, and sometimes it doesn't.

"But as I work this through as I get into maturity, in some ways I'm looking at a set of behavior that's linked to my great-grandmother. She was Native American, so she was very ramrod straight, very laconic. Her authority came through her persona, tight and silent. I would always be attracted to a woman who would come into a room and kinda not say much—which generally came in a butch package." Grandma clones? So much, we noted, for the stereotype that women are attracted to butch women because they remind them of a guy.

Jewelle described her lover to us: "[She] fits the stereotypical butch look, but, in counterpoint, is an extremely sensitive Cancerian person who likes to talk in very minute detail about how she feels and how I feel. She's my prince! She moves fast and kind of unapologetically, and some people would say abrasively, and she's New York Jewish, which I think is grating on people out here [in the Bay Area]. She's got this toughness. It's like a sense of otherness, an understanding that she is different than what people perceive women should be. As a young person, I always admired that, because that would be the lesbian you'd recognize on the street. I admired that outness, although there wasn't a word for it then."

The typical femme often thinks that men couldn't possibly cut it as butches, rather than the other way around. "Gender is contextual," said a femme from Eugene, Oregon. "I experience myself as very femme in comparison with butch women. In comparison with straight men, I really *don't* experience myself as femme. With straight men I feel aggressive, bitchy—not particularly female or sexy. Because I've never experienced this innocent, passive femaleness that I was supposed to. And I *wanted* to be female. It's only within butch/femme with women that I feel femmy in a female way that is really powerful. My femaleness is not in relationship to maleness or masculinity. I've been femme-on-femme and I may yet become it again, but at this point in my life my femaleness is in relation to butchness."

Most of all, butch seems to put romance in lesbian life. "There are some social gestures which used in one way are pointless and overbearing and chauvinist" when done by most men, "but if used in another way are flirtatious and seductive," said Susie Bright. "And I think it stands out more for you when a woman does those things, too, because she's violating her gender script. So when a woman sends you a drink or opens the door for you or pays for the meal or pulls out the chair, you go, 'Oh, wow.' It's hard for men to compete with this. It's like *The Crying Game,* one of the soppiest love stories, and you never would have believed it between a man and a woman, but between two men it was heartbreaking. One of the ironies is how our love stories can epitomize parts of hetero love stories that heteros are too cynical to believe in anymore."

Butch/femme in the nineties tends to be playful and even fluid, something that adds spice, not something that diminishes women's options. Karena Rahall, a twenty-six-year-old New York University prelaw student, looks from a distance like a tall, gorgeous, probably gay man. One night when we were hanging out with her at a trendy SoHo bar, she was refused entrance to the ladies' room by a scandalized straight woman. ("I have to start walking in with a Tampax in my hand," she mused.) Karena explained that her boyish appearance is actually utilitarian. "Women know I'm a dyke when I walk down the street. It's a lot easier to attract women when you're marked, and I love that. What I look like now makes it much easier for me to meet lesbians than it was when I had really long, curly hair. I didn't get called 'sir' when I had that hair."

Karena added, however, that the way she looks isn't predictive of much of anything. When she goes out to the Clit Club and Café Tabac, she always lets the other woman make the pickup moves. "Femmes are intimidating to me. They always make me feel like a geek, until they flirt or something. Then all is well."

In bed, it's a mixed bag. "In terms of top and bottom, I'm a little befuddled at any investment in either category unless we're talking about s/m. Otherwise I find it more fluid; I like both positions. I will usually let my lover decide, unless she wants me to—but that's the same thing as her deciding, isn't it? Most of the femmes I've slept with consider themselves tops. This could just be the type I attract. But the whole notion of butch/femme and its relationship to top/bottom and feminine/masculine is so muddy. There's no rules with any of this. There are feminine butches and butch femmes. There are femmes who like to strap it on and butches who like to get fucked with dildos and on and on. At a certain point I suppose one just throws out the whole notion of butch/femme because it seems devoid of any hard definitions. So why does it survive?"

Well, we asked Karena, what do *you* like about it? She thought for a moment. "There are certain theatrical elements I like playing with—wearing a suit or a tux and flirting wildly and lighting women's cigarettes. But I think what I like most about butch/femme is just that it re-marks gender. I know that many women find it constraining and think of it as some kind of hetero-sexual paradigm, but really, it's closer to a paradox. And I find that very subversive."

One of the reasons butch/femme has had a bad rep with lesbians is that during the fifties and early sixties, roles were sexist and set in cement. (Of course, so were Ozzie and Harriet's roles, and no one uses them to bash heterosexuality.)

"In those days when I came out there was a lot more rigidity than now," said Kathleen Saadat. Kathleen, fifty-three, lives in Portland, Oregon, where she has worked as executive director of the Oregon Commission on Black Affairs, as state director of affirmative ac-tion, and, most recently, as a staff member of the Portland City Commission and an activist in the No on Nine campaign. Back in the bars in Missouri in the fifties, "The first question I got was 'You butch or femme?' You didn't wanna be called a pancake, somebody who flips over—or a sooner, that would "sooner" be one thing as another.

"So you did some things because they were the role, not because you believed in them. Like how you treated women. Sexism. You learned to objectify women, in the way men do. You walk in and stand a certain way. You look at them a certain way, ignore them a certain way. You'd disappear for two days and let them worry about you. And this is what you did if you wanted to be a 'stud,' which was the word we used at the time. Girls were 'fish' or 'bitches.' Like 'Where's your bitch?' Friendly.

"As a butch, you developed this untouchable attitude. I remem-ber once a young man who worked in the bar dared me to go across to the shoeshine parlor across the street and get a shine, like the guys. I went. Just sat right down, put my feet down, and read. Never cracked a smile. I was absolutely terrified. But I had to do it, to prove I was a butch. It let me know a lot about what men do and why they do it. And some of it's because women let them."

The oldest of four children, Kathleen was the only girl in a family of teachers, journalists, and civil rights activists. But she wasn't without strong female role models. "Members of my family were protesting way before the sixties. Stuff like the fact that women who were teachers in the Missouri school system could not be married. My mother, who is now ninety-four: Recently we went to Lane Bryant, because she was going to buy me some things. They asked if she had a store charge card. She said, 'No. When I first got married, you wanted me to put my charge card in my husband's name. You wouldn't let me keep it in my name. So I sent it back to you.' " Kathleen felt "gay for as long as I can remember. I loved women. I knew who I wanted to be close to. So I was going to be a boy when I grew up. I didn't know how that was going to happen, but it *was* going to happen. And my fantasies would pretty much fall into that butch/femme framework. Being a hero. Taking care of the woman. As I got older, I realized at least I was not going to be the person who stayed home. I wanted *adventure* in my life. I had boyfriends. And I liked 'em! But I didn't want to get married to them and have kids."

Even before she turned twenty-one, she was in the bars every night, "in men's shoes, socks, undershorts, slacks, shirts, jacket. Cut my hair short like a man. If I was dressing up, a man's tie. In the summer, I wore Bermuda shorts, like the guys were doing. But I had two outfits, because I couldn't wear that to work; I was working at Washington U. as a lab technician. On Saturday night I'd go to Bill's with my friend, because she had a car. Bill's wasn't very big. You'd open the door and there was a bar running from front to back. Tables in the middle, a tiny dance floor, a jukebox, and a kitchen behind that with the best hamburgers and fries in the city. He'd cut the fries himself, fresh when you ordered. It was dark. And I spent a great part of my life then—I laugh at this now—dressed all in black, sitting on the end of that bar, staring into my drink (whiskey straight; I don't drink whiskey anymore), looking mysterious . . . and catching girls. They'd want to take care of me! They wanted to know what was bothering me, to heal me."

For all the butch bluster, it was the femmes who did the footwork. "No matter what anybody butch wants to say, when you get in the bedroom, you're a *girl*. I don't care how many suits you own, how many ties you have, I don't care nothin'! It feels safer to take the chance in a gay bar, but still, the few times I approached a woman stand out in my mind. I just wanted to run, I was so scared, there seemed to be so much at stake. The safest thing to do is sit there and be however you have to be to make people come to *you*. And when I was very young, whoever came, that was what you were gonna respond to."

Eventually, the butch role became a kind of prison. "I can remember arguing with a woman and saying, 'Don't talk to me like that. I'm a man!' And I watched those words fall out of my mouth and thought, What the fuck does *that* mean? It took me a while to analyze it. What I meant was, I'm somebody to be respected. But it was in that paradigm of man/woman. When I figured out I didn't need to be a man to be respected, that was another move along letting go of being so immersed in the idea of butch/femme. I think what it did to you most in the old butch/femme culture, what it does to men still, is distort your view of what you are or who you could be. You made sure lots of women were crazy about you, and therefore you were a man by virtue of having another thing to check off on your list."

Between 1957 and 1970, when Kathleen moved to Oregon, "I'd had more than a hundred women. Either one-night stands or three-day things. It was like *the* apartment. If you came in, you didn't get out unless you slept with the apartment owner. And there were very few with whom I wasn't successful. It was a whole seduction thing: powder in the sheets, music, courtship. Girls love it! And they don't get it from guys, okay?"

About a third of Kathleen's conquests were straight women. "You give her a present. I've met women who'd never been given a birthday present. You get a split of champagne for someone who's never had champagne, and two glasses, and you're standing there in your white shirt, grinning at her . . . I still had my teeth then. You say, 'This is for you, baby.' And she cries. I've made love to women who started to cry, and I've said, 'What's wrong?' And they'd say,

'No one's ever touched me like this, no one's loved me like this.' That's what they were after: the touch, the gentleness, the kindness. Somebody who was going to be involved *with* them, not somebody who was gonna do something *to* them. See, because even with all this butch stuff, I never believed that you *make* a woman come. That's not your prerogative. That's hers. When you go in with that attitude of, We're going to do this together, that's different from someone who goes in to prove himself a man on your body. Which is what I think had happened to a lot of these women."

In 1968, Kathleen began a four-and-a-half-year relationship with a woman who had seven children. "It takes a while—a lot of exposure, I think—to come to a consciousness that you don't like what you're doing, and you don't want to do it anymore. And then you have to figure out how to deal—how to stay on the street, but make changes of some kind. But for me, some kind of change had to happen. Because I genuinely *like* women. When I got with Ginny, I looked at her kids and thought, I don't want them to think I'm like this. That was the beginning of the change. I stopped wearing men's clothes so much. I wore slacks, comfortable clothing, but not the tailored men's things. You see, I liked the children and I wanted them to like me. I wanted something different than the kind of relationship that left me as sort of the step*father*, instead of someone who was playful and interesting and who was interested in them. I didn't want to be who I saw men be, or treat women the way they do.

"And the more I learned about myself, the more I was able to let go of a lot of it. Still, there's also a part of me that retains what I call the butch element, that might be defined later in my life as 'style.' Looking people in the eye. Being direct about what I think. People see that as male. I don't. I'm attracted to it in women.

"Then I went back to school, Reed College, in 1971, and feminism was all over the place. So the transition was two things. One was what was happening in my personal life. And the other was butches moving towards a feminist perspective. I see them as connected." She also changed sexually. "I was pretty hardass about all that—where you could touch me, when you could touch me, if you could touch me. And *don't* touch me, mostly. I touch you, you don't touch me."

When she and her lover eventually broke up, it was not because of butch/femme considerations, Kathleen said, but because of pressures that were put on the relationship when she went back to college. In subsequent relationships, and on her own, she's tried to negotiate an identity that feels authentic, but not restricting. Her last lover "was very feminine—but not. She wears high heels, makeup, is very flamboyant. And I like that. At the same time, she's a person who . . . Well, when we were first together she was downstairs building something. And when I said, 'Do you need me to cut that?' she turned right around and said, 'I've had a carpentry class. I've got my own saw. I don't need your help.' I liked knowing she could fix the furnace. She's the best cook I ever met, but I'm a good cook, too.

"We dressed up one night to go to a drag queens' bar. I said, 'Okay, I'll put on a dress and you wear the pants.' Sondra put on a tux, bowler. I put on a long black skirt and a feather boa. She'd never gone out like that among the lesbian group. We walked in, and I was promptly seated and had my cigarette lit for me. She had to stand up! And it all had to do with what clothes we had on.

"Younger lesbians have more options in everything—dress, hair, how they act. When I was coming out, I didn't feel I had any options. They can go butch-on-femme, femme-on-femme, butch-on-butch. We couldn't have. My very good friend Goldie, who was very butch, I just loved her and thought she was beautiful, truly gorgeous, from the first time I saw her. But we would never've slept together. It would have been just outrageous. And we'd have been put down a lot."

But Kathleen sees something similar happening today, to lesbians who step outside the fold in other ways. "It's interesting to me that we spend so much time discussing the label. When women I know who have been lesbian part of their lives come to me and say, 'I know you'll be upset, but I'm sleeping with a guy,' my question is 'Is he good to you?' Because the revolution I'm working for is one where you get to do what you want to do with other consenting adults. What is this compulsion to dig ourselves into little slots, like men and women do? I think it's about arranging yourself so that you don't feel beyond certain limits. That's what guys do. I know what it means to have sex with most of your body shut down, so even when you're having a sexual encounter there are limits to what your body's gonna feel. You're talkin' to somebody who wore boxer shorts."

We wondered what Kathleen wears now. "White cotton underpants." She grinned. "Basic J. C. Penney. And white socks."

Could she ever be attracted to another butch? "Highly unlikely," she shot right back. Then she considered. "I figure it's back to the old thing—somewhere in me, that germ of being afraid of being submissive in some way. But that's a good question. I like that question; it leaves me something to consider, because I never think of it that way. Even when [my most recent ex] would put on jeans and a belt and a shirt, she always looked femmy to me, very womanly. The butch things about her, certain gestures and all, were not outstanding. Her *thinking* sometimes was. That's why I get back to style. The deeper question is, What makes us attracted to other people? I don't know. I don't think I've ever been with anybody who looks like me. Most of the women I've been committed to have been browner than me, smaller than me. . . . I probably just wouldn't be attracted to another round-faced my-color black woman. Even if she was femmy, I probably wouldn't. Unless she was truly dramatic in some way. Because I consider myself very reserved."

"Let's do lunch!" said Sharrin Spector, yelling slightly to overcome a bad phone connection from her Pacific Northwest base to our Atlantic Southeast one.

"Great!" we agreed. "Where?" This won't be our first interview trip to Seattle by any means, but we aren't really familiar with lunch spots where it's quiet enough to talk and tape.

"Why don't you just come over here to the house?" Sharrin suggested. "We can eat in my dungeon."

Sharrin is a professional dominatrix. We hadn't yet met her, but had connected through a listing in a Seattle gay-business directory for Powersurge, an international lesbian s/m conference. As well as being a Powersurge producer, twenty-eight-year-old Sharrin is a longtime member of Outer Limits, the biggest s/m group in town—

but far from the only one. Although Seattle is far better known for camping equipment (the outdoors stuff, not the gay kind), its lesbian leather community is actually one of the oldest in the country, Sharrin told us. "When I joined Outer Limits, you had to be sponsored by someone in the group, go through a three-month waiting period where you attended events with your sponsor but had no voting privileges, and then you were put on probation for a year. It was cloak-and-dagger, a secret organization, to protect members. This was before Madonna.

"Now it's easier to get involved. We have public forums and talk about what we do. I think what happened with lesbians into s/m is several years ago, with the rise of lesbian visibility, lesbian s/m has gotten very trendy and chic. So there's a lot of access, if you live in a somewhat cosmopolitan area. Here there are three clubs that have s/m fetish nights, meetings, educational forums, so much going on that every weekend there's probably *something* s/m-related going on."

Including private dungeon luncheonette parties. "I'll bring my lover," Sharrin said. "Bear. Bear Thunderfire."

"We'll bring a picnic," we said, rising to the challenge.

Sharrin and Bear's house was indistinguishable from any of its neighbors in their working-class neighborhood, and Sharrin, who answered the door, looked similarly suburban-normal. Naturally redheaded, with matching all-American freckles, quite short, and perhaps a hundred pounds overweight, she was wearing a below-the-knee rustic print cotton housedress that needed only a couple of chocolate-mouthed toddlers grabbing the hem. This was not Barbarella.

We could not help but note, however, that lying prominently across the floor right inside the door was a humongous mace, one of those spiked iron-volleyball-on-a-chain things you always see in pen-and-ink illustrations of good knight–versus–evil knight fights. Saintly Sir Galahad is never the one carrying it. (Guinevere wouldn't even have been able to *lift* it.) Clutching our brown picnic bag from Seattle's Pike Place Market, we stepped over it, very carefully.

"These are my *other* work clothes," Sharrin noted, smiling. It turned out that she wasn't just a professional dominatrix; she also counseled terminally ill women. This was the job she had trained for; her master's, from Antioch College, is in whole systems design, with an emphasis on women's health care. Domination was just her day job. "Between the time I began graduate school and the time I got out," she explained, "I found the job market had changed. When I started school, a degree was all a therapist needed to get work. By the time I got the degree, everyone was demanding experience. I looked for a job seven months."

Fortunately, Sharrin had meanwhile picked up experience in a somewhat different field. "To put myself through grad school, I took phone sex. So I'd sit there writing papers, and I'd be going, 'Oh! *Ohhh! Ooooohhh!!* F1, footnote.' Finally, a friend who knew I was personally into s/m said, 'Sharrin, you have a dungeon. You have the equipment. Why don't you try it?' So I took out a few ads."

The rest is history. At this point, Sharrin frankly admitted, the domination business pays for the therapy practice. Shrinking is approximately $60 per session. Spanking is $175 an hour. "And for some domination clients I do overnight sessions." Even with the multihour discount ($250 per hour and a half, $325 for two hours), it adds up. But does Sharrin have to stay up all night? "Oh, no. *They* do. Come on in and meet Bear."

A former corporate executive at Nintendo, Bear was now a professional piercer at Sin, a local fetish store. Unlike Sharrin, Bear favored the classic s/m lesbian leather-and-denim look; but, like her partner, she was very heavy (she looked to outweigh Sharrin by twenty pounds or so, and breathed alarmingly audibly even climbing a flight of stairs), and very friendly. Several local lesbians had described Bear to us as formidably butch, but she actually had the same ingenuously open facial expression and gently high-pitched, super-accommodating, good-as-gold vocal tone that children adopt about three weeks before Christmas. It was hard to see what was so scary about Bear, unless it was simply, as she explained, not jibing with the usual PNW look. "The Northwestern dyke image is not butch/femme. Up here, it's androgyny. And softball. And cats." Cats are the only listed item that Bear and Sharrin do. (And they don't do just the nine-tails kind. Also present for the interview, especially the lunch portion, were Princess, Boxer, Little Bear, and Minnie the Moocher; many additional felines were running around the backyard.)

Well, to be fair, the local lesbians were possibly swayed in their assessment by Bear's personal piercings: fourteen of them, most of them metal studs, rings, and barbells, quite thoroughly adorning her nose, eyebrows, lips, and ears. There were more, but some were not visible. Clearly, this is a woman who always has to get to the airport an hour early.

"The tongue thing is the greatest piercing ever invented, as far as I'm concerned." Sharrin grinned suggestively. "Very functional."

Just don't eat ice cream before going down on your girlfriend, we cackled. Bear frowned, perplexed. "Why not?"

Oops, forgot you're into s/m. Silly us!

"So let me give you the tour," Sharrin said cheerfully, leading us down into the cellar, into a large central room whose centerpiece was an antique wooden school desk. "This is the dual-purpose room, as I call it. It works for naughty schoolboys, because we have this little classroom setup." The "boys" reference is literal; though Sharrin actually has sex only with women, virtually all of her paying customers are men—and they don't know about her private life. "I identify as a lesbian, except to my clients. To them I identify as bisexual, because to identify as lesbian would threaten them. Only three clients know I'm a lesbian, and it's taken a year to build that trust to the point where they won't run away."

We were puzzled. With "lesbian" porn videos so popular with straight men, what's threatening? "Because when my clients walk in that door I'm totally in charge. And the main illusion straight men have about lesbians is that lesbians hate men. And are gonna chop off their dicks. And when you're in the position of wielding a whip, with that stereotype in someone's mind . . ." Got it. Not great for business.

"And by some lesbian standards," she added, "I *am* bi, because I touch men—though not sexually. I'm very careful about that. The law is very specific in Washington: Someone can masturbate in your presence, and/or ejaculate, as long as you're not touching them. So I don't. The only way they could bust me is possibly for assault. What I do is entirely legal. I have a client who's a D.A. And the person who owns this house is a vice cop. He's a cool guy. He's lived upstairs. He knows this all exists."

Next to the desk was an unidentifiable but very traditional-looking piece of furniture that looked as if it had been constructed from a colonial-era sailing ship's knotty-pine hatch cover. "This has a great history to it. It was built by a sixty-year-old blind carpenter, a woman, who does all her woodworking by hand, by touch, just feeling the curves." What it is: "A horse. You lay someone over it, and then tie them up on it." Aside from dungeon equipment, Sharrin explained, the olde craftswoman earns a living building miniature scale-model replicas of yuppies' yachts. Her shipshape high-gloss varnished finish is ideal for Sharrin's clients: no splinters.

"My main woman client is an ex-nun, forty-five years old, who's into heavy flagellation. She comes in, takes off her clothes, except for this little teddy; she bends over that horse, and I paddle her. Her whole gig is she takes care of this ninety-year-old woman, and every time she yells at her employer, she puts five dollars in a jar. Then when she's collected enough five-dollar bills, she comes here. She's a virgin, asexual. She sees me because I'm not as threatening as a man—and there won't be any sexual contact; she assumes I'm a straight woman, so why would I be sexually attracted to her? So I say things like, 'I'm going to punish you for being bad to the old woman. You should have kindness in your heart towards her.' And she says, 'I'm sorry, I'm sorry, I'll be better, I'll be more kind.' So much of the dominatrix business is total illusion. It's like a cross of being an actor and a social worker."

We trooped across the dark cellar to a smaller, sheet-partitioned cubicle. "This is my cross-dressing room. An amazing amount of my business, about seventy-five percent, is men who want to be dressed up as women and treated abusively. And they identify as straight—yes *all* of them. They come and see me because it's safe, they can live out their fantasy and then go home to their wives. I encourage a lot of them to talk to their wives. But a lot of my clients gave their wives copies of *Mrs. Doubtfire* to see how they'd react to the cross-dressing, and"—she shook her head regretfully—"they all, like, went, 'Eeeuw.' "

Sharrin took an absolutely fabulous white-lace-trimmed black maid's costume off the rack. "This is authentic right down to the buttons, custom-made by a seamstress I work with, for a client I see two or three times a month. He's really into being a French maid. Yes, he does speak French."

There was much black latex and PVC vinyl, mostly bustiers and miniskirts. There was even an Alpine milkmaid dress. "Yes, Heidi. And this is the big fetish." Sharrin held up a bra. "Lingerie. Female underwear. Don't ask me why." Any women clients who want to dress as guys? Sharrin shook her head. "Nah. They can do that by going down to Goodwill and buying a suit."

The next dark alcove held a physician's examining table, complete with stirrups, trays of medical instruments, a bedpan, and traditional Nurse Ratched operating-room garb. "This is the medical room. I bought all this from a gynecologist; I even have all the old diaphragm rings. You know, the whole fantasy of the nurse coming in with the mysterious formidable equipment . . ."

Any women clients who like to do this medical stuff? No? None at all? Sharrin snorted. "Give me a break! Would *you* pay someone to get in the stirrups, for *fun?*" She sighed. "I'd love to have more women clients. But I'm unusual in that I've seen regular female clients at all; that's a rarity in the domination business. And I have no gay female clients, that I know of."

Not even one paying lesbian customer? Why not? Sharrin smiled. "Because they can get it for free."

"We *play* with lesbians." Bear smiled bigger.

"There's one more room down here, our sling room," said Sharrin, opening the door to a smallish space that actually looked sort of cozy, for a dungeon. "It's got a bed in it which I sometimes bring out, to tie clients to. But I don't bring clients in here. Ever. That's sort of our sacred space, Bear's and mine, because we both do s/m—for ourselves, I mean—and we need a space to do it that's not connected to my business."

Not only does she keep separate physical spaces for business and pleasure, Sharrin said, but also the whole dynamic is different when she's doing s/m for pay rather than play. "And my play has changed as a result of being a professional dominant. The illusion with clients is, they're the bottom, I'm the top. The reality is, they're paying me to be anything they want me to be. So privately, when I play for *me,* the first thing is I want to design the scene, instead of catering to someone else's pleasure.

"And I play much harder than I work." Clients can't go home with those telltale handcuff burns.

"And I want to play with people I know and trust. So I've tended to trick less; I have many, many paying clients, but only seven women I play with regularly."

Sharrin and Bear are in what Sharrin terms "a committed non-monogamous relationship." What that means is that "intrinsically I know who Bear is and that I can't fulfill all her needs, and I accepted that from the beginning. So that gives us an ability to create a different kind of partnership. Not that it's easy. I think it's the hardest kind of partnership there is, because we're constantly bringing in outside forces. There are jealousy and insecurity issues. Sometimes other people fall in love with one of us. Sometimes one of us falls in love with other people, a little bit. But in a different way. I know her heart lives here."

"Sometimes we fall in love with each *other* all over again," added Bear. "That's happened often."

"And we do have rules," said Sharrin. "The basic rule is, if either of us feels threatened by another person, the other of us doesn't do anything with that person."

Certain sexual dynamics, too, are reserved only for each other. "I came out as a bottom, but now I am primarily a top. Bear and I bottom to each other, only—we're an unusual couple in that respect, because we are both tops. But our bottom space is kind of sacred to us. We don't do that publicly, with anyone else. Because I got fucked over as a bottom in this community, both physically and emotionally. Even though there are supposed to be rules in s/m, I found people let their own issues get in the way. The thing about topping is, there has to be a lot of responsibility. There has to be a lot of after-care."

"Once you take someone out there emotionally and physically, you have to be a cushion they come back and fall into," Bear added earnestly.

"Especially because when you're in the realm of s/m, you're dealing with a lot of possibilities for emotional baggage, so sometimes . . . *things* . . . happen," Sharrin said carefully.

Traumatic childhood flashbacks, triggered by s/m's intense power (and being-stripped-of-power) play? "Yeah. Often sexual abuse . . . It's amazing to me how many people involved in the s/m lesbian culture are survivors of some sort of abuse." Sharrin and Bear's circle of lesbian acquaintances includes women who have lived through incest, several who believe they were the victims of ritual abuse, and three multiple-personality hostesses.

However, Sharrin hardly espouses the old view of lesbianism as a booby prize for pathetic male-wounded casualties who now can't handle the rigors of the real thing. She sees lesbianism as the winner's position (to the very limited extent, that is, to which it results from negative feelings about men rather than positive feelings about women). "It makes perfect sense, when your trust is broken as a child with the male authoritarian figure in your life, that you turn to other, safer kinds of emotional support!"

"And s/m does seem to help women work through these issues," claimed Bear. "But you have to be careful. Sometimes tops are emotionally unavailable after a scene—which is fine *if* that's what you've negotiated; it's not a necessity after a scene. But so many tops don't talk about after-care, don't take responsibility for negotiating that in advance. And then people who do need it get left feeling used"—as Sharrin did.

"Being a bottom is like lending someone a piece of yourself for a period of time. And it's the top's responsibility to give the gift of that submission back, by taking care and reempowering." This is something Sharrin and Bear trust only each other to do, and why Sharrin became, otherwise, a top. "Being a top is like being a therapist . . . sometimes."

There are also specific acts Sharrin enjoys with Bear and other female playmates that she will not do with clients. "I don't do any nudity with clients. I usually wear a floor-length skirt with a slit up the back. I have about eight of them in different colors and fabrics—it's just what I'm most comfortable in. It's sexy but not revealing. And some sort of lace top with a corset—I always wear a corset. And four- or five-inch heels. That's how I came up with what I charge. My attitude is, it's fifty dollars for me to put on a face full of makeup. It's another fifty to put on a corset and, like, not breathe for three hours. And then the shoes are seventy-five dollars right there."

Despite the Dykes on Spikes price tag, Sharrin identifies as a lipstick lesbian and a femme. "But I came out as a butch dyke, because of where I lived and who I was with," she explained. "My first lover was a femme, and I met her in northernmost Arizona, where they were into that old butch/femme role stuff in a pretty traditional way." "Traditional" meaning each couple has one of each; and since Sharrin was only fourteen, her lover had already gotten first dibs on roles. "So identifying initially as a butch was really mostly circumstance. Then I moved to the Hudson River Valley, and the atmosphere is not about butch/femme at all. It's about survival. You wear flannel, because it's warm. So I did. Then I moved out here and came out as a femme."

Bear is a butch . . . or at least, that's what her friends tell her. "I've liked to wear a bow tie since high school, and my role models have always been Humphrey Bogart and Fred Astaire," she explained. "Having this gentlemanlike quality, I think, shows respect to other women. But it's not like I even identify myself as butch. To me, it's just how I'm comfortable." We noted that even here, among women whose sex lives are theoretically the most structured in lesbiandom, there's a fair amount of fluidity.

That reminded Sharrin of something else she doesn't do with clients. "No water sports. It's too intimate to me. And I don't *like* doing enemas for clients." She sighed. "But I get a lot of call for them. Well, should we do lunch? We can pull this table over and use it to eat on, if you'd like. It's wipable . . . as every surface in this dungeon is."

Okay. And *heeeere's* lunch! Half a dozen menacingly crimson armor-clad denizens of the deep tumbled out of the bag, which came from a waterfront fish stall. We had decided to bring lobsters—not the relatively soft-shelled Maine kind, but those virtually bullet-proof West Coast native tough guys—to see what these tough girls were really made of.

Sharrin and Bear recoiled six inches. "Oh! How . . . fun," gasped Sharrin, looking dubious. "I wonder how we can crack these open."

What? Hey, we pointed out, gesturing around us, you've got a whole *cellarful* of instruments of torture. How about that big spiked mace in the front hall? "No!" they both hollered, in scandalized unison. "That's our *doorstop!*"

Collecting herself, Sharrin scooped up the lobsters and disappeared. Much slamming was heard from the kitchen. Within minutes, she reappeared with a piled platter, the perfect hostess.

Obviously Bear's name is not quite the one her parents bestowed on her, we suggested. "That's true. My last name, Thunderfire, came from a vision I had. To me Thunderfire is something that's created in a moment of passion." She interrupted herself to speak to Sharrin, who was serving her lobster pieces. "Um, I really don't want a head, where all the brains are. A tail would be nice," she proposed, her voice even more super-accommodating than usual. "And 'Bear,' it came to me that was my clan."

Evidently, the lesbian leaning toward alternative spirituality—particularly, the emotional tie to Native Americana—is not restricted to the Birkenstock Bunch. Bear first discovered her clan, she explained, "as a kid, running around in the woods."

In Washington State? "Well. No. I was born in the Bronx. And then I was raised, um, in a semi-rural area . . . near the Delaware Water Gap . . ." Bear cleared her throat. "Within thirty miles."

Ah, a Jersey girl.

"Yeah," she said. "Dover." Plainfield and Montclair, we confessed. We are everywhere—and we understand; considering the relative likelihoods of gay-bashing and "Garbage State"–bashing, it's really much, much easier to come out as a gay person than as a person from New Jersey.

And Bear's original name? "Um. It's not like I'm ashamed of it or anything," she explained. "I just . . ." She looked to her dominatrix girlfriend for help. Sharrin, however, was preoccupied. Poking gingerly inside her lobster bod, she had uncovered two bright-red roe sacs. "Eeeuw, there're little baby lobsters in here."

"Well," Bear conceded reluctantly, "when my mom was carrying me, she went to see—you know the movie *Bambi?* Well, you know how the mother deer is really very strong? And independent, really. Yeah. So my parents decided to call me, um, Bambi. My birth last name is Lustgarten. Garden of Joy."

What was especially nice about watching Sharrin and Bear together was that both of these women, whose combined weight would make up at least five of the average fashion-mag cover girl, obviously feel their chosen partner is as hot as a Scotch bonnet pepper. When they first met two years ago—at a leather event, Bear related, visibly puffing up a bit at the remembrance of herself suavely striding around the conference, "I was told by a number of women that a flaming-red-haired woman with no underwear on was making inquiries about me." Later, at the convention dungeon, the redhead "play-pierced" Bear (surface piercing) and taught Bear how to do it—though no more.

"And the next day, I got a phone call," reported Bear.

"And I want to tell *you*," exclaimed the dominatrix, looking practically on the verge of the vapors, "I've *never* done that before." Never made the first move, that is. (Punching holes in strangers: No problemo!) But that's the big problem with two women; when both people in a prospective couple have been raised as bottoms, as all women are, no one's willing to risk just saying, "I wanna go out with you," much less "I wanna fuck."

"Yeah. Women don't know how to be aggressive that way," Sharrin agreed. "But s/m kind of takes care of that, because the roles are clearly delineated and defined." Meaning, s/m gives structure, so if you're into it you don't have to stumble around trying to figure out what to do because you don't have those handy prescribed girl-and-boy roles but there's no other structure in place?

"Right," said Sharrin. Nonetheless, when she threw herself at Bear, Bear said no.

"I don't do sex with strangers." Bear shrugged.

Consequently, Sharrin went on, "we did something I don't think lesbians know how to do. We dated. I think lesbians never get acculturated to learn it in straight society. And our own lesbian culture promotes serial monogamy, so we never have any reason to learn. You meet someone; the U-Haul pulls up, and you move in; you live together for two or three years. Then someone goes, 'You know, Jo on my softball team is kind of cute. It won't hurt to have coffee with her. . . .' And then the U-Haul's pulling away."

"We talked for four or five weeks before we went to bed. We did the dance." Bear beamed. "It builds up anticipation, heightens sensibilities. . . . When you get to the final act, it's so much better. And in the morning you wake up and have someone to talk to, and not go, 'What's your name, here's your coffee, leave.' "

Bear had very enjoyable sex with men when she was younger, and Sharrin is obviously more than capable of attracting and exciting scads of straight men; so why is it, we ask (not because we don't know, but because it seems to so confound a large portion of the general population), that they opted for women?

Bear considered. "I think women are mysterious, complex, multifaceted. Men are simple. I'm sorry." She shrugged, looking apologetic, but not very. "Men are boring, I figured them out a long time ago. When I figure something out, I drop it. I like that complexity. That's what attracts me to women. It's a challenge—and I don't mean a challenge to conquer. I mean a challenge to explore. It keeps you interested longer. It makes you grow."

"I don't know. I imagine I could fall in love with a man," Sharrin mused. "I just wouldn't have the partnership thing. But . . . well, this may sound shallow: For me, men *smell* funny. Maybe it's a testosterone thing." Mainly, she feels, "being a lesbian involves a deeper level of intimacy than I've ever had with any man. I mean, even on just a physical level, okay, so I'm PMSed. I'm having a really shitty day. And Bear knows what it feels like, because it happens to her own body . . . *and* she knows I'm gonna probably want a chocolate sometime in the next twenty-four hours. So it magically appears—that thoughtfulness women have with each other. I mean, Lillian Faderman, in her book *Surpassing the Love of Men,* defines lesbianism as something like a spiritual and emotional connection between two women—and she leaves out the sex. But I think a lot of lesbians live that life."

Surprisingly, this was not said in the judgmental tone one might expect from a professional erotica worker and personal s/m practitioner—someone most people would consider to be on the sexual cutting edge. Rather, in evoking these relationships where emotional connections increasingly supplant the sexual ones, Sharrin dripped respect.

And actually, both she and Bear believe it is not bondage, bruises, or any other standard sexual hot stuff that prevents bed death—or, ultimately, overcomes it. "We have friends in the s/m community that have suffered it. I don't think it's like s/m is intrinsically so much more exciting that bed death doesn't happen, where in vanilla relationships it does. I think it happens because people stop listening to each other. For us, our relationship is a separate entity. There's the you, the me, and the us. And the only way for it to be successful is [for us] to be two wholes putting active energy into a third, rather than two halves making a whole by rote, like the heterosexual model. I think lesbian bed death happens when two people stop paying attention to the third, the us."

Why isn't there "straight bed death," then? "There is," said Sharrin. "It's called divorce."

"Having affairs," added Bear.

"Cheating," said Sharrin. "There just isn't a *dedicated* term for it with heterosexual sex."

The two of them, Bear acknowledged, "do have phases, periods when we don't have sex, because of various things: stress, medications, focusing on work. We'll say, 'Let's have sex,' and then look at each other and go, 'Nah. Too tired.' Or maybe it's one of us; I'll be in the mood, and Sharrin's like, 'Get *away*.' It's just that it's okay that she can express her desire not to be desired. So sex gets put on the back burner for a while."

"Whereas in a straight relationship, perhaps the woman would just do it," suggested Sharrin, partly because it simply involves less trouble. But also, "I think in a lot of straight relationships, sex gets mistaken for intimacy. So when the sex dies, they're strangers." When lesbians experience bed death, in contrast, "we still have the intimacy."

"So then suddenly we'll look at each other, and we're bunnies!" Bear exclaimed.

And not just s/m sex, either, added Sharrin. "I mean, we do sometimes have vanilla sex. . . ."

"We do?" Bear looked stunned.

"I think so."

"Not according to the lesbian definition: index finger only, no penetration."

"What lesbian community are you talking about?" Sharrin demanded in disbelief. "The lesbian community of the fifties?" The idea of penetration as patriarchal is actually something many lesbians mentioned to us, but mostly just as a recalled remnant of pseudo-separatist extremism that died a decade ago, not as present reality. Today's thinking seems to be more along the lines of: As long as the penetrator is a woman, the purely physical sensation of having something up there can be pretty big fun.

"Well, my first relationship with a woman, she was very much into clitoral orgasms," Bear persisted. "And I wanted penetration, and she told me, 'If you want penetration why don't you sleep with a man?' "

Sounds like the classic guy line, we noted: Why would lesbians prefer dildos to the "real thing"?

"Maybe because I get to choose the size, shape, and color?" Sharrin suggested sweetly. Besides, there's that female force driving the thing. "I know so many gay women from Outer Limits who do sleep with a man periodically, once every six or seven years. But that's just to remind themselves why they're a lesbian."

Probably the major misunderstanding the rest of the world has about lesbian relationships has to do with total bafflement over how two people manage to couple without . . . Okay, let's not overdignify this. How it's always expressed is some variation on "So which one is the boy?" And every other erotic variation is lined up accordingly. The "man" is also the butch of the butch/femme, the top of the top/bottom, the "s" of the s/m: the "active" partner. And vice versa. The conventional straight world defines excitement as male/female, and assumes that lesbians therefore must be imitation male/female. In her experience, we asked Sharrin, did top/bottom and the other opposite-role dynamics have any relationship whatsoever to boy/girl?

Sharrin considered. "I think the relationship it has is not what most people think it has." Namely, the roles are neither intrinsic to lesbianism nor imitative. And they're not 180 degrees apart, either. "I think butch/femme and top/bottom are something lesbians *create* to have difference." Sharrin does feel relationships require some degree of difference to stay hot. "Yeah, I believe that. I think we either create the difference, or relationships die. But for some women, more subtle tonal differences work" than the programmed polarized opposites men and women have to work with. "Like one woman's a light gray and one's a darker gray, and that's enough." In other words, it's not a matter of some lesbian couples being butchy/femmy masculine-feminine (or any other type of one-of-each polarized opposites arrangement), and other lesbian couples opting for merged androgynous sameness. Rather, in the blessed absence of a mainstream societal definition of how the proper lesbian should be, each lesbian is free to move back and forth between poles, playing with various degrees and interpretations of these opposite roles. Then she can pair up with another lesbian who is similarly fluid, and eroticize . . . whatever. (Heterosexuals, of course, are free to do the same—but there's a lot of cultural baggage working against them.)

Another factor is that in lesbian culture, none of these opposite roles is necessarily for keeps, as Sharrin's shifts between butch and femme and the couple's shifts between sexual topping and bottoming illustrate. As we do with nature versus nurture and het/bi/homo, lesbians often place themselves somewhere along the top/bottom, butch/femme, continuums . . . and then, with what's perhaps the only "typical" lesbian trait one can count on—a natural, virtually irresistible urge to confuse all hard-line categories—refuse to stay put. Hence the rash of butchy femmes, tops who sometimes flip, masochists who sometimes grab the whip, and even lesbians who have some degree of sexual involvement with men.

About the only thing that *is* clear is that pairings even among women in the sexual fringes of the 1990s lesbian community are not, contrary to popular yahoo belief, pseudomale/female or anything else similarly unimaginative or rigid. Sexually, we constantly reinvent ourselves. And "as different as individual women are from one another, we're still," Sharrin feels, "like with like" in some deep, bottom-line ways.

For instance, she explained: "I have always been attracted to a more butch dynamic. But I've also had relationships to femme women, as both a butch and a femme. I find my relationships with femme women as a femme are more like sisters. You go out shopping together and you have sex."

Why, that sounds . . . well, it's undeniable that the vast majority of lesbians are sexually vanilla; but frankly, this couple didn't seem all that chocolate. We were kind of feeling a little fudge ripple bond here. In fact, we couldn't think of very many *straight* women in this country who wouldn't be tempted by sex 'n' shopping. As we declared to the professional dominatrix and the perforated professional piercer, two very nice girls: You've just recruited thousands.

Slippery Slopes:
What We Do
in Bed

In the last decade, while the mainstream veered to the right and gay men were preoccupied with AIDS, the wild-experimental-sex baton was passed, almost by default, to lesbians. Most of the ferment began in the Bay Area. If Northampton, with its women's colleges, is the lesbian Athens, San Francisco is the lesbian Sparta. Transsexual lesbians, "lesbians who sleep with men," lesbians who work in the sex industry, and other women who would be on the sexual fringe in other communities are pillars in San Francisco.

It was there, in 1984, that Susie Bright and several other women founded the raunchy lesbian sex magazine *On Our Backs*. At the time, Susie was doing erotic poetry readings and working a day job at the women's sex-toy store Good Vibrations. Lesbian erotica "was new territory," she explained. "Six years later I was saying that I never wanted to write another story about the G-spot, but then, there was so much stuff!"

The lesbian-feminist movement of the previous decade had frowned on butch/femme and even penetration as somehow "male-identified." The same crowd, to be fair, wasn't exactly puritanical; they thought that monogamy was a patriarchal capitalist plot to keep women as property. By the eighties, however, the national feminist movement was devoting increasing energy to combating pornography, often allying with the same right-wing forces that were working to quash gay rights legislation. *On Our Backs* thumbed its nose (and virtually every other body part) at antiporn feminism. Even the name was a takeoff on a Washington, D.C., feminist newspaper, *off our backs* (which threatened to sue).

"The hardest thing about that first issue was finding women who would let their faces be used," Susie recalled. "Not their pussies, but their faces and names. Later on, we'd get letters saying, 'Why can't you show someone more like me—I work in a bank—instead of all these punk girls with piercings?' But of course it was the punk girls who had told their parents and the world to fuck off. Sometimes we'd say to *them*, 'How would you like to dress up as a bank teller?' and they'd go 'No way, I've got to be *me*.' "

The centerfold of the first issue was a *Playboy* takeoff, showing Susie's very butch then-girlfriend as "Bulldaggcr of thc Month." Reader reaction was fierce, but divided. "One-third had the reaction that this woman was a disgusting pig, how dare you, blah blah blah. The second third were, like, 'I'm wet, what's her phone number?' It had been a secret that butch women could be hot, that being butch wasn't just about buying sensible shoes because they were on sale. And then the last third thought they *should* be turned on because it was so politically right on, but in fact they were attracted to femme women."

We were interviewing Susie at her and our favorite San Francisco restaurant, Zuni. The two of us once scarfed down twelve dozen oysters at Zuni as part of an experiment, which later became an article in the national gay magazine *Out,* to see if the briny bivalves were truly an aphrodisiac. They sure seemed to be, though it might have been the several accompanying bottles of champagne that did the trick. At any rate, we rolled back to our hotel room, had great sex, and lived to tell the tale.

But in the ball-and-blab department we cannot hold a candle (or any similarly shaped instrument) to Susie, who has shared every twitch with her public. A 1995 *Vanity Fair* profile showed her cupping her bare breasts and wearing a sort of horse-bridle arrangement with a chain between her teeth. And this was soft-core stuff to readers who had been following her sex life for years. At *On Our Backs*, she also dished out advice to the lustlorn as Susie Sexpert, the lesbian Dear Abby. She told a rapt audience that dildos weren't pseudopenises (that, in fact, penises should be so lucky: any size you want, hard forever, no pregnancy or nasty diseases); that fantasies were just fantasies, not plans; that butch/femme was part of lesbian culture; that desire, by its nature, is too boundless to remain politically correct all the time. The magazine was often tasteless (usually deliberately so), featuring photos of things that had never appeared in *Ms.*, from clit jewelry to dildo blowjobs. A large number of its readers were male voyeurs. But it had struck a nerve among lesbians who were ready to trade up from processed sex into something rawer.

Within a few years of the magazine's appearance, there were so many newly visible s/m lesbians that you might have guessed someone was giving out frequent flayer miles. In certain quarters women who *weren't* into butt plugs and leather were even written off as "vanilla." (In other words, the same putdown we'd been hearing from straight men—that basic lesbian sex was a big snore—was now being tossed around by lesbians. Bedfellows do make strange politics.)

By the late eighties there was a subtle shift, at least among young urban lesbians, from an explicitly feminist orientation to one that looked more toward gay men. Girls who made political common cause with ACT UP and Queer Nation began partying like the boys—or at least like the boys had before AIDS. The result is sometimes a little hard to keep up with, for us pale-flavor Häagen-Dazs types. We remember a raucous late-night party at the downtown fashion photography space Industria in New York during the Stonewall celebration in 1994. We had just watched bisexual performance artist Annie Sprinkle do a strip routine to "America the Beautiful"; for the finale, Sprinkle, clad in almost nothing but a Statue of Liberty hat, pulled a giant American flag out of her vagina while holding aloft a sparkler.

In the least-populated corner of a sardine-packed room normally used for glossy magazine shoots, we were trying to shout above the din to Alix Dobkin, the fiftyish folksinger who was one of the most unyielding lesbian-feminist separatists of the seventies. Just then a pretty girl in a Mohawk walked by with a big red dildo on her forehead. A baby-dyke unicorn!

We all gaped stupidly, three remnants of an era in which the worst thing that could happen to a woman was to be treated like a piece of meat. "This is really okay," Alix said gamely. "I think what it's about is challenging phallic supremacy."

Kris Machado and Beth Rubin are working on their ejaculation skills. Although Beth hates the word.

"But it's the only word there *is* right now," Kris sweetly tells her. "And I learned how to do that by making love with her," she says, pointing to Beth.

They weren't the only ones. There are lesbian videos (by Sprinkle, for one) about the joys of squirting and how to achieve it. But in the beginning, Kris acknowledged, "we had a problem with it because we got the bed all soaking wet. I want the message out there that it's okay! You're not peeing in your bed! Be proud! Get plastic sheets!"

Beth, who is thirty-four, and Kris, who is forty-six, were in the process of becoming full-time residents of a rural woman-owned community in southern Oregon when we met them. They had become lovers seven years earlier, when Kris was a housewife and mother in the San Fernando Valley. Kris had seen the film *Desert Hearts* and realized she was dying to sleep with a woman, but she had no clue how to make it happen. She knew Beth was a lesbian, and took her aside one night to pick her brain. "We'd been giggling and laughing and talking for about an hour, and the electricity was charged. It was like the room faded away, and all I could see was her face. And then she took her finger and slooooooowly moved it all the way up my arm. My God!"

For months, all they had was stolen moments. "We'd go to parking lots and turn on the radio and dance," Beth recalled. The first time they made love was in the room of one of Kris's children.

("There were all these surfer pictures all over the wall.") Kris announced that she would, of course, never leave her husband.

"In the beginning, I was just so excited about being with a woman, I just wanted to have sex all the time," said Kris. "I was really into it, but sometimes she wanted to do other things. I was so hurt! I was used to being with a man who was constantly after me. I thought she didn't love me, didn't find me attractive. Then Beth said, 'Kris, if you want to make love, *initiate* it.' I was like, 'What?' My initiations are so timid. If she's tired, that's like *it*. That's been an ongoing struggle for seven years, because I felt it was so difficult for me to initiate; and if I did, and she turned me down, I was so devastated that I decided not to initiate at all. And then she felt like I wasn't touching her."

Meanwhile, there was the E-word. "We were making love so often, we'd just throw the covers back and let the bed dry. And [Kris's adolescent daughter] would come in and see and say, 'Did you pee in the bed, Ma?' "

"I told her one time I did, so she wouldn't think it was about sex," Kris admitted.

"So now she thinks you're incontinent?" Beth gaped.

"Well, anyway," said Kris, sailing right ahead, "I think it's a real lesbian thing—because of the time it takes to do it . . . and the care it takes."

Time for the jackpot question. After all the flirting and the courting and the assignment of roles or lack thereof, what *do* lesbians do in bed?

Pretty much everything.

"I think most lesbians are doing what they always did—which is tribadism, mutual masturbation, i.e., outside rubbing on clit and lips, finger-fucking, and oral sex, in that order," said Susie Bright. "If we're going to talk in sheer numbers of what people are doing, that hasn't changed. But there *is* a very visible minority doing all kinds of other things, so what is *talked* about in lesbian sex is so much broader and wilder than what was talked about before. Emphasis on *talking* rather than doing."

In 1995, *The Advocate* surveyed thousands of its female readers, a self-selected group who are presumably more activist and hence more interested in answering sex surveys than the average lesbian. Still, that vanilla staple, oral sex, was a winner: Some 48 percent of the respondents had been on the receiving end in their most recent sexual encounter; 70 percent "love" giving it and 75 percent love receiving it. Nongenital sex acts like kissing and cuddling were even more popular. When asked which of ten kinkier acts they had engaged in over the past five years, the most common, with 43 percent of the survey, was "use of a hand-held dildo with a partner." (In second place, with 35 percent, was "use of food as part of having sex.") Twenty-seven percent had used a strap-on dildo with a partner.

But 26 percent had done none of the above and none of any of the lower-ranked sex acts: bondage and discipline, fisting, three-way sex, use of double-ended dildo with a partner, s/m, nipple clamps, and water sports.

Large majorities of both single and coupled lesbians griped that they wished they had sex more often, but the quality of their sex lives stacked up well against a control group of heterosexual women from the University of Chicago's 1994 National Health and Social Life Survey. When asked about their most recent sexual encounter, 39 percent of the lesbians (versus 15 percent of the straight women) reported that it had lasted for more than an hour, while 32 percent of lesbians (as opposed to 19 percent of the heterosexual sample) had more than one orgasm.

After spending months hearing older lesbians enviously grumbling about how the young chic lipstick girls were getting it on nightly in politically incorrect lesbo-a-go-go clubs, and hearing younger lesbians enviously grumbling about how the old unchic Chap Stick crowd had already gotten it all back in the seventies when monogamy was politically incorrect, we ourselves had started wondering if anyone in the lesbian community was even having sex anymore.

"We can vouch that they are," Claire Cavanah assured us. "Or at least they're buying the accoutrements."

Claire, twenty-nine, and her friend and business partner, twenty-seven-year-old Rachel Venning, are the owners of Toys in Babeland, a Seattle sex boutique that is open to one and all, but is particularly geared to lesbians. (The mother church of stores like Babeland is Good Vibrations, where Susie Bright got her start and where Claire worked for a month as a kind of lesbian sex-toy apprentice; there are similar operations in Boston, New York, Portland, and Provincetown.)

Both Claire, a Brown University women's studies major originally from Casper, Wyoming, and Rachel, a religious studies major at Wesleyan who'd grown up in Oakland, had moved to Seattle after college. Rachel was "a housepainter, a cocktail waitress, a rafting guide, and a chocolate packer, and then I decided I wasn't going anywhere professionally, so I went to business school." Claire "did some film work, some publishing work, coffee-pulling, chocolate packing. Then we had this brilliant idea, to start the store. Rachel was about to graduate from business school, and I was doing films. I could just switch in a second. That's the whole Generation X thing, right? Girl/boy, top/bottom, filmmaker/sex-toy store owner . . ."

"Claire and I were sitting around one day and I saw this bottle of Probe on her table. It's a sexual lubricant which is not a favorite brand for either of us. It's stringy, sticky, gross. I knew it wasn't for her. So I was harassing her about why she had it. And the reason was, she'd gotten a gift certificate to a regular sex-toy store in town, and had gone in there and there was, like, *nothing* she wanted to buy. This gross lube was the only thing even close.

"And there was all this icky packaging with vacant-looking women on it," Claire added. "And butt plugs so large that they were, like, you've got to be kidding! Everything just assaulting my limits; it assaulted me to go in there. So my idea was to have a place where women could go in comfortably and have access to these toys that really improve your sex life a lot. One thing about our vision of the store is definitely that it's for women, and not lesbians specifically. That's a little bit different because I think with a lot of lesbians now, politically anyway, the alliance is with gay men, and bi and transgender people: 'queer.' I think we're a bit more traditional feminists in seeing sex as a women's issue, and not just a lesbian one."

They borrowed money from their Ivy League classmates and opened their doors in the summer of 1993, on a side street in the city's very gay Capitol Hill neighborhood. The shop is a surprisingly homey place, despite the slings and arrows of outrageous s/m equipment and a dildo display that looks like a Popsicle field at harvest time. The checkout counter is a bar of the sort that were de rigueur in New Jersey "rec rooms" thirty years ago. The idea is that customers can belly up, put a foot on the rail, and chat. "It's hard for people to admit they don't know about sex," said Rachel, "because there's such a value placed on knowing about it—like that's all supposed to be instinctive if you're cool, you know? So you have to figure out how to tell them stuff without suggesting they don't already know. It's kinda tricky."

Claire added that the pseudo-sophistication operates in tandem with the fact that "absolutely no one is writing about sex. Or talking about it. That's one of the unofficial functions of the store: to get women to talk about what they like in the sack."

Well, what *do* they like? What single product sells best? Dildos? "Books," said Rachel. "Almost everyone can find a book they like, and they can feel comfortable buying a book. And a dildo and harness, like eighty to a hundred and twenty dollars is pretty standard, so that's a lot of money."

Vibrators are ever popular, too, Claire noted. But the Magic Wand—that super-solid seventies standby whose motor could, in a pinch, substitute for the engine in a Volkswagen Bug—has been supplanted. Claire demonstrated today's favorite: the Rabbit Pearl, a bunny with suggestively rotating bead-stuffed ears.

Another technological marvel of the moment that was flying out of the store was the Thigh Harness. We had interviewed its inventor, former oil company geologist Susan Lankford, at her booth at a crafts fair at the Dinah Shore Golf Classic. "This product comes out of the fact that two women together naturally make this position"— she clasped her fingers together in an X—"with intertwined legs. So why not put the dildo where it's gonna do the most good?"

We watched as customers filed past the booth doing double-takes. Because this wasn't a—ha ha ha—*natural* dildo? "At least with a conventional harness folks feel they know what this is about," Susan explained. "With this, it's sort of like a gender fuck within a gender fuck."

The United States Patent Office had also been a little taken aback, Susan added. "I wasn't clear on exactly how to categorize this device. They had me looking in the section on bedpans, and similar stuff. The whole thing is, they considered it to be dirty, therefore it must be in these other categories."

At Toys in Babeland, the thigh harness was right up there with the cotton gin and the electric light bulb. "It's a great concept," enthused Rachel. "It's right there on your thigh, which is really powerful; you've got a lot of bone and muscle supporting it. You can move around a lot. It's kind of a natural position you're in. That missionary thing? That's *hard.*" And if you get tired, you just use the other leg, which is not an option for people with only one pelvis.

As for the dildos themselves, "straight women tend to go for the realistic-looking dildos," said Claire. "So do some lesbians, but more lesbians buy the Goddess-y, water-mammal kind." She brandished a sleek purple silicone dolphin.

We noted that there actually seemed to be a complete about-face from the old antipenetration pressuring to a virtual pro-dildo Mafia. "Well, a lot more lesbians are using them, and feeling okay about talking about that," Rachel said.

"And women do seem embarrassed to admit if they've never used one," added Claire, "like they're a lesser lesbian." Somebody's always in the out-group.

"I think it's like that with s/m now, too," Rachel reflected. "There's this sort of contempt, like if you really knew yourself and your desires better, you'd admit you were kidding yourself about just liking vanilla sex."

One product that people talk about more than use, said Claire, is the dental dam. "Well, some do. More than used to." As well as a slight improvement in safe sex awareness among lesbians, there was, she explained, a major improvement in dental dams, which, several years back, were apparently constructed from the gauge of rubber used for inflatable riverboats (sharp boulders no problem). "There's very good dental dam technology now. There's a very thin one from Australia we carry. There are even a couple of flavored blue and purple ones."

And no, Claire and Rachel agreed: Straight people, though presumably still engaging in oral sex, aren't buying dams. We had noticed in our own research that most lesbians: realized that lesbians aren't immune from HIV (even though we're statistically at far smaller risk than gay men or straights); wished there were more research on woman-to-woman transmission; and were aware of safe sex . . . and didn't practice it. It's apparently difficult for lesbians to evaluate what's a necessity and what's simply an inaccurate equation by the gay male–identified lesbian sex radicals at the forefront of the raunch renaissance: Hot sex = gay male sex = layers of latex. If going down on—or digitally touching—a vulva is really risky, why aren't the Centers for Disease Control telling straight men to use dental dams and finger cots?

Some women are downright *offended* at the idea of injecting plastic and latex into their relationship. The president of the Los Angeles chapter of NOW was quoted in *LN* as saying that she, for one, wasn't about to go out and buy the thigh harness or anything like it. "The whole idea of using an inanimate object in the first place moves you away from the intimacy of being with a woman."

We actually wonder about the opposite problem. It seems next to impossible for lesbians not to complicate fucking with feelings—in particular, with prolonged precoital anticipation, followed promptly by the postcoital U-Haul. When we were writing our previous book, a set of travel essays about gay and lesbian Europe, we were fascinated to hear about a backroom sex club for women in Amsterdam. But by the time we tracked it down, it had come and gone. It seemed that although the concept had been an initial smash hit, most patrons had met, paired off, rented the U-Haul, and disappeared. By and by the owners regretfully began to feel that they really couldn't spare the space. Rather than close it down completely, they let the room double as a storage area, forcing all the wild future nesters to make their hot contacts next to the mops and brooms.

In our own extensive collection of gay male and female bodice-ripper "summer vacation reading," it's hard to find a gay male cow-person tale where the lead bunkhouse buddies aren't out of the saddle and riding the foreman by page five, at the latest. In Kim Larabee's 137-page *Behind the Mask,* in contrast, the damsel desperados fall madly in love on page 21, but don't get it on until page 64—and the covered moving wagon has pulled up by page 72 (the tumble in the hay having evidently caused the heroines to immediately recognize "a bond between you and I that was forged in the beginning of time"). And this is pretty quick in the dirt department and slow in the commitment department for female-to-female sexual dynamics. The heroine in Sarah Dreher's 204-page *Stoner McTavish* falls in love with a *picture* of a woman on page 17; is deeply in love by page 21 (still not having met—the photo's grown on her); falls in love at first sight of the actual woman in the flesh on page 38 . . . and doesn't fall into bed until page 187. In Doris Grumbach's *Chamber Music* (213 pages, first sex on page 167) the heroines are already nesting on page 161, *before* bed, but after much intensely intimate verbal and eyeball communication. Even in Victoria Ramstetter's very promisingly titled *The Marquise and the Novice*, stern Ms.tress Annelise de Rochelle, dark raven tresses whipping wildly in the wind as she gallops off in riding attire, is not coaxed off her color-coordinated raven steed into bed until page 86 of 101. And yes, she and her gentle, spunky governess are merged in a woven "tapestry of love" in the cohabitation castle by page 99.

Perhaps not surprisingly, a lot of Babeland's customers, both lesbian and straight, read gay male porn. "But that should go further," Rachel said. "Sometimes I think we should put up a sign in the store that says, 'If you're a straight man, read gay male porn. If you're a straight woman, read lesbian porn. If you're a gay man, read lesbian porn.' You know? Cross-pollinate the ideas!"

We mentioned debates we used to have back in the early 1980s with our friend AIDS activist Michael Callen. (Michael died in 1994.) At the time, after over three thousand sexual encounters, he had decided lesbian monogamous merger should be the model for gay men. He argued that total noncommunication of everything except body parts was central to the excitement of gay male casual sex, the idea being that if one so much as exchanged names with a tearoom trick or asked him out for coffee afterward, the hunky garage mechanic one had been picturing behind the glory hole might be exposed as a pencil-pusher for Merrill Lynch.

Personally we did—and still do—see our own decision to be monogamous not as universally more right, but purely as more realistic for us as an individual couple of jealous bitches (monogamy being definitely preferable to murder). And, while agreeing with Mike that the virtually institutionalized anti-intimacy of anonymous sex sounded tedious, we also regretted lesbians' inability to have sex without signing a lease on an apartment as foreplay. So it seems odd, we suggested to Claire and Rachel, that lesbians comparatively rarely get into the casual but friendly fuck-buddy kind of thing some gay men do—not glory-hole anonymity, but just having sex with a pal when you're horny. Like, why didn't the two of *them* ever have sex?

"Hey, that's an idea!" Rachel snapped her fingers breezily. "What are you doing tonight?" She laughed. Claire didn't.

"Actually, I wanted Rachel," she said casually. She turned to her buddy. "I never told you that."

"That's okay," Rachel mumbled, looking aghast.

"Rachel's blushing," noted Claire. So was she. It was actually kind of cute to find there was *some* sexual subject that can embarrass these women.

"No, actually, at that time she was already with her partner, who she's still with." (And happily/typically merged-monogamous with.) Claire sighed.

Had their own sex lives been affected by spending days surrounded by new toys they can take home and experiment with? Rachel and Claire exchanged brief glances. "Yeah," said Rachel. "But not the way you think. I do get so sick of false assumptions we run into all the time in this store. Like, 'I bet you hot babes personally use *every one* of these implements, every night.' "

"Right," Claire agreed. "And assuming we want to be a part of their sexual experience when they come in here: 'Well, you know what *we're* going to be doing later,' nudge-nudge-wink-wink. I'm like, I don't *care* what you're going to be doing, just give me your money and go *do* it, willya?"

Okay, ladies, "Twenty Questions" it is. More or less? "Less," Rachel groaned.

"Numb, numb, numb! That's what it's done," Claire admitted. "Only a couple of days ago I started feeling sexual again, after *nine months.*"

Well, they say that's what happens to people who work in bakeries. You think you're gonna be scarfing those pastries all day long, and then almost immediately you lose your appetite for sweets. "Yeah, you'd think, Whooee, honey, sex machine!" Rachel snorted. "But it's not like that. A couple of months after we opened I felt my whole desire for sex really dropping. *Everything:* sex with my girlfriend, masturbating . . . I think I may be getting some of my libido back, finally, which is a relief. I was like, 'Does having this store mean I'm gonna be asexual the rest of my life?' "

Claire, who's single and looking, added: "One thing I've noticed is I have a definite anticruise orientation in the store. I don't look at *anyone* in a sexual way. You'd think it'd be the best place in the world for that, but it's *the* anticruise zone. Not only am I busy, but I'm trying to tread this line where I'm selling them sexual things in a nonsexual way, so they don't have to feel exposed and leered at. I just cleanse the air of that sort of thing, so more information can be exchanged." She shrugged. "Then I end up having to go to the opera or something to cruise."

And the ultimate sicko kick: "Sometimes in the store, I feel like masturbating," Claire confessed, "and . . . " She gestured at walls and tables hung and stacked with every kind of jerking-off aid imaginable. ". . . I use my *hand.*"

One anticipated problem that hasn't arisen, so to speak, is flashers and other perv-type fellows. "Some straight guys do come," according to Rachel, "but nice ones who have girlfriends they want to please, not those ones in raincoats who want to leer and so on."

"There's some kind of positive force that keeps those people out," Claire mused. "Like they're a lot more afraid of us than we are of them. I think fear of men's uncontrolled sexual aggression has been virtually bred into women, with good reason; but the truth is, these guys whose sexuality is sick are really pathetic. So it's like having a healthy sexuality is the best medicine for dealing with them, the best antidote. It just turns them away."

There must be something, too, about coming into a store with a wall full of dangling dildos . . . "Yeah." Rachel chuckled. "We have this straight guy friend who's been coming in to use our computer. When he came yesterday, we'd just gotten this new dildo in that's really *humongous.*" Actually, we kinda couldn't help but notice it ourselves. Mounted so that it protruded from a mirror, it looked the size of, roughly, the Chrysler Building. "And he's at the computer, trying to look anywhere else, and going, like, 'I'm feeling a little bit threatened right now. . . .' "

The previous year, Claire "wore a big purple dildo for Halloween, to a very straight party. And I swear, every guy there, except one who made a mile-wide circle around me every time he crossed the room, came up at some point and said, 'That's . . . um . . . kind of big, isn't it?' And I go"—swaggering and booming—" '*I* dunno. *Is* it?'

"But I'll tell you," she added, "straight men are certainly bending over a lot more. We sell *so* many dildos and harnesses to men who are going to give them to their girlfriends, to use on them. As wedding presents! I'm serious! There was a guy one night who shopped around for one, who had been wanting this . . . Well, I think it's gonna be a little bit of honeymoon punishment, ya know: 'I need a *bigger* one than that.' I love it! That's the alliance with *queer* sexuality, where everything—male and female, straight and gay—is just falling apart, and coming back together different ways."

"I really feel we're helping people," said Rachel. "It's like they've opened this little hidden place in themselves, and we've seen it and sort of validated it. And then they don't feel so ashamed of who they are."

Given their vantage point on the literal underbelly of the community, we asked them what they liked most about being gay. "It's so brave," said Claire. "When I think about women together, it's just so daring to do that. Because there are so many sensible reasons to be with a man: money, security, position, approval, normality—just fitting in. So to be with a woman you've got to really be in touch with your desire, and want to live your life accordingly."

"There's something sentimental about being a lesbian, too," added Rachel. "Like in a strange city I go to a lesbian bar or café, and here's all these women I don't even know, and coming from wherever different places they came from, and we have something in common." There is indeed something in sexual identity that goes way beyond sex, we agree. It's ethnic, in a way, the community bond. "And heartwarming, I think, sometimes."

She considered a moment. "And then other times, I think: Trashy broad. Stop hogging the pool table."

Sprawled close to each other in a circle in the woods, about two dozen women were slowly and caressingly feeling up . . . apricots? Oh, *yessss.*

Here at the "Sensual Foods" workshop at Michigan, we were also feeding each other orange sections, swapping recipes, and listening to tips from facilitators June Sahara and Oleyna Richman on how to fully explore, exploit, and enjoy the food/sex connection: dinners where both women eat with their hands; Sunday morning oranges-and-chocolate brunches in bed; fabulous food fights that increase intimacy; even how to turn klutzy accidental spills into seduction.

June and Oleyna should know. Both just over forty, they have been a couple for fourteen years, and both have worked extensively as professional chefs. While June's career was now rehabilitation counseling for disabled people, food foreplay still figured in their sex life together, as it always had. In fact, they met through food, which also played a fat role in their falling in love and first sexual experience.

At the time, only June was a chef. Oleyna, just out as a lesbian (having previously slept with "men, a lot, maybe a hundred of them

. . . maybe two percent of them at all satisfying"), was a politico—
with a hunger. "I was working for the state legislature in Columbus,
Ohio, and I found out through the women's community that there
was this women's restaurant collective, which June was involved
in. This was something I was interested in; my job was just a job.
And I was intrigued about meeting June, just because she was a
professional female chef, and everyone talked about her. So I had a
break-the-fast dinner after Yom Kippur.

"Well, she brought a tuna-salmon mold that was, to me, died-
and-gone-to-heaven." She gazed at June in total adoration and ad-
miration, remembering. "It was not only molded salad, it was
coated in *chaud-froid* and decorated with cucumbers and olive and
pimiento—jeweled! *Very* exciting. It was like, 'Who *is* this
woman?' "

Though it was obviously a case of love at first bite, June and
Oleyna didn't sleep together until about a year later, because both
had girlfriends, "and I was chefing so many hours," June explains.
Their first real date was at Ziggy's Continental Restaurant, in
Columbus. "It was a hundred and twenty dollars! That was a lot in
1980," exclaimed Oleyna.

"It was this really staid, formal kind of restaurant," June said,
nodding. "And we're all dressed in dyke chic, both butch: slacks,
blazers, ties. But the waiters were all gay. They treated us very well.
They thought it was terribly romantic."

"We had foie gras, and champagne. And I had smoked eel for the
first time . . ." Oleyna murmured huskily.

". . . and then we went back to Oleyna's, and she finally let me in
her bedroom." June smiled.

"Not only that, she took command and seduced me. I was, like—
wow!" Do we have to explain? And the great sex continued—along
with great meals; Oleyna trained, and was soon cooking professionally, too.

From the intimacy apparent as Oleyna and June sat on a Michigan log feeding each other citrus slices, it's clear (unless that
dreamy look is produced entirely by the smoked eel) that there is
still a good deal of *wow!* in their sex life today. What isn't clear, un-

til Oleyna helps June get up from the log and transfer herself laboriously to a wheelchair, is that June has multiple sclerosis.

The real trauma of the MS came because although June was sick enough (with symptoms including gallbladder and vision problems, as well as loss of strength and energy) to have to quit work in 1986, she was not correctly diagnosed until 1989. "It was so bizarre," she explained. "I knew I was sick. But I couldn't get anyone to take me seriously. I was seriously depressed, and scared shitless, because they're telling me it's all in my head. So I withdrew, a lot. I, who'd been this gregarious outgoing extrovert with lots of friends, became totally introverted. It was a major thing to get up the courage to go out on the porch and get the mail. And a lot of emotional damage happened during that time."

Their sex life suffered too. "She'd been a hard-drinkin', boot-stompin', cigar-smokin', motorcycle-ridin' tough dyke. And suddenly she wouldn't even talk on the phone, to anyone," said Oleyna. "I wasn't getting any emotional response from her; she was just going deeper and deeper into herself, and I was angry and scared. Oh yeah, if you're with someone and they withdraw that much . . . I'd say it had a major impact."

The most major was Oleyna's affair—with a guy. By this time, two years into June's nondiagnosis, Oleyna was working all day, every day, with a male pastry chef, whom "I was totally in tune with. While June was withdrawing, he was teaching me everything he knew from since he was a boy. It was very exciting for me to be there. We were making everything from scratch! Danish, croissants, puff pastry, learning how to use marzipan, making chocolates!"

So the cake decorating was so thrilling Oleyna decided to have a sexual relationship with the decorator, even though he was a man and she identified as a lesbian by then? "Yeah. A three-month relationship. I made that decision," Oleyna said sullenly. These are not happy marzipan memories. But although it took years, and a lot of couples counseling, "we mended our relationship," she added. "The commitment was still there."

"We've worked through the, um, the Eric thing," June said, still not entirely at ease with memories of the pastry Twinkie. "It's been a process for both of us. I came out of my shell, too, somewhere along the way."

The lesbian community "recognizes that all kinds of women are really beautiful," June says. "And that is very obvious to me here at Michigan. I have a friend who's paraplegic who's very attractive, though she wouldn't be considered conventionally pretty by straight-world standards even without being paraplegic, and I know a couple of women who are extremely attracted to her. And when I come across a woman here who sees I have a disability, oftentimes, yes, she finds me attractive. She may even hit on me, in a flirtatious way. She finds me energetic, assertive. She likes that. She doesn't make the assumption, as happens all the time in the 'real' world, that I'm stupid because my body doesn't function normally; she doesn't assume anything, except what she can tell about a whole person. And I *am* a whole person to her."

This attitude is in 180-degree contrast, June maintains, to society's inaccurate but near-universal belief that disabled folks are asexual. And that misconception intersects with the general rube view of gay folks as *only* sexual. "It drives the able-bodied heterosexual people that I work with crazy that I'm a disabled dyke. Because the general society thinks lesbianism is *all* about sex. So it's, 'How could *you* be a lesbian?' "

That's not to say that great sex is a piece of cake when one partner has multiple sclerosis. But clearly, a nice mocha butter cream dacquoise, properly used, does go a long way. Any sexual problems they personally have, June and Oleyna make clear, have far more to do with emotional residue from June's freeze-up and Oleyna's reactive affair than with actual physical problems resulting from June's disability. It's true, though, that physical deterioration raises plenty of barriers.

"Because I've lost so much physical strength and energy, there's far less frequency than in the first half-dozen years of our relationship," said June. "And every time we do have sex, it takes more preparation, physically, for me, so it's less spontaneous. It takes an extreme amount of stimulation for me to orgasm, *if* I can orgasm; I kind of build focus and then—" Her pursed mouth fizzles. "So I had this vibrator." June held her hands apart to indicate a magic wand approximately the size of a Saturn moon rocket. "*Rrrrrr!* You could probably hear it in Belgium. When I'd use it the whole house would shake."

As her MS has progressed, June's physical problems are, sadly, getting even worse. But she and Oleyna seem to handle the most embarrassing bodily function faux pas with good humor. It is hard to believe two people can laugh so uproariously and seem so sexually intimate when telling true-life tales about maintaining an atmosphere of glamour while wearing adult diapers. But honestly, if Lily Tomlin ever needs a funny yet truly hot catheter routine, we know just where to send her.

These women know the truth that has eluded both the body-image-obsessed gay male world and most of "normal" society (except a few, like paralyzed Vietnam vet Ron Kovic, who have learned through hardship): that the primary sex organ is the brain.

Politics

The Fire Will Not Consume Us (but Processing Might): On the Road with the Lesbian Avengers

Our right arms are lifted to the wall to wall Texas big sky. Our right hands hold aloft flaming torches. There are almost two dozen of us lined up like the Rockettes, right legs thrust forward in perfect synchronicity, left fists planted on backward-jutting left hips far more attitudinously defiant than the Rockettes could manage in their wildest dreams—or nightmares. Damn, we look great.

We're the Lesbian Avengers. We're here in front of the city hall in all-white Vidor, Texas, dubbed "Texas's most hate-filled town" by *Texas Monthly* magazine. We're on the first stop of our ten-day "Pride Ride" from Houston across the Deep South to New York, for the massive twenty-fifth-anniversary celebration of the birth of the modern gay movement at Stonewall. And we're about to do what Lesbian Avengers do best: kick butt.

And, of course, eat fire. This is *the* showstopper act of the Avengers, a political direct-action group founded two years earlier in New York City. If it seems flaming-hot chic to be a lipstick lesbian these days, that is in no small part due to the Lesbian Avengers, whose lipstick, necessarily, is SPF 36, and whose logo is a ticking bomb.

According to its plentiful press releases, the organization is focused on lesbian survival and visibility. The Pride Ride has been deftly organized by the Austin Lesbian Avengers chapter with high-profile publicity in mind; indeed, reporters are here from all over the state. Additionally, the Pride Rider contingent itself contains seven other media persons, including two part-time journalists with assignments from gay publications and a reporter from the San Francisco *Chronicle*.

We are also there, of course. (But in this case, because of work scheduling, "we" are actually only Pamela. Think of the pronoun as a royal "we," if you must; we prefer to think of it as a typically lesbian merged "we.") So is a three-woman part-activist, mostly student-pursuing-grad-school-project video crew. On the national Lesbian Avenger official pre-action checklist, right before "Do you have bail money?" and "Do you have legal observers?" is "Do you have a video person?" It is recommended that a video team tape all actions. The results will provide ready-to-run footage to TV networks if the action isn't covered; more often, it's used to assemble internationally shown Avenger information-and-recruitment videos. Admittedly, the circuit for these clips is somewhat more underground than Cannes. Still, lesbian visibility has never been a problem for Lesbian Avengers.

Lesbian survival is another story. After all, a lot of us just learned to eat fire earlier this morning.

"God I'm scared," sighs Regina Valdes, a twenty-six-year-old half-Mexican native Texan with a drawl and a definite Southern-belle streak. Regina teaches college English and is out to her students, "educating them about gay rights even when it bothers them." But as an activist, she's a virgin. "As a rule, I don't like being involved in organized political group things. The power-control dynamics. The drama."

The flambéed noses.

"Oh my God. Don't say that. I made an exception to the rule for this ride because I just thought, it's the trip of a lifetime—the twenty-fifth anniversary of Stonewall, marching on Independence Hall, fire-eating: something I could always remember. That is, assuming I survive the next five minutes." She fans herself like Scarlett O'Hara as Atlanta burns. "Seriously: Can *you* eat it?"

Well. Let's see. What *was* it they said just hours ago, at the gay-friendly warehouse–alternative art gallery–occasional Lesbian Avenger boot camp in Houston, where our adventure began? Oh, right: The main trick of fire-eating is DON'T inhale. Your lungs explode if you do. Instead, you're supposed to gently exhale as you bring the torch, a homemade device made from half of a straightened-out coat hanger with a head of tightly wound strips of old T-shirts or sweat socks, toward your mouth at a 45-degree angle. Clamping your teeth shut as soon as the torch enters your mouth cuts off the flame's oxygen, allegedly extinguishing it instantly.

There might have been another trick, too, but it's hard to remember in the heat of the moment, so to speak.

Veteran Austin Avenger fire-eaters have assured us that there have been no major accidents anywhere. However, there do seem to have been a distressing number of minorly—but mighty darned inconveniently, for lesbians—singed lips. So several newcomers and one lightly seared veteran who have big sexual plans for Stonewall weekend in the Big Apple have opted out of the personal pyrotechnics.

"Well, I surely am not getting on the end of the line. I wanna be between people who know how to do this," Regina declares. We squeeze in next to Lisa Davis, one of the main organizers of the ride, and Frida, a Mexican-American Austin Avenger who, as one of the few dark-skinned women on the Ride, has more than singed lips to worry about in Vidor. A year earlier, the federal government had seized control of a local public housing complex after nine African Americans—the first black residents of Vidor since the twenties—were driven out by hostile townspeople and the Ku Klux Klan.

As we dip our torches in the Coleman lamp fuel the Avengers use instead of traditional carnival fire-eater kerosene (it's less toxic), Lisa reads a statement for the press. A plentiful supply of printed statements is another media must at all Avenger actions. A broadside distributed by the Avengers at the 1993 March on Washington places "Access to Resources/Xerox Machines" first on the list of official

216

"Top 10 Avenger Qualities" most sought in new recruits. (Runner-up traits: Good Dancer, Pro-Sex, Fighting Spirit, Righteous Anger, Fearlessness, Informed, No Big Ego, Leadership, and Compassion.)

"There are lesbians in this community whether Vidor chooses to acknowledge them or not," Lisa proclaims. "We're here to show our support because they can't be out. To be an out lesbian in towns such as Vidor is to risk losing your home, your job, and your well-being." Then she reads several anonymous statements from local, closeted lesbians. "I don't feel safe coming out because the well-known expression of racial hatred here is only part of the hate problem," says one. "Anyone considered different from the norm is subjected to anything from slurs to violent acts in Vidor. The reason I have for not speaking out is the fact that I have a young daughter in a Vidor public school."

Lisa raises her torch to the crowd. If they can burn crosses, we can gobble flames. It's been the Avengers' trademark action since the 1992 campaign to defeat Oregon's Ballot Measure 9, which declared homosexuals "abnormal and perverse" and, had it passed, would have invalidated all gay rights ordinances in the state. In September of that year, skinheads tossed a Molotov cocktail into the Salem home of Hattie Mae Cohens, an African-American lesbian, and Brian Mock, a disabled wheelchair-bound gay man, killing them both. At a Halloween memorial in New York City a month later, the original Lesbian Avenger chapter, coached by a sympathetic circus performer, ate fire for the first time.

We chant, "The fire will not consume us. We'll take it and make it our own." We hope.

"Oops, everyone turn ninety degrees to your left," Lisa says. Right! *That's* the other trick: Always make sure the wind is blowing *away* from you.

"Okay." Regina sighs and takes a deep breath. "Here I . . . Hmm. I think I did it."

"Very close," Frida says.

"Shit. How far away was I when I blew it out? Shit," says Regina. "Hey, light me again. I'm gonna do this."

Regina hadn't quite managed to guzzle the torch in our earlier practice session without an audience. "It's easier now that you're actually doing an action," Frida says encouragingly, "because you're hyperventilating. See? You did it!"

"Did I?" marvels Regina. "I couldn't tell. I had my eyes closed." Frida nearly faints.

Across the street, Lisa and several other riders are now chatting with a trio of locals who have turned out as Vidor goodwill ambassadors: a young, newly elected city councilman, half polished politician, half eager-to-please junior woodchuck; Vidor's beer-gutted, good-old-boy-but-apparently-friendly-to-fire-eating-lesbians fire and rescue chief; and a woman astonishingly dressed in a not-a-hair-out-of-place outfit that is totally purple, right down to purple nylons and very high-heeled purple shoes. Unlike the other two, she's not here in an official capacity. "I work next door, and just was curious," she explains. "You came in as people. And we're people. And that's what's important."

"I just wish we'd known you were coming," the councilman says. Avenger policy is to not get permits, Lisa explains. The trio nods politely, obviously a bit too establishment to quite get it, but really, really trying.

They also don't quite get the second half of our action, which is a shantytown we've assembled on the city hall lawn. It's composed of graffiti-covered corrugated cardboard. One of the cardboard "building blocks" reads, "Hips Tits Lips Power." The intent is to broaden today's focus beyond lesbian visibility into a "Poverty is a feminist issue"/antiracism support action. The Avenger statement cites various stats: Two and a half million women sixty-five or older live in poverty, compared to one million men: 36 percent of old African-American women, 25 percent of old Latina women, and 13 percent of old white women are poor.

The trio nods. They understand all this. What they don't understand (aside from the business with the tits) is, what the heck does it have to do with lesbians?

Indeed, while the lesbian community's farsighted instinct—indeed, almost a compulsion—to at least aim for political inclusiveness is what makes some of us proudest of our lesbian identity, it's easy to see why these very good-hearted but very straight Vidorians are puzzled.

"You wouldn't have any trouble from me if you lived here," the purple lady finally offers, gamely trying to narrow the focus to the folks facing her. "I'd think other people here'd react the same way. I support rights for everybody. I can hear your voice."

Meanwhile, cars roar by on the mall-strip highway that's the town's main street. They slow down to read our signs. Most of these commuting citizens don't appear to understand our demo, either, but it doesn't seem to be the political complexities that trouble them. "Lesbians, fuck you!" comments one male voice of the people.

"Like there's any chance!" an Avenger yells back.

After the welcome wagon leaves, we decide to have a picnic/processing lunch before we go. The parade of insults from passing cars continues. Finally one guy peels into the parking lot, jumps out of his ratty Chevy pickup, and demands, "What're you-all doing here?" We invite him to sit and talk. He refuses to come within twenty feet. We are sincere, even cheerful. He's close to chewing off his lower lip, in agitation. "When're you leaving?"

When we finish lunch, we reply. Maybe ten minutes.

"Make it five," he snarls, peeling out.

We stay half an hour, and then, still feeling feisty, stop on the way out of town at Gary's, the coffee shop where the local KKK leadership meets. Despite hairy eyeballs from big-haired waitresses and patrons, though, there's no trouble. "I thought Vidor would be our worst confrontation on the whole trip," says one of the younger Avengers, an all-American-girl type (except for the nose ring), practically giddy with relief. "This hasn't been bad."

"You don't know Vidor," replies Tish Parker, the only local lesbian who has shown up for the demo. "Like there's Bubba drivin' by." She points to a fellow roaring by in a pickup. She tilts her head toward a uniformed cop with a camera. "And there's Earl, takin' everyone's picture." As a Vidor resident who will not, like us, be quaffing Blackened Voodoo beers in gay-friendly New Orleans several hours from now, she is clearly not optimistic about the possible consequences to herself of today, tomorrow . . . and tomorrow.

Tish is "Vice President, Racial Diversity, Texas National Organization for Women," according to her business card—which bears no address. "You can't do that here if you're lesbian. You don't want general people to know where you live. I do have a silent group of friends, so there's some support. Still, it's always a risk here." She has been a Vidor resident for only three months, and only because "I just happened to fall in love" when she came to a demo protesting yet another recent Vidor gala event, a massive march of White Power neo-Nazi skinheads. "My lover always lived around here. Otherwise, I never would. She works in Port Arthur where it's more liberal, and keeps a low profile here in town."

Blond, petite, thirtysomething, and prom-queen cute, Tish could easily pass for straight, too. When it's suggested, however, that demonstrating on Main Street today with the Lesbian Avengers might majorly blow her low profile, she just shrugs. "If you can't stand for somethin', what's the use of livin'? I'm too damn old to play games. There's nothin' wrong with bein' what I am."

More typical is the young supermarket checker, who notices our shantytown while she's walking to her car. She crosses the highway to talk. "Tell you the truth," she says hesitantly, after about twenty minutes' conversation, "I, I'm a lesbian, too. I think. I mean, I don't really know. I haven't thought it all out yet. But I'm at least bisexual. Shit." She glances at the reporter from a Houston daily newspaper, who's furiously scribbling, and back at the supermarket. Then she shakes her head.

"Ah, who cares. They'll know something's up just because I'm here. Wonder what it's gonna be like going back to work tomorrow." She laughs. "I really can't even believe I'm out here talkin' to you."

Most gay (or questioning) women like her, in Vidor or countless other towns throughout America, wouldn't dare. That's the point. And that's why the Lesbian Avengers are here today—and will, in the next ten days of the Pride Ride, be in Ovett, Mississippi, Birmingham, Alabama, Cobb County, Georgia, and half a dozen of the other most notorious locales of this decade's gay rights struggle, and of black civil rights movement actions thirty years ago.

Besides, as the official Lesbian Avenger slogan notes: "We Recruit."

• • •

The Lesbian Avengers began with a bang in June 1992 at the march New York City lesbians and gay men have held annually to commemorate the 1969 Stonewall rebellion. Eight thousand fluorescent-green cards were distributed by the group's six founders (the best-known being novelist Sarah Schulman). "Lesbians! Dykes! Gay women!" the cards read. "We want revenge and we want it now!"

It was an odd political moment. The presidential primaries were in full swing, and the gay establishment was putting its money on Bill Clinton. Openly gay U.S. representative Barney Frank was urging gay folk to be "more like the NAACP and the AARP." But lesbians were still reeling from *Basic Instinct,* and feeling decidedly invisible, un-chic, and powerless.

At the first Lesbian Avengers meeting in New York City, fifty women showed up. By the summer of the Houston–to–New York Pride Ride two years later, the group was close to four dozen chapters strong—thirty in the United States, the rest in Canada, England, and Australia—and growing. (Well, also shrinking. "In Toronto, all the Avengers were sleeping with each other, and it tore the group apart. No one is talking, and the more prominent members have migrated to British Columbia," according to one of the Canadian Pride Riders.)

What was most important about the Avengers isn't their numbers—there are probably more lesbians in the NAACP and the AARP—but their goofy, galvanizing spirit. For most aware lesbians, political demonstrations are a necessity, a responsibility, an obligation; they're something we do regularly, but reluctantly. For Avengers, they're a good time, and, as their original broadside noted, "a great place to cruise womyn." And as the broadside also made crystal clear, the Avengers regard going up against the Christian right as a blood sport: "WE'RE NOT WAITING FOR THE RAPTURE! WE ARE THE APOCALYPSE."

Early in 1993, following Colorado's passage of antigay Amendment 2, the New York City Avengers chapter dogged Denver's mayor, Wellington Webb, when he came to the Big Apple on a tourism-promo trip. Though Webb's schedule had been carefully guarded, roughly a dozen Avengers burst into his power breakfast and marched around the posh Regency Hotel dining room chanting, "We're here, we're queer, we're not going skiing."

New York Avengers also occupied *Self*'s offices, after the women's magazine announced a Colorado ski week–promo meeting. As a result of the actions, reporters asked Mayor Webb about Amendment 2, not skiing, and his scheduled Toronto tourism-promo trip was canceled. So was *Self*'s Colorado ski meeting.

For Valentine's Day, the Avengers installed, in Manhattan's Bryant Park, a gold-painted papier-mâché statue of a floppy-hatted Alice B. Toklas, stretching for a clinch with the park's existing statue of her lover, Gertrude Stein.

Then on April 24, the night before the official March on Washington, an estimated six thousand to twenty thousand women (depending on whether you accept the D.C. police crowd count or the Lesbian Avenger count) showed up for a "Dyke March," which climaxed with fire-eating in front of the White House. It was leather-jacket weather, but many participants threw caution and brassieres to the wind, marching topless. The event—featuring such catchy slogans as "We're dykes! Don't touch us! We'll hurt you!" and "We want Hillary!"—spawned many more Lesbian Avenger chapters, as marchers returned home to Yellow Springs, Ohio, and Tucson, Arizona, with the New York Avengers recruitment broadsides, fifty thousand copies of which had been printed for the D.C. march.

Along with dozens more Dyke Marches, new chapters sponsored actions every bit as imaginative as those of the New York mother-house. East Lansing Avengers managed to sneak an Avenger bomb float into the 1993 Michigan State Homecoming parade, masking their intentions with a sign reading "Bomb the Hawkeyes" (MSU's football rivals). That's how *one* side of the sign read. The other side, unveiled for judges at the city hall parade reviewing stand: "1 in 10 MSU Women Is a Lesbian!"

In response to Jesse Helms's denunciation of assistant secretary of Housing and Urban Development Roberta Achtenberg as not just "a garden-variety lesbian" but a "mean, militant, activist lesbian," Avengers in Raleigh/Durham, North Carolina, marched through the streets in a "Garden Variety Lesbian" demonstration of truly cultivated Southern womanhood, with large flowered hats, flowing dresses, and appropriate signs, such as "Helms Is Too Mulch."

San Francisco Avengers burst into the offices of a Christian right organization that purports to "cure" homosexuality and released a "plague of locusts"—actually, a thousand crickets—on the reception desk.

There have also been less flashy Avenger organizing campaigns in Christian right strongholds like Idaho and central Maine. Naturally, all this action costs money, but don't expect one of those fund-raising letters listing an all-star gay board of dignitaries down the side. The standard Lesbian Avenger fund-raising tool is a good party, publicized in a fashion better known to power rock bands than power politicos: massive grassroots-politics paper routes, urban underground trails of wheat paste and posters. One particularly effective New York Avenger New Year's Eve party paste-up featured blaxploitation star Pam Grier with big hair, a bigger shotgun, and tiny hot pants, bearing the slogan "Activist A-Go-Go." Over a thousand women showed up.

The Austin Lesbian Avengers chapter was formed in January 1993, when Sarah Schulman came to Texas on a book tour. The following May, while more establishment groups like the Lesbian/Gay Rights Lobby of Texas and the Austin Lesbian and Gay Political Caucus lobbied legislators against Texas sodomy laws, Avengers stink-bombed the state capitol building.

About a year later came the Austin Avengers' crowning glory: the "Manure Action" at Cedar Park Baptist Church in nearby Williamson County, where Apple Computer had a much publicized run-in with local right-wingers. Outraged at the passage in Austin of an ordinance enabling live-in spouses of gay city employees to obtain the same health insurance benefits provided to legally wedded spouses of straight city employees, the church was inspired by Christian love to put a huge marquee on its front lawn: "Don't Be Deceived. Homosexuals Commit the Most Heinous Crimes in America."

At 4 A.M. on Sunday, April 17, 1994, Austin Avengers responded to the billboard by dumping a full pickup-truck load of horse manure in the church parking lot. "It came to about three foot high," one of the dumpers recalls admiringly. "A beautiful pile." Scattered on top, like nuts on a sundae, were flyers reading "Homophobia stinks," "Jesus was a homeless hippie who loved everyone. Why can't you?" and "You eat shit. We eat clit."

This time, Austin's ruling gay political queens were, like Victoria, not amused. Openly gay Texas state representative Glen Maxey called the Avenger action "inappropriate" and apologized to the church, even offering to personally clean the mess up.

This will be a recurring motif in the history of the Avengers, needless to say. The actions that seem fresh and fierce to some seem alienating and tasteless to others. Of course, for those who remember the sixties, all this means is that the déjà vu of reckoning is at hand.

It's June 15, 1994, the night before the Pride Ride officially begins. Strewn around the elegant upper-middle-class Houston house belonging to Lisa's parents are nearly two dozen rather less than elegant-looking lesbians. Well, we're pretty darned scuzzy, truthfully, since some of us have traveled to Houston from California, Florida, and Pennsylvania; the Toronto rider has been on a bus for days. But this *Architectural Digest* cover–ready home is tonight's rather improbable Lesbian Avenger crash pad. (The ride's brochure has made clear that most accommodations will be the floors of lesbians who live along the route. Riders can spread our own sleeping bags. There'll be nothing like this basketball-court-sized living room.)

On a white piano, next to Lisa's sister's wedding photo, is a high school graduation photo of Lisa herself, looking longhaired, girlish, and preppy, with a very sweet smile. She is now a thirty-one-year-old, crew-cut, deliberately downscale-dressed hard-core dyke— with the same very sweet smile. Lisa is really the main Pride Ride organizer, main responsibility-taker, and main organizational shitworker. Naturally, by the end of the ride, everyone will have turned on her.

Lisa's dad is a distinguished gray-haired ex-pilot. Her mom has long blond ringlets and is wearing, for some reason, a long black evening gown. She has cooked a turkey for the group. Lisa is the first to admit that her coming out to them two years earlier was a bit of a bomb drop. "I had been an ardent Gerald Ford supporter and college business major, who had what I considered then to be perfectly fine sex and relationships with guys," she says. "I didn't even have my first conscious attraction to women until five years ago." Dad's response was to go off to a meeting of P-FLAG, Parents and Friends of Lesbians and Gays. Mom, on the other hand, "hasn't said the word 'lesbian' to me yet. Her attitude is, 'If you murdered someone, we'd help you bury the body.' Meaning, she loves me, but she doesn't want to talk about any of it. When the big *Newsweek* cover piece on lesbians came out, I thought this would be a good way to broach the subject. So I gave it to her, and sort of made myself available for questions and discussion. The article *after* the lesbian article was on suburban lawns. She said, 'Hey, that was a really interesting article on turf grass.' " Even tonight, Lisa maintains, Mom "is not really dealing with the fact that there are twenty-five radical lesbians in the house. It's more like, 'Oh, you have twenty-five friends coming over; I'll cook a turkey.' " Whatever, Mom and Dad are both trying hard to be good sports.

We're circled in the ancestral split-level for our "Getting to Know You" meeting, or, as political dykes would call it, "affinity session." More accurately, this is the first—and second, and third—of many, many, many hours of Pride Ride processing. Processing is kept to a minimum in the Lesbian Avengers, according to their P.R. releases. But Lesbian Avengers are, after all, lesbians. Processing is *required,* possibly genetic.

The session begins with us going around the circle, each rider sharing her name and her reasons for going on the ride. To our great relief, we are not required to run down our astrological pedigrees. (As it turns out, our relief is premature. Astrology is just being saved for the next night's processing session.)

"I'm an Austin Lesbian Avenger," begins Carrie, who is twenty-four and, like Lisa, one of the original organizers of the ride. "I feel very identified with the Lesbian Avengers. I *am* a Lesbian Avenger. I avenge, therefore I am. 'I am a Lesbian Avenger, therefore I am a lesbian' is, I think, how I feel."

She is also feeling nauseated. Carrie has a dreadful stomach ailment—we suspect it's stress-related—that almost prevented her coming on the trip. It's been a long year of planning, with splits over such issues as how long the ride should be (the winning side wanted to keep it under two weeks, so more working women could participate) and what to ride in. (A lavender bus? A rented regular bus with a giant lavender slipcover?) The group settled for three regular old blue rental vans, with giant Lesbian Avenger Pride Ride banners (painted sheets), complete with about-to-explode-bomb logo.

"I guess I got involved because of feeling dissatisfied with the way other, more establishment-liberal groups reacted to things," says Sara, a lesbian mom in her mid-thirties with an earnestly responsible brain and the super-femme looks, mannerisms, and squeaky Valley Girl voice of a stereotypical beauty parlor bimbo. "I like to be involved in a group that views radical actions in the same way I do, that does actions that don't strictly follow the letter of the law. Because most of the laws don't respect us."

"Being an Avenger makes me feel better about myself," says Frida. "Before, there were things I didn't do because of fear. This ride, this visibility in places like Vidor, marks a turning point in my life, where I can say I'm not afraid to do anything." (That said, it should be noted that "Frida" is a pseudonym. Frida is, in fact, not entirely out. Neither—oddly, given the high-visibility focus of this Pride Ride and its consequent potential for outing disasters—are several other riders.)

"On the ride I will be doing smudging with sage each day, after our morning circle," announces a cute thirtyish Midwest transplant whose bandanna looks permanently grafted onto her forehead in downwardly mobile hippie style. She is actually an ex-Avenger (now primarily committed to Native Americana and to her mixed-gender activist Texas commune, which appears to support itself largely on food stamps), but set on assuming Pride Ride leadership nonetheless. "Smudging is a very important thing," she assures us. "I do smudging in a traditional Lakota way. It keeps you safe. It's also for purification. I am not religious. I am spiritual. I am sure other people have fundamental opinions about that. Now, about the vans . . ."

Many of us have Van Issues. "I just want to preface this," says

Sara (pronouncing it "pree-fayce"), "by saying I really expect to have a good time in the vans. However maybe everyone should talk about that." She consults a voluminous list on her lap. "Like, are there ways we could have our own space in the van?" Everyone who's not an Austin Avenger and therefore has not been processing van intricacies for months looks blank. "Well," Sara prompts, "like, you could have a Walkman."

"Right," seconds a woman named Shana. "And we have CBs. But the directions say the antennas shouldn't stay up. So I suggest every half-hour we put the antenna up, in case people want to stop, or go in the quiet van, or something."

"Right," the Smudger jumps in. "We could also use white flags."

"Right. For a fallback, we could use white flags," Lisa says, a bit tensely. One of the few Austin Avengers with a freelance rather than a punch-the-timeclock job, photojournalist Lisa has turned down all pay-the-rent gigs for three weeks in order to work full-time on organizing ride details. She therefore feels, essentially, that said ride details are *organized,* not up for grabs by anyone who arrived on the scene half an hour ago.

"Right, and you're not stuck in one van," the Smudger adds. "You can move. Like to the quiet van."

"Right," says Lisa. "But we're going to have quiet times in *all* the vans."

"Right," says Sara. "Well, but personally, I don't know how the group feels, but I myself feel that if people in a van reach *consensus* that they don't want quiet time, they shouldn't *have* to have one."

That settled, we go on to the smoking-in-the-vans processing, a mere twenty-minute session to establish who smokes (but is trying to quit, and wants to talk about it at length); who doesn't smoke (and due to the usual astonishing assortment of lezzie environmental allergies can't be even in the same county, much less the same van, as smoke, and wants to talk about it at length; the most allergic rider, of course, is in the smoking van almost immediately); and who, like Regina, doesn't give a shit and wants everyone to stop talking so she can go to sleep. Regina will spend most of the trip's traveling time under her Walkman earphones, trying desperately to block all on-the-road processing.

"There will be some exercises we can do in the van to relieve stress, if there is stress," Sara announces, checking another item off her list. "Like role-playing. Or the 'Love Thy Neighbor' game, which is great fun. We've been doing it at meetings. It's like musical chairs. One extra person is always standing, and tries to get another person standing by saying, like, 'I love women who have labia piercings.' Or something. Then everyone with labia piercings runs to get a seat. I'm not actually that sure it would work in the van," she reflects, chewing her pencil. "Okay, the driver definitely shouldn't do it. Maybe at rest areas."

Another game is "I Never," which has become a classic in our community since serving as a plot device in Rose Troche's low-budget homo home movie cum Hollywood smash success, *Go Fish*. "You go around the van," Sara explains, "and someone says, like, 'I've never been penetrated.' Then whoever *has* been penetrated puts their finger up."

And . . . oh yeah, Sara reminds us. "No overt sex in the vans."

"Is discreet sex allowed?" somebody asks.

On an early Pride Ride guide mailed to all riders, one of the packing don'ts (along with alcohol, drugs, and weapons) was "No 'educational models.' " The Avengers were concerned about a Texas law that says possession of more than six dildos proves intent to distribute, Lisa explains. "But after getting, um, considerable rider feedback, we decided if you can fit 'em in your bag, you can bring 'em."

Major laughter, many raucous dildo jokes, a little loudly verbalized melodrama from a few device-dependent younger dykes who left their "toy bags" at home and can't conceive of how to get it on without them. "Geez, guys, will you keep the sex shit down?" Lisa hisses. "My mom is in the next room!"

"So should we go around the circle again?" Sara inquires. This would be round three. "Like, to express needs? To make sure everyone has a voice? Are there particular concerns we haven't addressed?"

Luz, who is half of one of the ride's monogamous couples, raises her hand. "Do we *have* to have discreet sex in the vans?"

"I'm too stressed to talk," Lisa explodes.

"So, um . . ." Sara frowns at the list, pencil poised. "Does this mean you need your own space in the van?"

"I am a board member of Ellas, a very big San Antonio Latina lesbian organization," explains Luz. "And to tell you the truth, they tried to convince us not to come on this ride. Because they thought it would be a danger to us. They're very closeted to the outside world. Most are teachers, and with kids. They don't want a bad image. They don't want an image, period.

"But one true thing they did put up to us about this Pride Ride is, we could get arrested. It's the South. And more likely me, being darker, I could be a target." Though both she and her lover are Chicanas, Veronica (a.k.a. Vero) is light-skinned, light-brown-haired, Spanglish-looking; Luz is very dark with black hair and flat features, appearing to be of Indian rather than Spanish descent.

But "being taken to a police car and them doing what is said they often do to darker women" would not be Luz's only problem if she were busted as a radical troublemaker. Born in Mexico, she has lived in America since the age of four and works for the federal government as a child disability specialist. But she has just applied for citizenship. "If they tag me, I am afraid I won't get it." Luz has told the Anglo Avengers that if there's any kind of police problem, she's going to run.

Vero also faces consequences, less dramatic but no less real, for being visible in such a public way as this major media-grabbing event. A registered critical care nurse for ten years, she is not out at work. While being outed could cause Vero to lose her job, "the problem is much worse. In critical care nursing, it is very stressful. You work in a team, and it is crucial to establish a good, trusting relationship with your coworkers, to make good teamwork. I know it would be a big problem if they knew I was a lesbian, just from the way they treat other people who have been out. Even a guy there who is a very, very good nurse, they talk about in terrible ways;

they don't like to be with him, so they do not work well with him. You are supposed to be there for the patient, and good teamwork is what it's all about. But being out makes it very hard to have good teamwork."

Why, then, risk it? Vero looks down at her hands. "This ride is for a good reason. It is worth the problems," she says. "I've been thinking about being out for a long time, anyway. And this lesbian visibility is more important than what I could risk myself on my job."

"It's our turn," adds Luz. "You can't just let other people always do it."

Luz is thirty-seven, Vero twenty-nine. They fell in love two years ago, after each had a lover leave them for a man. In fact, Vero's lover before *that* left her for a man, too. "Me and Veronica, we've been gay all our lives," says Luz. She is still a little nettled about the ex, who actually upped and married a guy, out of the blue, during a work-related separation. At the time, Luz was caring for the woman's young son, whom she had helped raise and is still extremely close to.

"When he was in first grade, a friend of his once said, 'Ha ha ha you don't have a daddy.' " Luz crows. "Tony goes, 'Why do I need a daddy? I got two mothers, you only got one!' So that was no problem."

What was a problem: Vero was upset because she didn't think Luz and the ex had properly processed the end of their relationship. "Because do you know, they were married?" Vero exclaims. "They had a ceremony, in a church. A *big* wedding! Bridesmaids. It was one of the biggest weddings in San Antonio. And it was still not dissolved. That was very serious for me. I told her, 'Luz, you have to go and get a paper, and sign it.' "

"The way I felt," Luz protests—still, obviously, smarting that her ex's meet-in-a-disco-one-night-get-hitched-the-next wedding to Mr. Maleperson was legal, while the *big* church wedding to her was not—"was she married this man. That automatically dissolved it."

"No, no, Luz," Vero counterprotests. "The way I felt, she was still married." Legalities notwithstanding, she explains, "I take this serious. If you were married to a man in church, you would have to get divorced. I didn't want to be involved with somebody if they're still married." The ex refused to sign the "divorce" papers. Finally, Luz got the minister who performed the commitment ceremony to grant them a lesbian annulment.

Despite all this attention to form, Luz and Vero have no interest in traditional roles. The hard part about being an out lesbian in Latin culture, says Luz, is "how can you not want Mr. Macho, who's going to take care of you, who's going to support you?" When she came out to her father, "he says, 'Ohhh. You think you can support a woman?' You know what he did? He gave me a wallet!"

"We even have that problem with my parents," says Vero. "Because my father thinks I'm still his responsibility because I'm not married. I'm his daughter and I'm not given to a man." Vero is going back to school in September, "and my mom says, 'Who's going to feed Luz? Who's going to be there to cook for her? You better lay out her clothes for her, take care of her, or she'll leave you.' " When they see Luz waiting on Vero, they don't know what to make of it. "It upsets me that some people think Luz must be the butch, but I'm very close with my family. I'm totally out to them. They help me with all my personal stuff."

"Her grandmother, she's like seventy-five," adds Luz. "On Mother's Day she's like, 'Get over here, Luz. You have to be in the film with us because you're with Veronica, you're in the family.' "

"So it's confusing," says Vero. "If a seventy-five-year-old Hispanic lady can just throw away homophobic behavior, why is it so hard for other people to do it?"

The Ride departs from Houston only after major fashion consultations. Human rights may be of prime concern to the Lesbian Avengers, but style is no small consideration. Many of us have opted, this first day, to sport the official Pride Ride T-shirt: on the front, a picture of a stern, upward-gazing World War II–era female armed forces gal in a tailored uniform, riding a motorcycle. The accompanying motto: "This is no time to be frail." On the back is a map of all our action stops from Vidor to New York.

"I was thinking I'd wear my 'Love Is a Basic Human Right' T-shirt," obsesses CathyAnne, a motormouthed activist from Philadelphia, who has a verbal riposte for every situation, and the perfect slogan-bearing shirt to match. "But do you think it goes with this 'Smear Me with Honey and Throw Me to the Lesbians' button?" The back of CathyAnne's T reads, "Sodom & Gomorrah Tour Guide—This Ain't Kansas."

There are Birkenstock lesbians and (especially in Texas) cow-person-boot lesbians, but the Avenger footwear of choice is thick-soled Doc Martens, which are certainly useful for stamping out stray sparks. "We do *everything* in our Docs," one of the Austin women swears. Second in popularity are what used to be referred to in our personal New Jersey high school days as "fuck-me pumps," for after-action wear. Regina alone has brought five pair.

For CB communications purposes, the vans have been tastefully christened Diesel Dyke, Car 69, and Snatch. In Diesel, the nine or so riders plunge immediately into demonstrating their dedication to official Top 10 Avenger Quality Number 3, "pro-sex." Totally tacky sexual sharing begins ten miles out of Houston with a game of "I Never," and doesn't stop until virtually within spitting distance of the Statue of Liberty.

"I never had sex with more than one person at a time."

CathyAnne's hand instantly shoots up from the backseat, to applause. *Of course* she has! Several other hands are raised, all belonging to the "older" (over-thirty-five) crowd—in fact, only one of the older women on the van can say "I never." Each of the other seniors racks up a point.

"I never had sex with more than two people at a time."

"Simultaneously?" demands an astonished younger woman. "You can't do more than two at once."

Sure you can! Points for all old-timers but one, again.

"I never had sex in an airplane."

One point, a high-flyin' older woman.

"I never have been to bed with a stranger."

"What counts as not a stranger?" someone wonders.

"You know her name," clarifies the Smudger.

"Whole name, or just first name?" First name, it's decided. More hands go up.

"What counts as 'to bed'?" niggles another older rider. "Does a dance club parking lot count?" Two younger riders gape. After all the parameters are set, this "I never" garners many "Oh yes I did" points, including all the older women.

"I never have been fisted."

CathyAnne's hand bobs up. "Does fisting somebody else count?" another older rider asks, reminiscingly regarding her very short fingernails.

"Um, no," says Shaila, the twenty-three-year-old woman who has started this round. CathyAnne's hand shoots down.

"Does trying count?" asks someone else.

"Only if it was an honest try," the Smudger arbitrates. "Past the knuckles." No actual points, but the discussion alone has finished off the young dykes.

"I don't think it's fair for women who were around in the early seventies to play without a handicap," one of them grumbles. The older riders laugh in delight. Until now, we had no idea we'd led such exciting lives. In fact, what with all those trendy talk-show glam gay girls, we thirty-five-and-ups had assumed that the thirty-five-and-downs were discoing home every night with lipstick on the flies of their 501s. They, on the other hand, seem resigned to the idea that all the truly hot lez sex scenarios got used up sometime around 1979. Anyway, the twentysomethings in Diesel have finer fish to fry.

"I never had a really nice female long-term lover. . . ."

Trailing off, Shaila watches wistfully as the old girls grab it again.

"I never had sex with a person unless I wanted a commitment."

"A commitment for the whole night?" Luz chuckles. This "I never" was from Vero, who gives her girlfriend a look of long-suffering patience. But neither of the devoted duo gets a point. Everybody else does.

"I never had sex with someone who was totally femme."

"Define femme," someone challenges.

"Oh . . . Big hair. Makeup."

CathyAnne's hand, which has been going up and down, remains up. "I didn't think I had, but now I remember, the first woman I ever had sex with was femme like that." She pauses primly. "But I can't say who."

"You *can!*" the whole van yells.

"Oh, all right," she quickly concedes. "She was a famous model. She's dead now. Supermodel Gia. I actually had to fuck her brother to get to her. But that was many, many years ago. I used to be bi, I thought."

"I think we *all* thought . . ." someone muses.

"I never slept with someone more than eight years younger than me."

No points. No one here has acted on this most common of male fantasies, straight and gay. No one even seems to get what could be the erotic thrill of cradle-robbing.

"I never slept with someone more than eight years older than me."

The erotic thrill of walker-robbing is a different story. Everyone but one rider gets points. (Remember, straight single women over forty who can't get boyfriends because the over-forty guys are all dating eighteen-year-olds: We recruit.)

"I never had sex with animals."

What about when your cat *thinks* she's having sex with you? someone wonders.

"I never had sex with a man."

This one's from Vero, and everyone scores an "I did so!" point except for her girlfriend, Luz. Luz follows up:

"I never had bad sex."

"That's because you never had sex with a man!" choruses everyone else.

"I never had sex with a straight woman."

"Oh, God," CathyAnne sighs. "It was the most horrible sex in my life. First there was this routine." She grimaces, and elaborately wipes her mouth. "Then she's, 'Oh no, I can't believe I've done it! And it's *all your fault.'* And then . . . her husband!"

She reflects. "Okay, here's one: 'I'll never *again* have sex with a straight woman.' "

Someone notes that the "I nevers" don't have to be sexual. Vero gives it a try:

"I never have been on a lesbian softball team."

It goes on. No one ever wanted to be a boy, except as a very young preadolescent. No one ever had sex with a transgender person. Astonishingly, three riders never cheated on their current lovers, even in daydreams. Only one point for anal penetration. One point for hemorrhoids. No one has ever done hard-core s/m sex. Although there are some fond memories of light bondage with handkerchiefs.

Where nearly everyone gets points is time travel, back to the good old days (real old: the Middle Ages); only the oldest rider has never wanted to go back in time. However, only the oldest rider wants to go forward in time. A vanload of radical activists on a mission to change the world, and nearly every last one is convinced the future's going to stink.

"Okay, I've got a new game," someone announces: "Stupid Comments Straight People Made When You Came Out."

" 'Which one is the boy?' " half the van shrieks.

"This one's from my mother," offers the Smudger, who is driving. "When I came out to her, she says, 'Well, now that you're a dyke, can I still change clothes in front of you?' My own mother!" The van weaves as she rolls her eyes to the roof. But almost every rider has a similar tale.

We move on to "Worst Jobs Anyone Ever Had." Having tried the full assortment of classic baby-dyke manual-labor jobs (underpaid housepainter, underpaid apple picker, underpaid foot messenger . . .), we personally have high hopes of winning this game. But the clear victor is CathyAnne, who dressed as Rainbow Brite for children's parties.

A passing car honks, and its four festive male passengers give us the high sign; fellow travelers to Stonewall. From the backseat of another car, a little boy waves wildly at us, and we all wave back. His mom turns around from the front seat, reads our Lesbian

Avengers banner, and yanks his arm down, yelling. He bursts into tears.

The CB crackles: There is a proposal that we stop at the next exit's Cracker Barrel. "No!" our van yells back, in outraged solidarity. Politically aware gay people have been boycotting this rustic restaurant chain since February 1991, when Cracker Barrel began a purge of gay employees, spurred by an outrageously discriminatory corporate policy: "It is inconsistent with our concept and values . . . to continue to employ individuals . . . whose sexual preferences fail to demonstrate normal heterosexual values."

"They say, 'Not to buy, just to pee,' " reports our CB navigator.

"Only if we pee on the floor," Luz suggests.

We don't, really. But after we use the regulation receptacles and are relaxing in rocking chairs on the Cracker Barrel's olde-tyme-y front porch, CathyAnne is overcome by nostalgia, activist-style. "The best pee action I ever did was during the National Endowment for the Arts Jesse Helms thing. A bunch of us got a five-gallon mayonnaise jar, went drinking, pissed in it, and put a picture of Jesse on the front with 'Piss Helms' written on it. Then we plastic-coatcd the whole thing, and mailed it to him."

There is much appreciation from the other rocking riders. "I've done upchuck actions, too," adds CathyAnne.

Sometimes we are thc Lcsbian Assholes.

In New Orleans, our designated action is to ride the St. Charles streetcar from the end of the line all the way into the French Quarter, passing out "Lick Homophobia" lollipops, chanting antioppression slogans, loudly singing old standards with "dyke" substituted for every possible word, and monopolizing two-thirds of the streetcar seats not only with our bodies but with our video equipment, as dozens of commuters stand.

Not to mention that this is all for no apparent reason, relatively speaking. Way back in December 1991, the New Orleans City Council passed an ordinance barring discrimination against lesbians and gay men in employment, housing, and public accommodation. New Orleans also prohibits discrimination on the basis of sexual orientation in city hiring and provision of city services. A Louisiana governor's executive order provides the same protection for lesbians and gay men who work in or do business with state agencies. The current mayor acknowledged gay people in his inaugural address. New Orleans can even probably claim the world's first lesbian "outing," pre-dating Michelangelo Signorile and ACT UP's visibility-encouragement efforts by almost a hundred years: On October 21, 1893, the scandal sheet *New Orleans Mascot* revealed residents Alice Mitchell and Freda Ward as sapphic sisters.

But here we are, singing, "This patriarchal image of our sex must die" to the tune of "Dixie." Most passengers take it pretty well. A young straight woman in a little striped sundress waves when she gets off. A black woman buries herself under a Walkman, but sucks a lollipop.

"Wham, bam, thank you, ma'am! Don't forget your dental dam," the Avengers chant.

A white-haired, white-suited Southern gent in an adjacent seat politely points out Garden District architectural sights to us, doing his best to ignore the kiddie show. However, when the Avengers get to "Battle Hymn of the Republic" (which they don't seem to realize, or else to care, was originally the civil rights anthem "John Brown's Body") with "the coming of the dykes" substituted for "the coming of the Lord," his mouth finally twitches downward slightly. "Patriotic bunch, ahn't they?"

Later Lisa admits that this particular action came about "sort of by default." In general, the Avenger policy is that "visibility equals survival." So lesbian survival "just sort of devolved into 'Let's ride the streetcar and be out.' The actions are as much for the women in them as about trying to change other people's attitudes. At this stage in the game, we're just sort of trying to form the army to march forward. Part of that is dealing with our own internal homophobia, so we can go from there. It's safe passing out lollipops. Singing proudly and loudly, especially when some people are kind of pissed off about it, isn't so safe."

In other words, the Lesbian Avengers is only part lesbian direct-action group. It's also part lesbian consciousness-raising–support group.

And, adds Lisa, "at the Texas Lesbian Conference a couple of months ago, one of the older feminists said she looked at us as the Black Panthers of the lesbian and gay movement, because we do stuff that's way out in left field, that's really offensive to some people. But what that does is push the envelope way out to here, so that mainstream gay politics becomes more legitimized. Like, if my mother was on a streetcar of women yelling 'Dyke!' every five minutes, then the next time I say the word 'lesbian' to her, maybe it's not gonna be so hard for her to take." In other words, the Lesbian Avengers is one of the extreme ends that justify the middle.

This is a valid point. But others besides us have also suggested that for maximum effectiveness as catalysts for political change, the Avengers could use a lot less *Ted Mack's Original Amateur Hour* and a bit more Modern American Poli Sci 101—with maybe a dollop of Ms. Manners, plus a Valium or two, for good measure.

A small example: In St. Louis, six Avengers who wanted to educate lesbians about gay-bashing reportedly leafleted in front of a popular woman-owned gay bar, rather than trying to arrange for a table inside. When the owners asked the Avengers to leave (on the grounds that their own anti-gay-bashing safety policy required maintaining a low pedestrian profile outside), the Avengers responded by arguing, then moving half a block away. Next morning, hundreds of leaflets littered the street.

A large example: Half a dozen Avengers from "Lesbianville, U.S.A."—Northampton—passed out candy and leaflets at a nearby West Springfield elementary school on Valentine's Day, 1994. The leaflets read, "Girls who love girls and women who love women are OK! Happy Valentine's Day." The leaflets also listed two local support groups for lesbian/gay teens, which later told the press that they hadn't been informed about the action and would never themselves advertise to elementary-school-age children.

Worse, the Avengers listed an 800 number, which was described as a national lesbian and gay hotline. The number was actually that of a gay sex line; callers got a recording advertising "America's wildest, hottest phone sex service . . . uncensored gay phone sex" (at a mere $1.98 a minute; have Mom's credit card number ready, kids).

A spokeswoman for the Northampton Avengers did later say that the group used the 1-800 sleazeline number "by accident. We are extremely sorry for any difficulties caused as a result." But one is left scratching one's head and wondering how such a mistake can *happen,* in light of middle America's worst fear: that we're after their children. It's a nonsensical fear, of course. (Like, with the recent lesbian mother baby boom, we really need *heterosexual* families' dirty diapers, too.) But it's a fear that the Christian right is exploiting with wild success. Given the sensitivity of the action, why didn't anyone bother to do their homework, as it were?

It's indeed hard, sometimes, not to wonder: Just what are the Lesbian Avengers avenging, anyhow?

In some ways, it comes down to the question: Which is the preferable form of homophobia: latent, or blatant?

Lesbian Avengers clearly prefer the latter, out there where they can fight it. They feel that the system has never worked for us before, so why would it now? "They" are not going to give us rights just because we're good girls. We have to *take* rights. Who needs to work to get gays a good name? The idea isn't to convince straights we're okay; it's to say, "We don't respect your rules and we don't follow them."

Mainstream gay pols, even activists, worry about alienating heterosexuals, making them uncomfortable. But, let's face it, most heterosexuals already *are* uncomfortable. Aggressive Avenger tactics tackle the homophobia lurking inside the heads of even liberals favoring "tolerance." This subtler type of homophobia is accepting as long as we "don't flaunt it" and "keep private things in the privacy of the bedroom"; it often morphs instantly into hatred and discrimination as soon as we become real, visible, successful, powerful.

It's harmful to allow heterosexuals to keep on thinking they're not as homophobic as they are, because what they say isn't always what they mean. They say, "What you do in your private life is your own business." But *they* have two standards for what constitutes a "private life," and theirs is very different than ours. For example:

What is more natural and routine than for a straight man to refer to "my wife" right after you first meet?

Pamela once responded to a band colleague's discussion of his fiancée—he'd been talking about her for the entire five weeks Pam had known him—by mentioning, for the first time, her female lover. Being a tolerant sort rather than an outright bigot, the guy did not actually barf, bash, or back off. But a while later, when she challenged Mr. Liberal about his telling an AIDS joke, his reaction was a hurt, indignant "How can you say I'm homophobic? You were throwing around all that stuff about being a lesbian the second we met, and I was fine with it."

Even liberal homophobes *don't* want to know what we are.

Worse, they want to keep *us* from knowing what we are. They want us to remain people who cobble our sexual identity together from scraps of *their* sexual identity. She's the boy, the real lesbian. The other one's the girl, the passive one. *That,* they understand. That's safe. That's not scary. But that's not us.

So Lesbian Avengers don't cajole. They confront. Frighten. Provoke people. Force a reaction out of them. Draw that old pus of prejudice out. It's an approach shared, of course, by predecessor direct-action groups that are either mainly male or mixed-gender, like ACT UP and Queer Nation. The shock of the Lesbian Avengers is in such impoliteness coming from the gender that has always been brought up to be the empathetically other-directed emotional caretakers of society. Avengers don't take pains to negotiate around delicate straight male feelings, or to be a credit to their own gay race. What in the world went wrong with these girls?

On the way from New Orleans to the next night's stop in Ovett, Mississippi, an Indigo Girls tape plays. It also played the day before. It will play for many, many days after.

Meanwhile, talk in the van turns to—surprise!—sex. Specifically, we're having a heated discussion about a hot subject: "bisexual women" versus "lesbians who sleep with men." It starts innocently, with Shaila doing a monologue on a subject we all know all too well, and completely agree on: the tediousness of straight women who hate men, assume that lesbians want to hear about it, and then get offended when we suggest an alternative.

"But I have one friend, a Smithie who lives in Northampton, who I feel really did try," Shaila says. "I think there are very few women out there who are entirely heterosexual, but she's one. She's distraught because she really wants to be a lesbian." She considers. "Well, maybe her stumbling block is she really just wants to get men out of her life.

"For me, I'd really prefer, sexually, to sleep with women," she adds, then sighs. "But I have trouble meeting the right women. So that's why, right now, I sleep with both women and men. It's more than sex. I judge a person for the person, and so far most of the right people haven't been female. If I had a good experience with women, I probably would be strictly lesbian. But I haven't had that yet. So right now I'd have to say I'm bisexual."

"I *don't* sleep with men, but I can't say I'll never sleep with a man again in my life," says the Smudger, who's driving again. "The problem is, people get into the negative connotation of 'bisexual,' so that's why people dislike the label."

"Well, I don't like labeling," declares a woman we'll call the Tank (a description of far more than her physique; this sensitive soul has already shared with the van the first of many *Screw* magazine–worthy "jokes" involving female body parts: "Man, if she clapped those things together you'd go deaf"). While she is not out about it in her hometown's gay community, the Tank explains, "I have a male lover right now, but I don't feel bisexual. I feel a bisexual is someone who's fairly equally attracted to women and men, and for me women win hands down. I could never be married to my male lover. He's gay and 'married' to a man. He's just what's happening now."

There is a long pause. Luz finally picks up the ball, albeit somewhat hesitantly. "I don't get it. You're a lesbian. And your main lover is a man?" Both she and Vero are obviously in culture shock.

"I find my sexual tastes are immensely varied and change with time," one of the older, almost-forty riders soothes, before zeroing in on the crux. "I just think there has to be some way to distinguish your political identity from what you want to do in your bedroom."

"Politically, I'm a dyke," declares the Smudger, banging the steering wheel for emphasis.

"So now we're saying it's okay for women who call themselves dykes to sleep with men?" Luz asks bluntly. "That's what we're striving for?"

"If you say dykes can't sleep with men it's the same thing as saying women can't sleep with women," declares Vita, one of the women from the video crew. "I don't wanna be fit into a little niche. I'm still trying to figure myself out and make up my mind."

"I don't care who anyone sleeps with," responds the Smudger. "I just want to know."

"This is about labeling sexual behavior, not limiting it," we second. "No one here's saying anyone can't sleep with who she wants. And no one's saying anyone's required to label herself—or, if she does choose to label herself, that she can't change her label if she changes her mind and her behavior. The point is just: A label should mean something, like any other word does; Birkenstocks aren't Docs."

"Well, I don't want, like, some self-appointed person to say, This makes you a dyke, this makes you not a dyke, and you're more of a dyke or a better dyke if you do this or this, and you're a lousy dyke if you do this," declares the Tank.

"Who's saying that?" we object. "Some of us just want accurate, honest communication about what's what and who's what, at any given time. Wanting information doesn't equal being judgmental. It's not a matter of someone being better or worse because of the gender of whoever she sleeps with. Birkenstocks aren't better or worse than Docs."

"Oh yeah?" someone challenges. Oops, bad analogy.

"Why it bothers me so much," says Luz, "is, when you are gay it is possible to pass if you want, by just looking a certain way and not identifying yourself unless it is safe."

"Not me, man," the Tank interrupts. "I always looked this way." She claims that she's frequently mistaken for a man.

"Come on," Luz objects gently. "Even you could dress different, you know? Us lesbians, we can survive. As a dark-skinned Latina, I have to be out. As a lesbian, I could just not look so gay and go on

242

with the straight world. And most of us did that, at some point in our lives. I mean, I have a regular job. It's safer to not identify yourself. The reason I finally did identify myself is because I wanted them to know I existed. I want them to know there is such a thing as a lesbian. And *you* want them to know there is such a thing as a bisexual. But when you go around and say, 'I don't want to identify or say nothing' . . ." She pauses, and turns her palms up in appeal. "Who are you?"

"I don't have any trouble with telling sexual partners, people who need to know or deserve to know, that I have a male lover now," the Tank blusters. "But I don't *feel* bisexual, I don't *identify* as bisexual, I'm *not* bisexual. If people say to me, 'Identify yourself,' I'm a dyke. 'Do you sleep with a man?' 'Yeah.' "

Got it. We have a cat who doesn't feel she's a cat, doesn't identify as a cat, is not a cat. If people say to her, "Identify yourself," she's a person. "Do you want some Friskies?" "*Meow.*"

"But what does this identification of 'lesbian' mean, if lesbians sleep with men?" Luz persists. "A problem I have with it is, I have met a lot of men who say about me, about lesbians, 'All you need is a good fuck.' It makes me very angry, this idea of theirs."

"Well, I defiantly refuse to identify myself as gay, straight, or bisexual," one of the video women says, "because I think what we're striving for is a society that allows more freedom."

"Right. But we don't live there yet," we point out. "And unfortunately in this society where we do live, which is not the society where we'd like to live, the concept of dykes who sleep with men falls right into typical X-rated video fantasies about lesbians where it takes a guy to deliver the 'real thing.' "

"And that's where I draw the line!" Luz insists, heatedly. "As a *lesbian,* I don't do that. I have no problem with other people being with whoever they want to be with. But *I* don't want to be thought of as a person who would sleep with men. And I feel I should be able to say that as a lesbian, I don't need it, I don't want it, I don't do it."

"Guess we're just old-fashioned lesbians—the kind that sleep with women," we say. "And we'd sure like to have a word—such as, say, 'lesbian'—to identify ourselves as women who do not, as a rule, sleep with men." And things are sure getting a tad tense here in the old van.

"Then I guess it's a matter of definitions," muses the video woman. "What does the word 'lesbian' mean? Or 'dyke.' "

"And are those two different this month?" someone mutters.

"Yeah. They've been changing so much, it's hard to know exactly what they mean," the video woman agrees. "Which is why I prefer the term 'queer,' because it's all-encompassing. At the same time I have to be very clear with whoever I'm with. It doesn't mean I'm confused. It doesn't mean I don't know what I want."

"And it doesn't matter whatever you are," says Vero, trying to peacemake. "But if you say, 'I'm a lesbian,' people should be able to know, 'Oh, there's women who sleep with women.' You say, 'I'm bisexual': 'Oh, there's people who sleep with both.' That's how you educate the public. It's all okay, it's no big deal who you're with. People should know what you mean, that's all."

"If it wasn't a big deal we wouldn't be having this conversation. Believe me, it *is* a big deal," insists the Tank. "That's why I'm not out about my male lover. You wouldn't believe the shit I've gotten."

What kind of shit? "People hassle you," the Tank explains. "Like, 'What are you doin'? Why are you with them? I thought you were such-and-such.' You know."

Uh-huh. Sounds pretty brutal.

"Or girls that probably would've gone out with you are sometimes like, 'Eeeuw,' " she adds, pulling out her ace.

"So it's sort of like wanting to cook, but not wanting to take the heat?" we push. Darn. There, definitely, goes our chance at the ride's Miss Lesbian Congeniality Award, and we really coulda used that toaster oven.

What we found in our research is that a fair number of "lesbians who sleep with men"—who insist upon the label "lesbian" and deny the label "bisexual"—were not saying their sexuality does not include both sexes. Often they meant they didn't feel as attracted to men as to women (that is, they defined "bi" as "*equally* attracted to women and men," rather than "attracted to both women and men").

Or their sexuality didn't feel centered on men, even if their primary sex partner was male.

But mostly, they just didn't want to deal with the negative connotations of the label "bisexual": that bis are sleazy, promiscuous, greedy, can't make up their minds. These "lesbians" who regularly sleep with men don't want to take on the admittedly formidable job of reclaiming the label "bisexual" and work, as gay activists have with terms such as "dyke" and "queer," on changing those negative connotations. Because their political life, if not their personal life, feels woman-identified, they also don't feel any compulsion to adopt some new label that would make clear both their similarities to and their differences from lesbians who *don't* sleep with men. For those of us who respect language and revere courage, this is a real problem.

"You know, there are some health risks that could cause these girls concern about having sex with a bisex—um, a woman who also sleeps with men," nurse Vero points out. "Like men carry a certain virus, HPV [human papilloma virus], that causes cervical cancer. This virus has a very long life."

"I wouldn't want to sleep with a woman who didn't want to sleep with me because I slept with men two years ago. That's separatism!" the Smudger declares from behind the wheel.

"She didn't say she wouldn't sleep with that woman!" cries Luz, exasperated. "She just wants to *know!* Like you!"

"Oh. Okay," the Smudger says mildly. "I can't hear very well up here. I just don't like other people telling me what I am. Like people are always going, 'You can't be a dyke, because you wear skirts and have long hair.' Fuck that. Am I a dyke now because I have short hair? I have short hair because a friend of mine totally fucked my hair up, and I had to cut it all off."

"Okay," announces the Tank, relieved to go on to any other subject—even the often sore one of dyke style trials. "Who wears underwear and who doesn't?"

Most riders don't. "I used to not wear underwear, but then I got pierced," the Tank reveals. "So now I have to wear underwear. Otherwise the ring would totally catch on all the seams of my pants, and be really ugly. I don't know if I'd have gotten pierced if I'd known. And they say it doesn't hurt? My labia didn't. But the hood of my clitoris hurt like a son of a bitch. I screamed like a girl, twice. Also, I can't pee standing up. It hits the jewelry and sprays all over the place. I feel really un-butch." For once, the van is speechless.

Outside the windows, spectacular bayous and moss-laden forests whiz past. "Is anyone noticing the great water?" Shaila finally asks.

"Between the bisexuality and the underwear?" the Smudger snorts. "Pfeh!"

It's probable that a certain amount of our increasing tension is due to our increasing proximity to Ovett, Mississippi. Six months earlier, homophobic terrorism by local right-wingers against Camp Sisterspirit, a fledgling retreat and conference center that was the home of lesbian couple Wanda and Brenda Henson, had escalated to the point that U.S. Attorney General Janet Reno sent in federal civil rights mediators. The Hensons and other regular camp residents (three volunteer caretakers, plus Wanda's Navy veteran son) found a dead female puppy draped over their mailbox, festooned with sanitary napkins. They have received hundreds of threatening phone calls, and been shot at many times. A February 27, 1994, *Mobile Register* article quoted Jones County deputy sheriff Myron Holifield as explaining: "We don't want [Camp Sisterspirit] here for the simple reason of . . . It's a known fact that all your violent crime comes from homosexuals."

About thirty miles from Ovett, the Pride Ride experiences its own first homophobic incident. Or maybe not.

Right off the thruway exit at Hattiesburg, we've stopped at Big Star Foods, a supermarket on Main Street. Part of the reason for the pit stop is to remove the banners from the vans; we're stopping in Ovett to work, not to agitate, and, according to the Austin organizers, the women at Camp Sisterspirit have asked us to keep a low profile. We also want to bring our own groceries. The camp can't afford to feed an extra twenty-four big mouths. Anyway, potlucks are another lesbian genetic thing.

Prices at Big Star seem unbelievably cheap: Glade Air Freshener is 19 cents, paper towels are 9 cents. The clientele seems very poor, and is entirely black. We, of course, are almost all middle-class and white, but we don't let that stifle us. The Avengers, in our usual flaunty-sloganed T-shirts, crew cuts, and Docs, basically take over the store. CathyAnne laughs loudly at a display of household cleanser whose brand name is "KKK." The Smudger loudly comments on the rotten quality of the produce. Still, the checkout lady seems perfectly friendly.

However, as we lounge out in the parking lot, the Tank comes barreling out of the market in hysterics, followed by other Avengers who yell that everyone should get in the vans immediately, if not sooner. Someone says the Tank has been "touched" by a guy in the store. Because the Tank is in no condition to talk about it, no one knows exactly what or where the touching was. But the scream of *"Don't!"* she emits at sympathetic arm pats from another Avenger certainly suggests serious sexual violation has occurred.

What actually happened, as finally revealed at a processing session next morning at Camp Sisterspirit: A black guy walked up to the Tank in the market, clapped a hand on her upper arm, and said, with what she described as "a kind of lisp," something "that sounded like 'Sister.'" While the fellow could have been the town's one black faggot expressing support, she figured he meant "Camp Sisterspirit," the lisp was fake, and he was being hostile. Further, though the Tank is an s/m dominatrix (and one of the main moaners about having to leave her bag of whips at home, because of the Avengers' one-suitcase rule), she's touchy about being touched herself, anywhere. So she flinched and grabbed her arm away. The guy did the same thing again. She decided she'd been assaulted. She fled the store. We fled town.

In the van, after this incident is dissected under the powerful lesbian processing microscope, it is decided that from now on, instead of everyone piling into places, only a few designated shoppers can go into grocery stores. Plus when we do pit stops at gas stations, we are to go in one at a time to pee. Given the bladder capacity of our group, which so far has topped out at about an hour and a half on the road, we are committing here to a major scheduling reallocation.

Nevertheless, we have survived our first serious, possibly homophobic confrontation. And the women at Camp Sisterspirit are very admiring of our nonconfrontational "fearlessness" (Number 6 on the official list of "Top 10 Avenger Qualities") and "fighting spirit" (Number 4). As soon as we arrive, the camp has each of us sign a "Liability Release Form" (including blood type and next of kin) before we can stay overnight. It includes a vow "not to take any action of rebuttal" to any violence that might erupt. Camp Sisterspirit, Inc., is committed to nonviolence, despite Wanda's collection of rifles.

After the ever-present video crew monopolizes the Hensons all evening, we corner Wanda to ask briefly, What happened here? The touchingly down-home leaflet posted at the 1993 Michigan Womyn's Music Festival, right after she and Brenda found this land, had sounded so excited. "I still am excited," Wanda declares, raising her chin. "Eventually we're gonna have laws to protect gay and lesbian Americans. You need case law. And ironically, these people are making that opportunity available. These officials who're gonna have us arrested for sodomy, arrested on cohabitation, they're gonna shit and fall back in it is what they're gonna do, and get it all over their goddamned faces. 'Cause I ain't afraid of them, I ain't scared a those bastards."

It's hard for an urban lesbian to understand why the heck any lesbian *would* want to stay in such a place, but the Hensons' reasons are simple. They think Mississippi is home. They think that, with one of the state's highest illiteracy and poverty rates, Jones County can use the help of a couple of community-spirited women who hold master's degrees in education and operated a food-and-clothing bank and an adult literacy program in coastal Gulfport for years. They have also produced the regional Gulf Coast Womyn's Festival since 1989, without homophobic harassment, for an audience averaging several hundred women. (This year, 1994, in Ovett, "we got fifty-three.")

Wanda believes that homophobia is the price one pays for living outside the gay ghettos of the big cities: "I think rural America's rural America. Ovett could be anywhere in rural America. It doesn't matter." We suspect she might get an argument from the

"10,000 kissing, cuddling lesbians" (as the *National Enquirer* trumpeted) of the Northampton area. Not to mention their kissin' country cousins from the dozens of women's "lands" in southern Oregon, along with the farmdyke enclaves in Vermont, New York's Hudson River Valley, California's Russian River, and other tolerant small-town spots that for decades have attracted so many gay residents that one suspects they must lie on some sort of magnetic lesbian ley lines.

But neither is the entire state of Mississippi a hopelessly homophobic backwater, as some gay commentators with big-city superiority complexes seem to think. The Hensons' adopted common last name, for instance, is the family name of Brenda's super-supportive grandmother. "Lots of people in this town," Wanda says, support the couple's right to remain in Ovett. Their attorney, for instance, is a conservative Republican Episcopalian. "I asked him why he should be on this case," Wanda explains. "He said, 'When your butts go, mine is next.' "

She then pulls out a local newspaper clipping that would be an eye-opener even in the San Francisco Bay area. Featured on the society page of the Biloxi *Sun Herald,* otherwise filled with straight married couples in wedding suits, is the Hensons' tenth-anniversary notice.

We'd tell you more, but six minutes into the interview, Avengers burst in to announce a required processing meeting.

"All of a sudden I feel like starting this like our regular Avenger meetings." Lisa chuckles. "Welcome tonight to the Lesbian Avengers. We're a direct-action group focused on issues vital to lesbian visibility and survival. Are there any members of the FBI, police, CIA, or media present?"

To our surprise, there apparently is a CIA operative present, and it's us. One of the video crew has noticed our red recorder light still shining; in a snit at being interrupted mid-interview with Wanda, we'd yanked out the mike jack but missed the off button. The dead mike's disconnected, dangling wire does nothing to convince the video woman and several others that this important meeting is not, somehow, being covertly taped.

What follows is an hour's worth of media-bashing (the quasi–house organ video crew being largely exempted) culminating in the assignment to all nonmedia riders of written essays on what's to be done about the media. These essays are to be handed in to and processed by the Ride's "peacekeepers," volunteers skilled at . . . actually, they're mostly the Ride's main loudmouths. Austin Avenger meeting facilitators also suggest that everyone on the ride should get to "review" all journalists' tapes and prepublication copy. We wonder why these supposedly media-savvy sisters allowed any professional journalists, whose tolerance for censorship is traditionally as low as Avenger respect for journalism seems to be, to come on the Ride in the first place.

We are getting pretty cranky, if you hadn't noticed.

The Pride Ride's third day begins with chores at the old homestead. For some riders, anyway. Most of the loudmouths sit in the house painting T-shirts for the next action—in Birmingham—and solving racism. Busy also with their own art are the video crew: Una, an energetic, eternally microphone-wielding, opinionated-about-everything ex–New Yorker skinhead femme with the tiniest tuft of hair up front; her girlfriend, Radclyffe, an academic sociologist who looks and acts like a flattop-cut adolescent boy, complete with much testosterone-esque fake wrestling-match action (she "identifies as a butch rather than a lesbian"); and Vita, who is Radclyffe's main wrestling partner. All three names, as is probably obvious, are pseudonyms; and we're not even going to explain what "Vita" signifies—except, naturally, to our CIA colleagues.

The rest of the gang builds protective fences around the camp's borders. With 120 acres surrounded by hostile homophobes, the camp needs a lot of protection. Our six-woman crew erects fifty yards or so of corrugated-aluminum barrier wall, schlepping rusted eight-foot-tall panels into woods full of icepick-sized briers and poison ivy, poison sumac, poison everything. The air's so humid we feel as if we're standing in a shower. The flying insects are the size of helicopters. The Camp Sisterspirit fence dominatrix does not schlep, claiming a bad back. Regina expresses distress at ripping her designer jeans, and the Hensons' fourteen-year-old baby butch sort-of grandchild (the informally adopted daughter of Brenda's daughter) tells her, contemptuously, "Get over it."

The Hensons themselves hole up in their offices, occasionally riding by on golf carts. They have two golf carts already, but want four more. Camp Sisterspirit's wish list also includes a hot tub.

The camp subsists entirely on donations, "the vast majority from gay men rather than women," Wanda says. "Many of 'em send notes along saying, 'This is our way of saying thanks to our lesbian sisters for helping with AIDS.' " But much of the actual physical work to erect protective fences and convert the camp's present derelict structures into conference and festival facilities has been done by visiting female volunteers, if the painted signatures on the fencing are any indication. Lesbians are, after all, issued power screwdrivers and *big* Swiss Army knives (the model with the built-in icepick) at birth.

Initially, there were a few construction problems, such as getting a septic system installed. "No companies would come in here," according to Wanda. "The state bureau of pollution control accused us of 'lesbian contamination.' "

However, things are moving along. The camp already has a big main community building, converted from a pig barn (the place used to be a major hog farm). This facility includes a still Sheetrocked, partially enclosed meeting hall decorated with various earth mother–female spirit dancer–wombmoon warrior postcards; an upstairs bunk room with a zillion mattresses; a big bathhouse with regular flush toilets and minimal recycling facilities; and a huge kitchen full of canned meat products. (The Southern-raised Hensons are skeptical of the idea that women can actually get up the energy to do heavy work on a vegetarian diet, which is what lots of the Pride Riders eat.)

After building the fence, and a refreshing swim in the camp creek—which features mud, water moccasins, and neighbor Jimmy Wade downstream with his rifle—it's almost lunchtime. With Regina, we volunteer for extra duty making the group's meal. Although we're both super-careful, thanks to a lecture during the previous night's processing session about how inconsiderate the ride's carnivores were of the ride's vegetarians, to plan a main course of lentil-veggie salad supplemented by the previous day's leftover lasagna, we get chewed out, with much melodrama and slamming by the Smudger, for our people-of-privilege wastefulness in using a box of the camp's lentils ($1.38, okayed by a caretaker) instead of pushing Lisa's mom's now three-day-old van-cured turkey.

All of this gives Regina more material for seething. "I am getting just a little tired of being judged as less-pure-than-thou by some people on this ride, because I work for a living," she fumes later. She's also feeling more than a little annoyed about, as she puts it, "being trivialized because I wear Joan & David shoes. When the lesbian community is criticized for being butch, fat, ugly, scummy-dressing people, *then* they point to dykes like me, who look sort of like your typical heterosexual female, to legitimize lesbianism as not unstylish. So in a pinch I'll do—just so mainstream society will think we're okay. Otherwise, these dykes are supposed to be feminists, and I'm on a Freedom Ride, and I have to get sexist, misogynist comments from women who are supposedly lesbians because they love women?"

Stereotyping of lesbians is evidently not strictly the preserve of establishment heterosexuals; even the most radical lesbians do a pretty good job of it, and they do it to their own. "Someone on this ride was trying to explain why I get this shit, and said, 'You just don't *look* like an activist.' Well, okay, I am a stylish woman," Regina concedes. "I like to shave my leg hair and wear makeup. But I'm intelligent, I'm very political, I have my Freedom fuckin' Rings. People say I look frail, but I lift weights; I'm a strong woman physically, and emotionally. I mean, my students read *Bent* and discussed it with their teacher, who they know is queer because I'm out at work—which lots of activists aren't. My students not only know about the pink triangle, they know lesbians wore a black triangle—which lots of activists don't know. So what *does* an activist look like?"

• • •

We spend the ride's third night in Birmingham, on the floor of the home of Jan Hughes. Jan owns the Agnes Gallery, an extraordinarily interesting experimental photo, film, book, and performance art space. Not what one would expect from one of the 1960s civil rights movement's biggest bigot backwater burgs. But then, not much else on this ride is turning out quite as expected.

After a potluck dinner, a group of local lesbians eagerly offer to take the Avengers discoing, though not to the city's lesbian bar since, as one cheery Birmingham baby dyke explains, the clientele is "all old. Like truck-driver types. I actually thought you would all be old."

It is pointed out that some of us are.

"Oh, not like you. I mean more like someone's mother. *Real* old. Aren't you coming?"

No. Suddenly, sweetie, we feel *real* old—and tired. After a couple of hours' conversation in a nearby coffeehouse with a Canadian Avenger (who, because of prior political arrests, is actually not supposed to be anywhere in the United States, much less on a visibility action) and (another Birmingham surprise) the best espresso we've had since our last trip to Italy, we crash under Jan's dining room table.

Several of the Austin Avengers also stay home, to write the following day's statement of purpose: "The Lesbian Avengers are here because the Alabama State Legislature recently passed a hate crimes bill that deliberately excluded homosexuals. We chose Birmingham because it's a historic site of the black civil rights movement, and the Avengers are particularly committed to lesbians and gay men of color who, because of the disproportionate amount of violence they encounter in their community, do not feel safe to come out. Exclusion reinforces the idea that violence against our community is acceptable. Lesbian lives are valuable lives."

Next morning, we set up on a picnic table in a crowded nearby park to make signs and new torches for the day's action, featuring a song adapted from the *Laverne and Shirley* TV theme. Several Avengers have written inspiring new lyrics: "Pride riding through the South now, / We're lesbians out and proud now. . . . And we'll do it Our Way, the Dyke Way; / Make all our dreams come true, for me and you."

They practice many times. They're very loud, very enthusiastic, very tone-deaf. Male onlookers stare. Trouble? Nah. The very big butch fellows on the adjacent athletic court turn out to be a local gay male volleyball team, who think we're a stitch.

On the short ride downtown to action central, a guy crossing at the traffic light in front of us reads our "Lesbian Avengers Pride Ride" banner on the side of the van, and lunges for his girlfriend's hand. "She's too skinny anyway," mocks the Tank, zeroing in neatly on the wrong target. "Looks like if you fucked her too hard she'd break."

At the action there's no local press whatsoever, and fewer than half a dozen local queer onlookers. The song bombs. The fire-eating, however, gets enthusiastic applause and whistles from a small straight crowd eating in a café next to the traffic island where we're demonstrating, plus several cries of "Encore!" The Avengers oblige with another flaming round, until two cops peel up, one of them a good-looking young African-American muscleman. Trouble?

"Oh, it's Cedrick Thomas. He's just so sweet." Jan smiles. "Really protective of the gallery."

Cedrick is suitably impressed by the Avengers' act. "I know some lesbians in town, but never had a bunch of 'em walk up and eat fire before," he marvels. "What do you *do?* I mean, y'all just get off work, and go traveling around the country swallowing flaming torches?"

Nevertheless, he and his partner warn us: No more pyrotechnics without a permit. Possibly they are wary of our official Pride Ride motto: "Ignite the South." We can, they decide, continue to demonstrate, even though we naturally have not notified them in advance. So we mill around chanting and chatting with Officer Thomas, who shakes hands and poses for pix with CathyAnne (today's T-shirt: "Lesbian Rights Are Civil Rights") and other Avengers.

"Well, I don't mean to rush you off," Cedrick finally says, politely, "but how long y'all figure you're gonna stay? I'm about ready to get in out of the sun myself."

"Just one more torch," pleads new fire-eater Alice Faye Love, a forty-one-year-old local lesbian. "Why, this is the best new thing I've done since my first orgasm!"

Despite the action's fizzle, the Austin Avengers are also looking on the bright side. One of the goals of the Ride is to help Avenger organizing in other communities—to motivate people, to keep struggling chapters alive and working on activism, to keep actions building everywhere. "New Orleans and Atlanta were easy," Carrie says. "They have chapters. We have a national Avenger list. We just called them up. The idea was to get together with local people and decide on each action, so it was not just like a bunch of out-of-towners coming in imposing our ideas. But there isn't a chapter in Birmingham."

"Well, we planted a seed of one," says Shana, glancing over at Alice Faye, who is stubbornly clamping her teeth around an equally stubborn flame, which refuses to go out. She conquers it on the third try, undaunted and somehow unscorched. "Though it's also an important goal to get media attention," Shana adds. "We figured if we can get it in small cities, more people will know lesbians are out there."

"And see what a diverse group we are," adds Sara.

Except, of course, for the fact that almost all of us on this Ride are white Anglos. "There were African Americans who expressed interest in the Ride, but felt they might be unsafe," says an Austin Avenger named Alix. "And some Avengers felt actively recruiting women of color was racist. Like tokenism." In truth, there has been bad blood between some black activists and the Lesbian Avengers since October 1993, when the New York Avengers held a ten-day caravan through the northeastern United States to work on an anti-gay referendum in Lewiston, Maine, and also to do general lesbian visibility actions. The Avengers called the caravan the Freedom Ride, a term some African Americans, including lesbian-feminists, felt had been disrespectfully coopted from the black civil rights movement.

"There's a Latina woman in her fifties in the Avengers, who was in the labor movement, who said, 'Hey, African Americans don't own the term "Freedom Ride." The labor movement was doing freedom rides before they came along,' " says Lisa, who went along on the New York trip to gather tips. However, this info did not placate angry African-American women from the Kitchen Table Press. They boycotted the Freedom Ride's Albany action and later leafleted Sarah Schulman when she did a reading at an upstate New York bookstore.

As we drive into Atlanta on day five, the Indigo Girls continue to wail on the tape deck, alternating with Melissa Etheridge and the Native American drumming and chanting ("Ooh-way oh-way, a-whine-a-way-oh") of the Minneapolis Buckaroos. Mellow, mellow, mellow. The Pride Ride is exactly halfway to Stonewall, and we've gotten this far without serious incident. But the Pride paranoids are so out of control about being stalked by evil truckers that we have taken to using less provocative code names on the CBs. The three vans that had been Snatch, Car 69, and Diesel Dyke are now Mother Teresa, Sister Renée, and Sister Mary Harper.

However, one trucker breaks the code. As it happens, it's during our personal tour of duty as Diesel's CB dominatrix. "This is Bearclaw. Ah hear voices of female persons. Respond."

Regina, incensed, is actually inspired to rip off her Walkman earphones. *"What?* Bearclaw? Fe-*what?* Oh, please." She indicates the CB. "Hand me that thing. Hey, Bearclaw? D'you hear me, Bearclaw? What makes you think I want to talk to *you* just because I'm a female person, huh, Bearclaw? *You* respond, Bearclaw." By this point, she's laughing hysterically, as are a few of the rest of us.

From the backseat comes Una's tight little voice. "You're *flirting* with that trucker, and I won't have that."

Immediate silent directional signals come, from the van ahead, to exit the highway. Oops.

At the nearest gas station, the Smudger walks up to our van. We say we're sincerely, more or less, sorry about Bearclaw, and will never ever do it again. Obviously tiring of being a control cop, the Smudger smiles and confesses she actually sort of wanted to get on the CB herself. We feel that does it.

Then *four* additional volunteer cops come over, separately, to scold. We finally explain to the last, CathyAnne, that we musta been uncontrollably overcome by residual hetero hormonal lust at Bearclaw's testosterone-laden tones, on account of not encountering enough straight guys the last week. No chuckles. She looks ominously back to her van. "Maybe you should get out and we'll have a meeting."

Our van unanimously, flat-out refuses to have another meeting. The Pride Ride drives on. "Progress, not process!" proclaims Regina.

There are two planned actions in Atlanta, the Austin Avenger brainstorm being a "die-in" at the headquarters of the National Centers for Disease Control, to draw attention to lesbian health issues. The action at CDC headquarters focuses on how—universally, and shamefully—government-funded medical studies, tests, and statistics concentrate on straight people and gay men, ignoring gay women. To dramatize this, riders lie down "dead" as an Avenger "CDC official" draws a white chalk line around each of us. We then label the corpse outlines "Died of AIDS," "Died of Breast Cancer," "Killed by Homophobia," and, this one two merged female outlines, "Together Forever: Died of Bigotry." We also chant (stuff like "Look, look, CDC: Lesbians get HPV," and, "The numbers are lying, lesbians are dying")—except, as organizers instruct, "not when you're dead."

The action gets all the public attention typically accorded to lesbian health concerns: none. No media, and no spectators, unless you count the CDC's security guards. But the chief of security is impressed. "This bunch is much more well-dressed than the average demonstrators we get here, your ACT UP types. They look pretty clean, too. And the action seems very well planned."

He is also not surprised that more than a few Avengers have to pee during the action. "Next time, let us know you're coming. During some of the larger actions here, we've set up Porta Potties outside for the demonstrators."

More successful in terms of garnering mainstream media attention to lesbian visibility is that afternoon's Atlanta Avenger–planned action in nearby Cobb County. Radical gay activists—and tolerant local liberals, too—have been in an uproar since earlier in the year, when the Atlanta Committee for the Olympic Games chose Cobb to host the 1996 Olympic volleyball competition. The reason for the dismay is that Cobb County commissioners have been known to publicly welcome neo-Nazis and skinheads to Marietta, the county seat, and in 1993 passed a resolution citing the county's "incompatibility with homosexual lifestyle units."

The Atlanta Avengers have already done several protests, the most recent and spectacular a thirty-five-mile Torch Run to Cobb, where their symbolic "Olympic" torch was extinguished. By mouth, naturally. "We vow that this is the last time that Cobb County will see the Olympic torch unless they rescind the resolution," read their statement. Among the Avengers' allies have been the Marietta Interfaith Alliance of fifty ministers and rabbis, Marietta High School's covaledictorian Kate McQueen, and Atlanta mayor Bill Campbell, who told a record crowd of 150,000 at June 1994's Pride parade, "We want you to come here, live here, and be a part of the city of Atlanta."

The Pride Riders' protest today is supposed to be a game of volleyball—played with a model Lesbian Avenger bomb—in Marietta Square, a small central park surrounded by the closest thing Cobb County has to a downtown business area. Unfortunately, the Atlanta Avengers have committed the faux pas of trying to work with the authorities, notifying them of today's demo. A contingent of Cobb cops meets us and nixes the game. Marching, chanting, and all the usual general radical obnoxiousness are okay, mind you. But no volleyball. Go figure.

Nevertheless, the action is covered by all three major Atlanta TV news stations that night, with one station dramatically inflating our band of about thirty-five (including local Avengers and a few sympathetic gay men) into "hundreds of demonstrators."

That night, we celebrate at a woman-owned (but largely male, in clientele) Atlanta gay club, The Otherside. It's drag queen night, which initially causes some of the more progressive lesbians to wrinkle their noses. The music is, like, "I'm Every Woman." The drag is from a similar era. However, the guys are nice to us T-shirted sapphic scuzzbuckets: They waive the cover charge. By the end of the night even a couple of the non–drag fans have tucked bucks into the queens' ample cleavages.

Also by the night's end, a Canadian Pride Rider has started a hot affair with Lisa's supposedly monogamous girlfriend—on the dance floor, no less. Tacky, tacky. Not to mention ungrateful to the lone dedicated politiholic organizer in the bunch. But as our long-time favorite historic lesbian political button asserts, "An Army of Ex-lovers Cannot Fail."

Two days after the Pride Ride's action, Shannon Byrne, the twenty-four-year-old daughter of antigay Cobb County Commission chair Bill Byrne, publicly comes out at an Atlanta press conference, demonstrating that us homosexual lifestyle units are not so incompatible with county life after all. Her father's first reaction to her coming out, she said, had been to tell her that she'd "chosen a hard lifestyle. You're going to be discriminated against." Her reaction: "Thanks, Dad, for making it happen."

The Olympic volleyball will be withdrawn from Cobb. And, nearly a year after our ride through Atlanta, the CDC will finally start meeting with lesbian health activists. Maybe we helped, a little.

In Durham, we converge on Our Own Place, a women-only place for social events and meetings. Most of the riders spend the night in the center, and stay up late having a slumber party. "The best part was 'Spin the Bottle,' " enthuses one party person the next day. "It was like being a preteenager all over, but as a lesbian!" They are all ready to go back to sleep, or to sleep, as the case may be.

A few of us are in somewhat better shape, having crashed in the nearby home of Kenda Kirby, who's on the Durham Human Relations Commission. Kirby considers herself "a more mainstream negotiator," but thinks less predictable, more volatile-verging-on-threatening direct-action activists have "a very important place. What I do is stuff like lobby the city council. The mayor thinks of me as a very credible person. But the mayor also knows, because of things like Avenger protests, that there's a huge population of all kinds of lesbians out there."

Between sleep-deprivation hangovers and the tempting presence in the center of a big washer-dryer, it is decided to cancel the scheduled Raleigh-Durham anti-tobacco-industry action. However, a few Avengers who still have clean underwear (or don't wear any) opt for an unscheduled "kiss-in" at Durham's Northgate shopping mall. They are immediately expelled, with official claims that "people complained."

"We got thrown out of the mall!" cries a jubilant returning rider.

"Good!" congratulates Lisa.

"We barely kissed at all, and security made us leave!" elaborates the j.r.r.

"Excellent!" Lisa exclaims.

En route to our crash site for the night in Washington, we stop in Richmond, Virginia, for an impromptu fire-eating action at the courthouse in support of lesbian parents Sharon Bottoms and April Wade. This one cuts close to the bone for the Pride Ride's three lesbian moms and stepmoms. As we douse our torches and discuss lesbian custody case law with the Richmond newspaper reporter who's shown up at the courthouse, it's hard not to reflect that as satisfying as it is to swallow fire, perhaps it's time to learn how to exhale it.

In Philadelphia, the Pride Ride's last stop before Stonewall, there are two actions scheduled: a joint effort this evening with Philadelphia ACT UP, and an Avenger parade to Independence Hall tomorrow, featuring fire-eating and the signing of a "Declaration of Independence from Compulsory Heterosexuality":

> *When in the course of human events it becomes necessary for all human beings to recognize themselves as sexual beings, these truths must be declared as self-evident:*
>
> *That all people are entitled to respect and dignity for the sexuality they claim;*
>
> *That the act of claiming their sexuality should take place in an environment of friendship and support;*
>
> *That every type of sexuality is equally valid, as is every expression of sexuality between consenting participants;*
>
> *That the forcing of sexual identity onto an individual or group by an-*

other is contrary to the inalienable rights of us all, which are life, lib-
erty, and the pursuit of happiness.

    We the undersigned vow to undertake to enshrine these rights in all
hearts and all minds, for all time.

Today's Avenger/ACT UP action is to express outrage over a recent state Supreme Court ruling on what constitutes rape. The
court's decision was that a former East Stroudsburg University student was not guilty of rape, because the woman he raped didn't
scream or physically struggle—though she did say no throughout
the act. Based on antiquated Pennsylvania sexual assault laws
which focus on use and/or threat of force rather than consent, the
decision, with its blame-the-victim-rather-than-convict-the-rapist
rationale (which forces women to physically resist rapists, even if
doing so results in further harm to themselves), has become known
as the "No is not enough" ruling.

Unfortunately, thanks to the previous two nights' party action, we
haven't fully processed our political action's chants yet. One particularly problematic polemic goes, "We won't break, we won't bend,
unjust laws have to end. Fight back, fight back, fight back!" No one
likes the ending, since the whole idea is that women shouldn't *have*
to actually do battle to avoid rape. So, while driving from D.C. to
Philly, we tackle alternatives via CB.

"Well . . ." Regina considers, with a classically schoolmarmish
frown. "How about: 'Fuck you, fuck you, fuck you'?"

Our navigator presses her ear to the CB speaker. "They're . . .
They're trying to reach a consensus in the other van about the 'fuck
you's."

"Let me talk to them," Regina says firmly. She grabs the CB. "Hi
there, y'all? What's so great about the 'fuck you's is, we're turning
the 'fuck' back on society, and the man. We're saying, 'Don't fuck
us; fuck you, and your fucking stupid laws.' See? It's a little bit of a
double entendre. Also, we like the fricatives. So it works on many
different levels."

The CB crackles. Our navigator concentrates. "They don't like
the 'fuck you's. They say, How's 'Just say no'?"

Regina dismisses this. "*Way* too Nancy Reagan. Too trivializing. We wanna be strong! I want the fricatives."

"I really don't think people watching TV are going to do a multi-level linguistic analysis of 'Fuck you, fuck you, fuck you,' " Radclyffe comments, sourly.

Regina ignores her. "How about 'Fuck you up the ass'? What do you think, y'all?" she yells into the CB. "I think it'd work, don't you? Because then they'd get a sense of what we're talking about."

Our navigator listens long, then announces, "They wanna know, how about *'No* is all we need'?"

"Oh . . . well . . ." Regina trails off, defeated.

Shy Austin Avenger Harper, who has uttered barely a controversial peep the whole trip, suddenly interjects, "How about 'Change your fucking laws'?"

Regina brightens. "Ah! And see—once again we have a double entendre!"

Our navigator holds out the CB. Through the tiny speaker, we hear the other van yell, *"No, no, no!"*

"I think they want to avoid the 'fuck's," our navigator notes.

Regina shakes her head. "They simply do not understand how these apparently small matters of grammar and style can make all the difference. Well, let's see. 'We won't break, we won't bend, unjust laws have to end. . . . Don't make me be your wench.' Ha!"

Very Chaucer, we decide. "D'you think?" Regina marvels. "Hey girlfriends! We have a Chaucerian one."

"Their navigator says you're getting her wet," our navigator relays.

Shanti, an eighteen-year-old Dartmouth student who is the youngest person on the trip, interrupts. "What I want to know is, do we have any capes on this trip? I want a Lesbian Avengers cape. Like Wonder Woman."

"You see how important style is?" Regina demands, triumphant. "Style is *so* fuckin' important, and it's underemphasized in the lesbian community."

Unstylishly, we protest that evening minus any fricatives. "No is all we need" is our battle cry. After about an hour of chanting and another couple of hours' milling around aimlessly, the Southern Pride Ride is joined by the equally ragtag Northern Avenger Stonewall Caravan, which arrives (with far less impressive transportation than ours—several ratty cars—but a far more impressive supply of illegal substances) just in time to miss the evening's Avenger action . . . but make that night's Avenger party.

It's the last leg of the Pride Ride, heading out of Philadelphia to New York City. And we're lost again. For no doubt complex emotional reasons, the lead van won't let in CathyAnne, who is *from* Philly and the only woman who knows where we're going.

"*Why?*" wails Regina. She is not particularly consoled by the suggestion that someone must be having *issues* with the one person who can get us out of town. "We have fucking processed every fucking pee stop on this whole fucking ride, and *now* the fucking van decides to make its own fucking decisions, based on who-knows-the-fuck-what?" she enunciates between clenched teeth. "Are we supposed to get to New York by *Braille?*"

Somehow, we manage to process our way to the Jersey Turnpike. Most of the overplayed former favorite tapes have bitten it. People will tolerate *one* Melissa Etheridge song and a compilation album of some excellently loud and obnoxious female rock-and-roll bands, some riot, some not, but all of 'em definitely *Grrrl* kind of girls. That's the kind of mood we're all in by now.

Within a few months, the Austin Avengers will be kaput. But the Pride Riders don't know that yet. We've survived the flames, the floors, the cops, the rednecks . . . and the lavendernecks: each other. We all roll into Manhattan in the midst of Stonewallmania, burnt out but still unburnt.

Trickling Up
and Spilling Over:
What Is a
Lesbian Issue?

*S*ince our community can't decide exactly what a lesbian is (or even what a woman is), maybe it's not surprising that we have trouble pinning down the definition of a lesbian *issue*.

For years, the lone, uniquely identifiable, important lesbian political concern that couldn't be subsumed under "gay" and "women's" issues was lesbian visibility. No more. Most of "our" issues continue to overlap the concerns of the feminist and gay movements, although there do seem to be differences in priorities. According to a *Newsweek* poll, for instance, lesbians feel that the right of gays to serve in the military is a more important issue than AIDS. But gay men say that AIDS is the prime gay issue. A survey by the Human Rights Campaign Fund's Lesbian Issues Outreach Project indicated that domestic partnership benefits are lesbians' primary concern by far. (Over two-thirds of the women surveyed cited them.) Next came gay rights in general, abortion and privacy issues, and lesbian mother issues such as custody.

But if there's any generalization that can be made about lesbian politics, it's that we tend to cast a wide net. For example, the various demonstrations along the route of the 1994 Lesbian Avengers Pride Ride were designed, according to an Avengers brochure, "to bring attention to discrimination faced by lesbians across the south." One action did focus on the need for lesbian-specific health research, and another on lesbians who had been targeted by violence. The other protests, however, ranged further afield to defend groups that might simply include lesbians: victims of poverty, racism, the tobacco industry, and unfair rape laws.

Looking beyond our borders is a habit that's by no means limited to political radicals like the Avengers. It almost goes with the lesbian territory—and sometimes operates to our detriment, at least in terms of getting quick results. If lesbians were able to unite and mobilize single-mindedly around any one issue the way gay men have focused on AIDS, we might have more mainstream political success. We don't simply *happen* to support a multiplicity of issues affecting a large number of people, however. Seeing the connections among all those issues and people is the *point*.

You would think we were secretly in charge of changing the world.

The clearest brief analysis of the difference in lesbian and gay male political approaches comes from attorney Liz Hendrickson, former executive director of the National Center for Lesbian Rights. During a debate at a high-level national legal conference about how to win domestic partner benefits, the gay men, according to Liz, favored the trickle-down theory: Get spousal benefits for the high-profile gay professionals in a corporation, and eventually the goodies would filter down to the rest of us. The lesbian strategy differed by 180 degrees: Figure out how to get spousal benefits for the poor African-American lesbian-mother cleaning lady in the same corporation, because if we can get *her* protected, we'll all be protected—the trickle-up theory.

One needn't be an expert in federal law, but merely familiar with the law of gravity, to realize trickling up is considerably trickier.

Lately there's been a growing emphasis on health concerns, which are just as difficult to pin down as "lesbian political issues," and for the same reason: Lesbians define the issues broadly and factor in principle at least as much as practicality. Gay women have always been on the front lines of the battle for reproductive rights, for instance, despite the fact that we're far less likely than straight women to need abortions. But most lesbians (ourselves included) consider abortion to be a "lesbian issue," because any attempt to limit women's options and keep us in our place impinges on lesbians. We see a link between those who don't want lesbians to share a bed and those who want to tell pregnant heterosexual women what they can and cannot do with their own bodies.

The same holistic view informs lesbian AIDS politics, since lesbians understand the part that homophobia played in the government's refusal during the Reagan years to so much as recognize that there was an epidemic. Some resentment has since publicly surfaced over the fact that lesbians have been vastly more active in AIDS work than gay men have been in, say, the struggle against breast cancer. But AIDS is still a lesbian issue because (a) lesbians can get AIDS, just as men can get breast cancer, and (b) the AIDS crisis has dramatically exposed the profits-over-people flaws in the medical establishment. Feminists had been talking about these for years, mostly in terms of unsafe breast implants and IUDs, forced sterilization, the rights of midwives, the overprescribing of tranquilizers to female patients, and so on.

Some lesbians see vegetarianism as our health issue, for anti-cancer and/or save-the-planet and/or animal rights reasons. (Lindsy has contributed to a nonprofit lesbian farm that rescues pigs from being turned into bacon.) The list goes on. Frankly, we would not be all that surprised to hear of a "Blue Balls Is a Lesbian Health Issue" movement.

But to try to narrow the definition slightly, Marj Plumb (who co-edits a lesbian health newsletter for the National Center for Lesbian Rights and directs the Office of Gay and Lesbian Health Concerns for the New York City Department of Health) feels that the most pressing health issue for lesbians is primary care. Lesbians often ignore it. Because of our relatively low rates of sexually transmitted diseases and our typical lack of need for birth control, many of us don't see a gynecologist and get Pap smears regularly. We thereby

266

put ourselves at greater risk for cervical cancer, particularly because so many lesbians do have sexual pasts with men. A 1992
study of 104 new clients served by the Whitman-Walker Health
Clinic in Washington, D.C., showed that, in contrast to a general fe-
male-population average of nine months between Pap smears, the
average interval between Pap tests for Whitman-Walker's overwhelmingly lesbian and bisexual clientele was thirty-four months.
Fourteen percent had either never had a Pap or hadn't had one in the
last ten years.

Then there's the fact that doctors can be hostile to lesbians; consequently, many of us avoid visiting the doctor unless we're in such
hideous shape that we must. In a 1994 survey of gay and lesbian
doctors, 67 percent reported hearing of substandard or denied care
for lesbian, gay male, or bisexual patients; 52 percent had personally witnessed substandard care; and 88 percent had heard colleagues make disparaging remarks about queer patients. Some of
the humiliations are subtle, like the forms that ask you what *kind* of
birth control you use. (The best!) We know a woman whose straight
male doctor asked her about her sex life in excruciating detail; she
later saw that he had written on her chart "not sexually active."

A controversial data analysis by Dr. Susan Haynes of the National Cancer Institute suggests that lesbians may be up to three
times more likely than heterosexual women to develop breast cancer. The reason is a combination of factors including lower child-
bearing rates, less frequent clinical breast exams, and a greater
likelihood of a variety of other risks. These include several that may
be linked to stress or low self-esteem, such as smoking (31 percent
of Whitman-Walker clients versus 27 percent of women in general); being overweight; and heavy drinking. (In 1989, *Alcoholism
Treatment Quarterly* reported alcoholism among lesbians to be two
to three times more frequent than in the general population.)

Haynes's theory is controversial because nobody, in fact, *knows*
if lesbians really do develop breast cancer at a higher rate than other
women. Nobody knows because nobody knows much of anything
about the general state of lesbian health. Until very recently, no one
cared enough to begin funding any studies.

Which brings us back to AIDS. Although lesbians are at low risk, female-to-female transmission is possible. Yet it wasn't until April 1995, a decade and a half into the AIDS epidemic, that the Centers for Disease Control, under pressure from activists like Plumb, agreed to start addressing the problem. Previously, no statistics were kept on lesbians and HIV, so there was a huge information gap.

In our own travels, we've heard about lesbians who never take precautions, even when engaging in sex that logically seems risky, like going down on a menstruating stranger. The rationale is that lesbian AIDS cases are few, and most of the documented ones involve lesbians who were infected through intravenous drug use or from having unsafe sex with men. (Perhaps the women having sex with men were assuming that lesbian *identity* is just as effective a protection as latex.) On the other hand, there are women who protect themselves in ways, like wearing latex gloves to touch a woman's vulva, that aren't even being suggested for heterosexuals, who are at much higher risk.

What *is* safe sex for two women? No one knows.

For every Lesbian Avenger breathing fire, there are countless women volunteering at their local women's or gay center, or writing checks to the National Center for Lesbian Rights, the Astraea Foundation, NOW, the National Gay and Lesbian Task Force, the Lambda Legal Defense Fund, the ACLU's Gay and Lesbian Rights Project, and other work-within-the-system organizations.

There are also women whose main political contribution is, quite simply, telling the truth about who they are. As far as we're concerned, Martina Navratilova was a lesbian politician on the tennis court.

Although "lesbians" are now relatively visible, individual lesbians still mostly are not. Even when they don't have to deal with outright discrimination, some lesbians fear that if they come out they'll forever after be singled out as "that *lesbian* doctor/lawyer/editor/actor/commissioner/whatever," rather than being known for their accomplishments. We ourselves have been warned that by writing this book, we'll spend the rest of our careers branded as "lesbian writers," as if we were living lavender Vuitton bags. (To which we say: "Feh." We figure some of our straight colleagues already pigeonhole us as "the bass player with the beer holster" and "that weird chick who writes about computers *and* makeup.")

In 1991, Sherry Harris was elected to the Seattle City Council. She called herself "a raging moderate," but she was better known as the first black lesbian elected official in the nation.

We followed Sherry around one evening, listening to her give speeches at two fund-raisers, one for a white gay colleague, another for an African-American heterosexual colleague. By the time we got her alone in Chau's, our favorite Seattle Chinese restaurant and hers, she was yearning, practically salivating, to discuss with us her real political passion:

Land use permits.

Don't get the wrong idea about Harris, though. Hazardous waste processing really turns her on, too. Ditto for mass transit and salmon farming using existing streambeds. Sherry may have been the firstblacklesbianelectedofficial, but before she was a politician she was an engineer, who worked at Boeing and U S West.

"I still don't want to make a big deal about my sexuality," she told us, delicately chowing down a Dungeness crab claw. "The thing is: What does it mean to be a lesbian? I don't know! I'm an engineer; I'm interested in technical things. I'm an avid sports enthusiast. I'm also black and gay, and I want to advance the civil rights movement as a whole, but that's not why I ran for public office. It's a side benefit, above and beyond what I wanted to do on the city council. It's very easy, especially for whites, to discount a minority person: 'Oh, you probably want to work on welfare reform.' If I tried to emphasize my being gay, I'd never get to talk to them about the importance of a regional transit project to our ability to grow as a city. I want the freedom to work on the issues I care about, just like the other council members."

But Sherry knew she was walking a tightrope. Even if you don't want to be a twenty-four-hour-a-day lesbian leader, she added, gay voters from all over Seattle "see you as their representative. And they will come to me for everything from the potholes in the street to the police officer that harassed them. You can run yourself ragged."

She had recently been gay-baited from the pulpit of a leading black church in town (she snortingly noted that the church in question has a choirful of queers). During her campaign, her house was pelted with eggs. There is a woman who phones her at intervals to "say things like how God doesn't like lesbians. What gets me is that it's one thing to feel that or believe that and another to pick up the phone and *tell* me that. That's what *I* think is weird."

Mostly Sherry was trying to go about her business, obsessing about land use but figuring that her very existence did some good for the gay cause. "The important thing is that [bigots] get to know somebody gay. It's one thing for someone to stand up and say all these things about gay people, and it's another thing to come meet me and see I don't look like or sound like or seem like anything he had to say." However, she had also "read the riot act" to reporters who insisted on mentioning her sexual orientation when it wasn't germane.

Sherry's resistance to being narrow-cast goes way back, as does catching shit for it. Growing up in Newark, she got her undergraduate engineering degree from the New Jersey Institute of Technology, where "the population was ninety-eight percent white. There was a black association for student engineers, BASE, and the only activity that was appropriate in their minds *was* BASE; if you were black, you went to BASE." Sherry didn't find it so simple. "I looked around at this school, and there was all this *stuff!*" she enthuses. "Skiiing, hiking, tennis, basketball, climbing, caving . . . I did it all, and I had the best time of my life. But I was incredibly ostracized by black students who thought I was a sellout. I thought *they* were the ones with the problem. I could never relate to blacks stereotyping themselves, saying that to be black means you have to fit yourself into this four-by-four box."

Still, Sherry admitted that as a high-profile lesbian, she had agreed to make some compromises. One of her most riveting features is a white-lightning streak of hair jagging from front to back. Before she went into politics, she also had a tail of hair down her back. It got snipped for the campaign, at the insistence of a political consultant.

The consultant also suggested high heels and makeup. "I hadn't worn makeup since I was a teenager; it's not that I don't like it, but I'm not a morning person, not at all, and you have to get up fifteen minutes earlier to put it on. I won't even get up fifteen minutes earlier to eat breakfast." And while Sherry has always preferred dresses to pants, the heels, she confesses, are a bitch. She had to agree, though, that image-consciousness is vital to a candidate forced to face dilemmas that straight candidates don't.

"I always have to look the part, is what it boils down to. It was like going to charm school. I think it's something *all* candidates go through, but if you're a minority person, you have to be the opposite of the stereotype. [The consultant] completely changed my look, and I wear these impossible shoes because of her beating it into my head that what you have to realize is that you're more than yourself. You're a role model."

This goes beyond just looks. "I'm now very conscious of where I appear. I remember someone wanted me to go to this lingerie party, where they were talking about safe sex for lesbians. Before, I never would have given it a second thought." Nor will anyone see Sherry on the Seattle nude beach known as Dyke-ki-ki. "Maybe because I'm an only child, I tend to filter everything I consider doing through a loom of correctness. Do I want young people to do whatever I'm doing? If I don't, I won't do it myself. I have a lot of friends who are part of the leather community, and they're the most wonderful people in the world and I really love them. But I won't go to parties that are heavily s/m. In a lot of ways you're estranged from normal social contact. You blow your nose wrong, and it's the talk of the town."

A year and a half after our interview, Sherry was defeated in a close race for reelection by a straight male African-American police sergeant. There are many issues in any campaign, obviously. But a major problem in this one appeared to be the candidate's failure to be all things to all people.

According to the *Seattle Post-Intelligencer,* black voters thought her primarily committed to the gay community. Much of the gay community, however, thought Harris wasn't committed *enough* to prioritizing gay-specific legislation; the lion's share of gay support went to the successful campaign of a white lesbian for another seat on the council.

The ex-councilwoman was especially criticized for not being accessible. Her staff, however, pointed out that because of her multiple minority status, she received five times as many phone calls as other council members.

"She pissed a lot of people off," one politico told us, but added, "If she'd been straight and white, she'd probably still be in office."

Let it never be forgotten that lesbians were the group that coined the phrase "politically correct." *Entre nous,* it never had the nasty put-down quality it later took on in the straight world. It was simply a way of poking fun at our knee-jerk "None of us is free until all of us are free" weltanschauung, rooted in the feminist movement.

One political difference between lesbians and gay men is that even the most potentially conservative members of our community—the wealthy, middle-aged, often closeted professional set—consists largely of women whose lives were shaped by the women's movement. That doesn't mean that no lesbian ever votes Republican, but it does mean that our community is philosophically grounded in the notion that "the personal is political." To lesbians, how you vote is but a tiny corner of what's "political." What you eat, where you spend your money, what you call people, how you dress, even what you do in bed . . . all of these things *matter,* because they have *implications* for the vast, intricate web of human life.

So, needless to say, all these intimate everyday decisions are subject to intense scrutiny under the giant Mount Galomar Observatory processing lens. Straights and gay men often just do what feels good. Lesbians analyze it, challenge it, justify it, wring it out and hang it up to dry on the village green.

If that sounds too grim, let us share with you a conversation we had with musician Gretchen Phillips (best known as part of the defunct gay women's band Two Nice Girls) and several of her friends.

The thrust, as it were, was that the ultimate politically correct lesbian sex act might be, well . . .

Maybe we should start with Gretchen's theory that to really understand the lesbians-who-sleep-with-men syndrome, you have to appreciate that lesbians are just more *imaginative* than straights. Straight women, she insists, *should be* so free and open as to try girls the way young dykes these days try boys.

It still sounded a little 1984-ish to us pre–Gay Nineties old-time lesbians-who-sleep-with-each-other.

"Well, I do think lesbians who are thirtyish or even younger have a feeling of increased options in that regard because of older-generation feminists," she acknowledged. "What they did and said—about men, and power, and fifty-nine cents, and the whole range of radical stuff—made things cushier for us, gave us more of a feeling of entitlement, so now we can go, 'Yeah I know that, and now I want to fuck this fag boyfriend of mine.'

"I understand how someone forty-five might find this hard to imagine as being a good idea," Gretchen concedes, "or even something she'd desire to do, because her life has been geared to fighting battles in a different way. But it's like making it so every successive generation of lesbians can imagine more. And the excitement of that endless range of imaginative possibilities, wanting to be a part of this beautiful timeline of passionate love, is one of the main reasons I decided to be a lesbian."

For Gretchen, a few heterosexual encounters after coming out, starting with a high school graduation-night orgy, were "just experiments, because originally, I thought I'd be bi. I knew I would sleep with girls first because girls matured faster, but I figured I'd end up with a guy. So that night my friends—me and my girlfriend, them and their boyfriends—got into a sort of wife-swapping thing, and I had sex with one of their boys." Rating the experience, Gretchen reminisces: "The fingers part: divine. The dick part: fifteen seconds. I would describe it as 'very supportive but brief.' I don't have a dick problem. I don't even have a dude problem. I just realized the guy thing wasn't happening for me. In terms of masturbatory fantasies, fine. But in a real feelings-and-talking sense, guys weren't as good as my friends who were girls. I decided, I'm going for love—and to be *seen*. I think sexism creates this rift where it's difficult for men and women to truly see each other, and I really wanted that. To me that's an important part of being turned on."

It's not a priority of most straight women, Gretchen is certain. And, she adds, she should know. "It was a big deal for me to sleep with straight girls for a long time. If I was at a dyke party and there was a straight girl in the kitchen: *Mwwwonk!*" She makes the noise of a humongous rubber suction cup, zeroing in. Why? "Well, a lot of things. But mainly, I think, my proselytizing nature. I was right on the front lines converting straight women. Some are Big Ol' Dykes today. I converted eight, only lost two. I'm pretty happy about that."

As for her two misses, "the problem wasn't the sex, believe me. That is *magical* for those straight girls—especially the look on her face when she fucks a girl for the first time. Because my experience with straight girls is: They wanna fuck! They wanna just get their fingers inside there, and plunge away! They love it! And they're totally into it. They're gonna do everything right, by golly. They're going to go down like they never got gone down on by a dude before.

"So there's the honeymoon period. But then it gets all very close. And that's when some freak out. I think they're totally threatened by the things that are so fantastic, that I love about lesbianism. Like the intensity of the relationship and the relating, the closeness, the exacting attention, the lack of separation, the ability to really see inside the other person, the questions."

Gretchen does admit that the intensity of lesbian merger can get overwhelming, even when the relationship in question is not sexual. "The separation thing can sometimes be a real relief, essential breathing space. That's why I'm now playing with two men in my current band, instead of women. The bonding I had in Two Nice Girls I just cannot do right now. So I understand making limits for a time. It's just not something I'd want to do forever."

However, "there are a lot of women who do want to skate through life," Gretchen insists, "who don't even want to ask themselves certain questions, much less have their lover ask them. I don't think these two ex-lovers of mine could handle having somebody absolutely knowing they faked it while making love, and going, 'Hey, sweetie, what's going on?' And a guy's not going to pursue it. I think these two girls were too fainthearted to be able to accept the challenge, not in terms of dealing with society's homophobia, but in terms of dealing with relationships that really required something of them."

There are nods all around. Four visiting lesbian friends, including Lynn from San Francisco, are also hanging out in Gretchen's Austin, Texas, living room. We had tentatively mentioned—maybe two minutes after sitting down, figuring a little warm-up time would be necessary before the conversation got hot—that one thing our book was going to cover is what women who identify as lesbians are doing or want to do, sexually.

"Well, I want to penetrate a guy," announced Lynn. Nervous "I can't believe this conversation" titters erupted, as the other three visitors leaned forward. Unlike Gretchen, they don't participate, but are thrilled to listen.

"One reason," Lynn continues blithely, "is just because I never have." Although she started doing what she terms "mainstream sex"—sleeping with men—when she was sixteen, Lynn had stopped by the time she turned twenty-one. "I don't do that heterosexual fucking thing anymore, and I don't want to. I mean, the physical reality's okay. But I guess the *idea* kinda bugs me. It annoys me, this penis-vagina power thing."

"Because you could possibly be fucking someone who, because of this world's screwed-up assumptions, thought he was better than you," agrees Gretchen.

"Right! That's why I stopped fucking men. Because it's what's in their *heads* I can't deal with," Lynn agrees. "Though, well, I don't know . . . sometimes dicks are pretty gross. That uncircumcised-dick dildo at Forbidden Fruit? Oh my God! Gnarly! The thing looks real. The balls are in the right place and . . . eeeuw! I didn't like it at all. Keep that away from *me!*"

Using such an implement on a guy, though, is a different story.

"At least, this specific guy, my roommate." While her roomie is heterosexual, Lynn explains, "the thing is, he's very cooperative. Very eager to please. My lesbian friends come over, he really likes to make them tea. He really gets into it. So that's another reason I want to penetrate him."

We were a little floored. "Um, this straight boy is the perfect lesbian hostess so . . . so . . . ."

"So you want to butt-fuck him?" Gretchen prompts.

"Ha ha! Yeah!" Lynn laughs. "I figure, he makes me tea, so—it's kind of a trade-off. Because he's into it."

Well, that sure clears things up. "See, I've fooled around with this guy just every once in a while if I'm horny and there's no women I want that are around," Lynn elaborates. "But the thing is, I can't think of anything I want to do to *him*. Like, the first time I'm, like, 'Well, none of this heterosexual fucking. I don't do that. Maybe there's other things we could do?' But everything I could think of was like, 'You know, I don't really want to do that, either. Because, like, *euuuw!* So actually, it's okay if you touch me, but I really don't want to touch you at *all*.' Oh, and one other time, I was like, 'I don't know, would you like to masturbate? I might be interested in watching you do that.' The thing is, I'd never seen a man masturbate before, because before I stopped being straight I just hadn't gotten to the point where I was creative or did anything interesting or unusual with guys. So he's like, 'Well, that'd be okay.' Like I say, he's eager to please.

"But butt-fucking this guy, I think, is the one thing I can do for him that I'd find interesting that he'll be into, too—because I don't wanna do anything else. So it won't be just like me having an orgasm and then getting up and leaving. He complained about that once. He said I split too fast afterward. Like, 'Thanks, honey—hey, gotta go . . .' "

Laughter. (Have we heard that one before? Somewhere?)

"And my main reason for wanting to penetrate this guy is, because I think it's"—Lynn rises, raising a proclaiming forefinger to the sky—*"important politically!"*

General hilarity. "Really! Politically speaking, I think all men should be butt-fucked. Although, that's not the number one reason with this particular guy, since he's already done that."

"Good," approves Gretchen. "The thing is, most dudes are dolts, really boring and really fearful, because they don't have that experience of receptivity. And I think their fear is based on misogyny: 'At least I'm not a woman, if I'm not getting fucked; I can fuck you.' They're killing us all because they think getting penetrated is inferior and contemptible and weak, and a 'real man' will kill you if you even insinuate he's getting fucked. And it's so dumb! I mean, sometimes I play a little game with myself: If I could choose only one thing, penetrating or being penetrated, which would I choose? And it's like heartbreaking to think of only doing one! I couldn't even imagine. Because I've been a lesbian, both penetrating and being penetrated, with women, my whole sex life."

So men need the lesbian sexual experience?

"Yeah! I can't even imagine who I'd be if I was doing only half the sexual experience. I feel different and changed because of the experience of being penetrated. And, just as a sort of gift to themselves, men need to know what that is. To open up wider and wider and take it more. And I don't mean it as 'Now *you* know how it feels, motherfucker.' I'm talking about a majorly loving experience, under ideal circumstances for feeling and knowing. You learn so much about sex and power—and pleasure; it's not about revenge—from getting fucked. And they *need* to learn."

"Exactly!" enthuses Lynn. "Because their whole role in life is to avoid that. You know, avoid 'getting shafted.' Really, the expressions: 'Get fucked!' "

" 'Up yours!' " Gretchen chimes in.

"And in football, you don't want somebody to 'penetrate your defense,' " declares Lynn, her face lighting up. "And spike the football in your 'end zone'—right? *End* zone!"

Now, that might be stretching it just a bit, we demur.

"It's *not!* It's *not!*" Lynn and Gretchen roar together, rolling on the floor in hysterics, but earnest. *"It's not!"*

Well, okay, we concede. They *are* all terms for humiliation, basically, but . . .

"Right!" Lynn beams. "So that's why these guys all need to be butt-fucked. And I, for one, as a politically responsible lesbian, wanna do my part."

"And that's why I'm with Lynn," Gretchen agrees—adding that, however, it's not something she's personally planning on doing, since she's currently in a monogamous relationship. "The real question is, Why aren't more *straight* women going, 'I want to butt-fuck my boyfriend, because I've never done it'? They don't even consider it. They just assume they'd never penetrate. All they've been doing is getting fucked, literally. They just don't know about that primal power, which is our God-given right, which they do not take advantage of.

"That's why lesbians are so important in women's music and why straight girls can't get shit done. Lesbians can save this fucking planet, man! We're the greatest cultural critics because we're on the outside. When you can't see the forest for the trees, lesbians can see it."

Taking the Law into Our Own Hearts: Family Values

August 6, 1994: There's a Ku Klux Klan rally in central Indiana later today, and a major antiabortion demonstration in the northeast part of the state. But in Indianapolis this sunny Saturday morning, most of the news is about the Brickyard 400 stock car run, "a race where guys who drive Fords and Chevys watch guys drive Fords and Chevys . . . a race where I can pronounce the names of the drivers," according to the *Indianapolis Star*'s relieved sports columnist. Despite decades of foreign formula car racing at the Indianapolis Speedway, names from paella/risotto-type countries are troublesome here in grits central.

It's also apparently assumed that there's an organic connection between the Carburetor and the Cross. Local Christian groups have been meeting with representatives of the ultraconservative Sports Outreach America, a ministry that distributed 600,000 evangelical booklets at the 1992 Minneapolis Super Bowl. (Their choice of sport seems pretty evangelically abominable, given the repeated prohibitions in Leviticus, the same Bible book that prohibits homosexuality, against toucheth-ing pigskin.) We are in deep Dan Quayle turf, the fount of the so-called family values movement.

For most of the conservative religious sects that have been growing in political power and influence in the United States since the Reagan years, the word "family" would not apply to the couple whose commitment ceremony is being celebrated this afternoon, with no newspaper announcements or similar public fanfare, at All Souls Church. One of the oldest Unitarian Universalist churches in Indiana, the beige brick building is large and light-filled, but not lavish. (The room in which the wedding reception dinner is going to be held resembles, more than anything else, a high school cafeteria.) And the sincerely spiritual yet practical Church Week Calendar signboard in the front lobby reflects the church's motto of being a place "where reason and religion meet": "Monday, Rational Recovery, New Men's Group, Weight Watchers; Friday, Bridge; Saturday, 'Congratulations Beth & Verlann.' " Today's wedding wishes are for thirty-five-year-old Beth Ernst and forty-three-year-old Verlann Major, both women, both ex-nuns.

Together as a couple since leaving their rural Indiana convent almost eight years earlier, Verlann and Beth have been planning the wedding for two years. It is not a real, legal wedding like heterosexual weddings, of course—although that "of course" may be inapt, considering how many well-meaning and otherwise well-educated straight people still seem stunned to find out that the gay church "weddings," more and more of which have been celebrated in the last decade, are not, and never have been, legally recognized marriages. They're simply ceremonies, mostly performed by liberal denominations such as the Unitarian Universalists, the United Church of Christ, the Quakers, some individual Jewish and mainstream Protestant congregations, and the Metropolitan Community Church, a national Protestant sect whose membership is mostly gay and wholly gay-friendly. After Hawaii took a baby step toward gay marriage in 1993, Utah immediately passed legislation similar to the Southern miscegenation laws of yore, explicitly refusing to recognize any legal same-sex marriages that might at some future time be performed elsewhere. By early

1996, South Dakota had followed suit and at least twenty-five other states were poised to do the same.

Verlann and Beth are fully aware that their "wedding" today will provide neither the legal nor the community support it would if one of them were the opposite sex, which is why they, unlike some gay couples who choose to recognize their life partnership, are calling their commitment ceremony a "celebration of blessing and union" rather than a wedding. But they aren't bitter. Whatever name the event goes by, they are thrilled. The quote on their wedding program's cover, from Jewish theologian Abraham Heschel, says it all about their humble expectations: "Just to be is a blessing. Just to live is holy."

Some radical queers think that same-sex unions are an unimaginative aping of heterosexuals. In middle America, though, not much could be *more* radical than what Beth and Verlann are doing. "For us, this public ceremony is as much a celebration of at last being totally out as being together. This is really something for us. When we moved to Indianapolis seven years ago, after leaving the convent, we did not even know one other gay or lesbian person," explains Verlann.

"We were somewhat isolated when we first got together. Our history, obviously, was not the bar scene," Beth notes dryly. "And because of gay people being ostracized by churches, even though I think there's a great spiritual hunger, you're not going to find many gay people through those. We found one magazine called *CCL,* [from the] Conference of Catholic Lesbians, and when it'd come in the mail we'd *comb* it. Actually, we did find in there the name of a contact person in Indianapolis. But we were too scared to call it, ever."

"We'd drive by her house, like some awful spy novel." Verlann, pulling an invisible cloak over her head, pantomimes a furtive stake-out. "Until maybe a year ago, we didn't even know the names of any of the gay and lesbian newpapers, or bars, or even any of the vocabulary. I knew that one bookstore in town, Dreams and Swords, had a gay and lesbian shelf way high up; I might wander over there, if no one was looking. But we still had a lot of internalized homophobia."

The couple did eventually meet a few other lesbians through Holy Cross, the Catholic parish where they first worked after leaving the convent and moving as a couple to Indianapolis. Beth taught fourth grade for four years, while Verlann spent five as a pastoral associate (with duties spanning everything from preaching and religious education to leading the buildings and grounds maintenance crew). "They'd all been there all along, really. But they were as under cover as we were, and those who are still members still are. We were not out," Beth declares emphatically. "We couldn't be, because even though it was a more progressive parish than many Catholic churches, we would have lost our jobs. It was very oppressive, the first years we were together."

"Your language, everything," Verlann adds. "I never talked about myself." She stops abruptly. "Well, maybe you know."

Of course. Closetyness is actually an area where our early straight-girl training stands us in good stead. ("Avoid talking about yourself. Ask about *his* interests!") But Verlann seems almost astonished that, for a change, she is having a conversation in which she doesn't have to be in the teacher/missionary role. These are people who clearly have many friends in their community—but not many who are other openly lesbian couples, with whom they can experience a simple reality check, based on shared experiences. "A woman I knew from Holy Cross once, when I was asking about her life, said to me, 'Tell me about *your* life. You never talk about it. Do you know that?' I just said, 'Yeah. I do.' "

"But finally, about two years ago," says Beth, "we decided we'd someday want to be completely out, and celebrate with our friends and families publicly . . ."

". . . and never, never have to live in that kind of fear and hiding again," Verlann concludes.

Like close-knit couples of any gender, Verlann and Beth tend to finish each other's sentences. But perhaps because of being "just married, almost," they haven't yet—except for their common earnest-educator manner—developed that old married pair lookalikeness. Beth is a classic compact, bespectacled schoolmarm (the kind of tiny terror who never has any trouble keeping a whole classroom of kids in line with one look); big, rawboned extrovert Verlann strikes one more as the kind of good sport kids can always talk into climbing the school flagpole, after hours.

For the ceremony, however, the pair is dressed alike, in matching

J. C. Penney pink-and-black flowered shirtwaists, with white puffy-sleeved blouses—very appropriately Julie Andrews–*Sound of Music* ex-nun wholesome.

Aside from Beth and Verlann, there are 135 people attending, and it isn't too challenging to pick out the other lesbians. They're the ones in pants-and-vest ensembles, or *very* tailored dresses. Oddly, all the straight women seem to have independently chosen to wear extremely large strands of pearls; possibly this is some secret straight agenda thing. And just for the record, almost all the guys, even the gayest ones, are doing ties. Extremist evangevultures who hang around San Francisco's annual Pride parade waiting with armed camcorders to pick out only the lezzies in loincloths would find no fanaticism fodder here; there's not a nipple ring or pierced nose in sight. All in all, the prevailing fashion statement is, "Hey, most of the time most of us are just as boring as most of you!"

In fact, that statement pretty much covers the rest of lesbians' lascivious lives, too. Let's face it: Far more of us lesbians have 2.2 kids (the extra .2 being the required two cats) than 22-inch dildos, and spend far less time in hot pants than over a hot stove.

"Homophobia." Beth sighs. "It's amazing the mind games people go through when they try to accommodate something they've been taught to believe, on the one hand, is so bizarre, into a reality they know, on the other hand, is so normal."

The union ceremony—which blends Catholic tradition with multicultural symbolism and much touching homemade creativity (heartfelt amateur artistic performances by friends)—reflects just that normalcy, right from the slightly shaky first bars of the live piano–folk guitar–nervous soprano trio's opening music: John Denver's "Annie's Song." Then the more traditional strains of Pachelbel's "Canon in D" ring out for the wedding processional.

Parading down the center aisle are Dr. Bruce Clear, All Souls' pastor; two Franciscan nuns carrying a Bible and a broom; and a nun from the Order of St. Joseph holding a copy of Robert Fulghum's *All I Really Need to Know I Learned in Kindergarten* (source of today's first inspirational reading; the second is from Isaiah). But the procession is dominated by the Oblon family: very serious seven-year-old Daniel, the ring bearer; his slightly older sisters, Sarah and Rachel, grinning flower girls in flowered pants suits; and their parents, Joe, a big shy guy who is awkwardly holding bread and a chalice (to symbolize the postceremonial reception dinner he's sponsoring), and radiant Danskin-clad Julie, carrying burning incense she beneficently waves over the crowd like a magic wand. Later in the ceremony, Julie does an interpretive "prayerful dance" to a tape of Barbra Streisand singing "Somewhere," something of a theme for gay people.

Like the Franciscan sisters, the Oblons are acquaintances from the ex-nuns' tenure at Holy Cross. These days, Verlann works as a counselor at the Indianapolis Youth Group. Beth is a respiratory therapist. When first discussing a commitment ceremony, the two decided to quit all leadership positions at Holy Cross in order to make their eventual public coming out less traumatic for their parishioners. "We purposely chose to give it a year of being away from those positions, quitting our paying jobs and then withdrawing from our volunteer positions, to recede into the background a little bit, before announcing our union ceremony," Beth explains. "It would have been much harder on the parish, emotionally, for us to be fired from our positions, as we would have been, immediately, because of this ceremony—the statement it makes about our relationship."

Being a traditional family, the Oblons didn't face the same situation. But they, too, separated themselves from Holy Cross, distraught over the Catholic church hierarchy's official inflexibility in accommodating a couple whom they had come to respect as highly moral, and to love as extended family. "Over the last year, Julie has grown in finding this patriarchy and sexism and stiffness just more and more unbearable, and Joe has grown with her in that process. So she recently wrote a letter to all her family, friends, the pastor, the archbishop. "Not a radical tract," Verlann hastens to assure us. "But just something saying the church does not hear her, so she could not be with it anymore." For both families (and a few other disenchanted Catholic female friends, along with their husbands,

284

partners, and children), alternative worship in each other's homes was now their sole spiritual solace—as such services have been for beleaguered believers throughout history.

"The Oblons might not have been so central to the ceremony if our actual siblings and nieces and nephews had been geographically closer, and/or more supportive and comfortable with our making this public statement. But they're not." Beth shrugs. "So Julie and Joe and their children, in the roles they've taken on to make this happen, have really been an extended family to us."

"But in a more open way," adds Verlann.

Pope John Paul II is on record as saying that efforts to allow gay couples to marry and adopt are "a serious threat to the future of the family and society." But despite the Catholic Church's rejection of them as a lesbian couple, Beth and Verlann are reluctant to reject its traditions. Enveloping the crowd in incense, for instance, is "a symbolic way of creating a space for ourselves and bringing everyone into it." This is a multicultural spiritual tool, Verlann explains, used by Native Americans and by numerous other faiths. "But for us, it comes out of Catholicism, incense being used in high holy times to lift us into the spiritual. One of the things I love about the Catholic Church—and there are many things I don't love—is that sense of symbolism. Beth and I both struggle with our Catholic identity because it's so much a part of our roots. I can easily give up the institutional Catholic Church; that, to me, is bizarre, it's so out of touch with my reality. But I have a hard time letting go of the richness of the ritual, which is what we tried to incorporate in our ceremony."

"Sometimes I feel more small-'c' catholic than big 'C.' That's the heritage of the church," adds Beth. "A lot of that gets lost in the narrowness of the political institution, but the heritage is not narrow; it's universal, and we're trying to reclaim that. It's very hard to find that sense of sacrament, for instance, in another denomination, and we don't want to let it go. But I think we're finding that we don't have to let it go, at least in a church like this one."

The pair found All Souls with a cold call to the Indianapolis gay and lesbian switchboard. "We didn't have any religious connections in town or anything." Verlann laughs. "We just knew we couldn't ask any Catholic church, although that's home to us. The

Unitarian church was marvelous. I'll never forget that phone call. I said openly who I was and that we wanted to celebrate our union. And the church secretary said, 'Oh yes, we do those same-sex ceremonies all the time. Would you like to talk to the pastor?' I couldn't believe it! I almost screamed. You ask a Catholic church secretary that question, and *she'd* scream. She wouldn't know what to do with that."

"Oh, she'd know what to do with you if you're lesbian and you think you're sick, you need help, you're one of the wounded they need to minister to," Beth says. "It's if you're a well-adjusted and happy lesbian, and you go with your gifts to help, and share your gifts on an equal par with other church members, that they don't know what to do with you. At least that has been our personal experience. If instead of a blessing of our union we'd wanted healing, I'm sure the Catholic Church would've dealt with us in a compassionate way."

While a number of elements in the ceremony of union are quite traditionally Catholic, cross-cultural and completely creative symbolic touches also abound. On the right side of the platform is a straw farmstand basket, the kind that's normally full of tomatoes. Next to it is a kerosene lamp, which Verlann and Beth light and place on a stand above the basket. The accompanying gospel reading, Matthew 5:14–16, is Jesus' lesson about the foolishness of placing one's lighted candle under a bushel, instead of letting the light shine from a candlestick so that the whole world can see one's good works.

"In a sense we have lived a great deal of our lives with our light under the basket," Verlann explains. "What we did in lighting the lamp and placing it on the stand, proudly, was say, 'No more.' "

After exchanging vows and rings (traditional gold bands, but engraved with flowers as a symbol of life), Beth and Verlann join hands and turn to face the congregation. Lying in front of them is a broom. Back in America's slavery days, many slaves were prohibited from legally marrying because of the biblical injunction that "what God therefore hath joined together, let not man put asunder"—an injunction Christian owners had no intention of honoring, if the price was right; so slave couples—forced, as gay couples still

285

are, to invent their own rituals to recognize their unions—"married" themselves, by jumping over the one item members of an oppressed toiling class were sure to possess: a broom. The nervous broom-bearer has placed it only about six inches from the front of the stage, a drop Beth regards as if it were the Grand Canyon. The couple hop over very carefully, to applause.

By the time Pastor Clear officially blesses the union and leads the recessional into the reception room for the traditional wedding buffet (featuring traditional gray roast beef), most of the crowd, including Beth and Verlann, are in traditional wedding tears. One of the older nuns in the audience rushes up and envelops the pair at the chapel door. The bear-hugger, Sister Mary Lynn, is from the Franciscan community where Verlann and Beth met and fell in love. She lived in the same motherhouse as Verlann for years—and taught Beth in high school on the same campus. "I'm so happy for you!" She beams. "It's been such a long time for you to come to this."

Even as a matter of mere practicality, the cost to gay couples of not being allowed to marry is substantial. In its 1989 "Gay in America" report, the *San Francisco Examiner* calculated the cost to a hypothetical employee of its own who was in a legally unrecognized gay relationship, and compared the costs facing a legally married straight employee. Both staffers were fifty years old, and both earned $40,000 a year. Findings included the following:

> Legal spouses got employer-provided medical and dental insurance worth almost $300 per month, while gay partners got nothing.
>
> Legal spouses automatically got $5,000 life insurance if their employee husbands or wives died, while gay partners got the money only under the same conditions applying to any stranger off the street—that is, if they were specifically named as beneficiaries.
>
> Legally married employees got up to three days' paid bereavement leave upon death of spouses, while no time off was guaranteed to employees whose gay partners died.
>
> Legal spouses of employees who died before retirement automatically got two weeks' severance pay for each year their employee hus-

bands or wives worked, plus an $800-per-month pension, while gay partners—again, *if* designated as beneficiaries—would get the severance pay, but no pension whatsoever.

In total, the report found that partners of gay *Examiner* employees who had worked for ten years would receive $55,890 less in benefits than straight employees' legally married spouses, and, if they outlived their gay partners by ten years, would lose $8,000 in pension payments. (Just a few of those gay "special privileges.") Activists working for gay marriage in Hawaii have identified some 160 rights built into state law that accrue to legally married spouses only.

The emotional cost of non-"real" commitment also takes its toll on gay couples, according to Fort Lauderdale Unitarian minister Liz McMaster. "I've done quite a few gay union ceremonies. And I've seen a fair number of unions break up afterwards," she explains. But while right-wing moralists are always pointing to the impermanence of gay relationships as though this were an integral gay characteristic, the pastor (who is straight) insists this isn't the case.

"The problem is not that gay couples can't love, or can't commit. The problem is reality: the nonlegality of these unions, and what that realization of second-class citizenship does to your sense of self-worth as a couple and the way you look at yourself as a couple; the pressure and difficulties caused by societal nonbackup, and how the outside world looks at you, treats you as a couple. And honestly, this nonbackup comes even from lesbian society; I know lesbian couples that *eat* on each other like psychic parasites. But I'm mainly thinking of the straight world. I remember a female couple I did a commitment ceremony for, who walked to church for the service. On the way, a car of young punks passed them and screamed, 'Hey, lesbos, get off the street!' "

Some of our own most humiliating experiences as legal strangers have come at the hands of the medical establishment. Pamela has a history of kidney stones. The first time she had an attack during our relationship, Lindsy got her to the hospital—but then wasn't allowed to stay with her because she wasn't "family." We were told that the best way to protect ourselves from this kind of humiliating treatment in the future was with a durable power of attorney.

Years later, Pamela suffered another kidney stone during an out-of-town band gig and was taken to the nearest hospital. Scared and in pain, she did manage to tell her doctor that Lindsy had power of attorney if she should become incapacitated, and was the person who would be calling to get test results and other medical information. The doctor was uncomfortable; he kept asking Pamela why she had to make a "big deal" about being gay. But at least we had, this time, done everything we could do without a marriage license.

That night Lindsy phoned the doctor from Pamela's hospital room to get an update on her condition. "How do I know you're who you say you are?" he asked suspiciously. (Hmmmm. Is this a page of the Gay Agenda that the Central Committee failed to pass on to us? The Secret Plan to ring up doctors and pretend to be some *other* lesbian?)

Lindsy handed the phone to Pamela, who was hooked up to a million tubes and in no shape to talk. "I thought I had explained all of this when you were in my hospital room this afternoon," she said tiredly.

The doctor, clearly out of control, barked back, "If I was in your room this afternoon, what did my tie look like?"

Sometimes what grinds you down the hardest are the people, often friends and family, who don't outright hate you but don't quite see you on their radar either. When the two of us first became friends, Pamela's nine-year relationship with another woman was in its final death throes. Lindsy's nine-year marriage to a man had ended two years earlier. It was sadly instructive to compare notes. Even people who didn't *like* Lindsy's ex-husband had regarded the breaking of a marriage bond as a tragedy, the dashing of hopes that had once been held for something that would last a lifetime. Pamela's equally painful breakup seemed to disappear into the ozone, thanks to the assumption that all gay relationships are transitory. Not a single straight friend or acquaintance ever thought to say, "I'm sorry." Even many years into our own couplehood, one or the other of us will often meet a heterosexual friend who, with no apparent malice, will ask, "And are you still with . . . ?" It's not a question married people ask each other, however high the divorce rate.

On the contrary, we have frequently heard straight people say

that they've finally decided to get married after years of living together, because "we wanted to show the world that we were ready
to make a *commitment*." Unfortunately, the mind-set that equates
marriage and commitment puts gay couples into a perpetual limbo
where no true commitment is possible.

Since we can have only a nonlegal celebration, the two of us
have opted for quantity over quality. The year after we became
lovers, we went to the roof of Notre Dame Cathedral in Paris, wrote
our names together on a postcard, which we shoved under an ancient door, and solemnly put rings on each other's fingers. The year
after that, Lindsy's children, then nine and six, decided that it was
time for us to get married; they spent weeks writing a ceremony,
making decorations, and figuring out what to put on top of the cake
(two tiny stuffed mouse dolls, both in bridal gowns). We've since
registered as domestic partners in New York City, taken part in two
mass commitment ceremonies (one at the 1993 March on Washington, the other on the island of Lesbos, with an all-woman Olivia
cruise), and, for yuks, twice been blessed by the King himself at the
twenty-four-hour automated storefront Church of Elvis in Portland,
Oregon. In 1989, we had a genuine religious ceremony, performed
in Paris by a defrocked Baptist minister who was then one of the
leaders of the gay movement in France.

We also stopped going to straight weddings. The institution of
marriage, we eventually came to believe, is like a restricted club.
We may wish our straight friends lifelong joy together, but if they
choose to join a club where some of us aren't welcome, at the very
least they shouldn't expect us to stand outside the clubhouse in the
snow with our noses pressed against the windowpane. Our decision
has caused some hurt feelings among friends and family who don't
understand that we're not just being "political" . . . that it hurts *us*
to be in a setting that underlines how little regard the world has for
the love we share. (It also touches us on the occasions that heterosexuals do seem to get it. When our dear friends Jane and Foster got
married several years ago, their wedding announcement invited
their friends, in lieu of gifts, to make a contribution to the Lambda
Family Relationship Project, an organization working for rights of
gay couples and parents.)

It infuriates us that in our new home, Florida, we're not considered good enough to adopt or foster-parent a child, despite the fact that two delightful, high-achieving young women grew up in our former home in New York. According to the National Gay and Lesbian Task Force, at least 21 percent of lesbian couples have children, and many academic studies have shown that our kids are pretty much like everybody else's.

But it would be wildly optimistic to say that our families are thriving in the current political climate; there are still women who, because they're gay, lose custody of their children, and others whose ex-husbands use their sexual orientation as a negotiating point to avoid paying child support. According to Liz Hendrickson, former head of the National Center for Lesbian Rights, "It's assumed that we don't value our children, because if you really valued them, you wouldn't become a lesbian."

Still, lesbian mothers *are* winning rights that were unheard-of twenty years ago. A lot depends on your resources, and a lot depends on where you live. For instance, the week Sharon Bottoms lost custody of her son in Virginia in 1993, the Massachusetts Supreme Court ruled that there was no reason why a child couldn't have two parents of the same gender. This decision allowed two women who were both on the faculty of Harvard Medical School to become the legal parents of the daughter of one of them. Such second-parent adoptions have also taken place in Alaska, California, New York, Washington, and Vermont.

When the two of us were raising young children in the late seventies and early eighties, most lesbian mothers were refugees from past heterosexual liaisons. But the desire to mother a child knows no sexual boundaries, and in recent years there's been a baby boom among lesbians who (like many single or divorced straight women) refuse to accept the traditional nuclear family as the only viable incubator for a child. Some women go to a sperm bank where they can choose the ethnicity, physical characteristics, and even college major of their donor. Others prefer to be inseminated with the sperm of someone they know—for instance, a relative of the non-biological mother in a couple, or a gay male friend. Some women

use the services of a doctor; others inseminate themselves, the
turkey baster being the delivery system of choice. Among those
who use a known donor, some want a peripheral uncle figure and
others want an active coparent. Looking for Mr. Goodbaster can be
a tricky business.

Samuel Austin Lowinger is sitting on the floor of one of his houses,
gnawing intently on a cordless phone. "His uppers are coming in,"
explains his mother, Sandy Seagift. He clearly thinks that phone buttons are the best toy in the world, and his mother keeps an eye out so
he doesn't inadvertently punch in a call to Helsinki. There's an article posted on the refrigerator pointing out that a child born today
will cost its parents $231,140 by the time it's seventeen years old.

But at fourteen months, Sam has pretty simple needs. Buh-bup,
bee BEEP. He's Gerber Baby cute, with the Woody Woodpecker
scruff of hair that his biological parents, both redheads, were hoping for when they decided several years ago to make a child together.

Sandy met Sam's father, Steve Lowinger, and Steve's partner,
Dave Dean, at San Francisco's monthly Sperm and Egg Breakfast,
a mixer for lesbians and gay men who are looking to become parents. Sam was the first baby born through the group, although there
have since been others. (And at least two lesbians met at the breakfast, became lovers, changed their minds about how to organize
their family, went to a sperm bank, and now have a child.)

He was delivered by a lesbian obstetrician, and he goes to a lesbian pediatrician. His father belongs to a gay group from the synagogue where Sam had his naming ceremony, and his mother
belongs to a play group made up entirely of lesbian mothers. Sam
also has two lesbian "grandmas," two women (one in her sixties,
the other in her seventies) who placed an ad in a gay paper in search
of an ongoing relationship with a child. If Sandy and Steve ever
have an irreconcilable disagreement about Sam, they've agreed to
go before a local gay and lesbian mediation board. Then there's
Dave's son, who also has a lesbian mother. He had lesbian teachers
for day care, preschool, and first grade, and he now goes to "Camp

It Up," a summer camp for children with gay parents. In the San Francisco Bay area, gay parenthood is as much of a quantum leap forward from our own fearful, isolated personal experience as Sam's cordless is from a plain black dial phone.

Sam's family also deals with baroque logistical problems that most heterosexuals don't face until they've been through multiple messy divorces. "I have him two and a half days and then Steve has him two and a half days, and then I have him for five, and Steve has him for five," Sandy explains. "It used to be three and four, but it changed because of Dave's son's mother's teaching schedule."

Sandy and the two men are not quite a family unit, but a lot more than a business arrangement, and there are delicate balances to be maintained. Sandy lets Steve come by sometimes when it's "her" time with Sam, but Steve and Dave tend to guard their own time together as a couple raising two children. Steve worries about Sandy feeling excluded: "Like, there's a weekend when we're going down to L.A. to see my parents. But it's a lot for them to have me, Dave, Dave's son, Sam, *and* Sandy. If I went down with just her, it would send the wrong message to my parents, who still haven't told their friends. Their friends think I just had this baby without marrying the girl. I want them to see that Dave is my partner, but I don't want to exclude Sandy." (The solution, reached after mucho processing: Sandy will come down for the day at the end of the weekend.)

We first met Sandy the month before Sam was born. She was forty-two, her biological clock in overdrive. Except for the maternity shirt, she looked like a stereotypical soft butch, with short hair and freckles. "I always knew I was a lesbian," she told us. "I can remember being in the first grade and standing on line and thinking, I'm different. I like these little girls. I always had crushes and thought I was the only one, and depraved, and weird, and that all the bad things that ever happened to me were because of that. But I always wanted to have kids."

Even more than most people, she also had an acute hunger for family. Her mother died after Sandy's alcoholic father had abandoned the family; she was raised in Omaha by an aunt and uncle who, she says, obviously favored their own children and treated Sandy like a Cinderella. Sandy's young adulthood was one of unrelenting misery: too much booze, too many drugs, a halfhearted suicide attempt made when she couldn't imagine life as a queer, and a few disastrous attempts at sex with men. "The first time it was because I had told a straight woman that I was in love with her. She reacted badly, and didn't even want to be alone in a room with me. I really freaked. To prove to myself that I could be sexual, that someone would want me, I got really drunk and slept with a man. I was maybe twenty-three."

A few years later she fled to San Francisco and got a job as a telephone lineperson. (She's since gone back to school and now works as a physical therapist.) It was then she took the name Seagift, to symbolize a new life away from her problematic biological family. The Bay Area was an easy place to be queer, but not such an easy place to nurture a relationship with a child. Sandy baby-sat regularly for a "woman who had gone straight and wanted me to be an auntie. But our parenting styles were vastly different. I'm stricter, and she and her husband were lackadaisical. When the kid was four or five, she was still not using silverware, and always interrupting people when they talked."

Thinking that maybe the solution was to have a more structured role in a child's life, Sandy made an arrangement with a lesbian couple to help financially with their child in exchange for caring for the child one night a week for several years. But when she had a falling-out with one of the women, she was cut off from the child.

Eventually Sandy got into a relationship with a woman who had a daughter—and when they had a bitter, nasty breakup several years later, the same thing happened. At that point, "I realized that if I wanted to be a parent, the child would have to be someone I was related to. By then I didn't even want to adopt. There were all these stories about parents who come back later and claim the baby." A rueful smile. "That would be me."

She went into therapy, and "was able to come to a place where I could provide myself with a family instead of trying to get it from somebody else. But I didn't want to do it completely alone. I needed support"—certainly financial support and, hopefully, other sorts, too. However, she was pushing forty and didn't have a lover. When she read about the Sperm and Egg Breakfast in a newspaper ad, it sounded perfect.

Finding Donor Right took some time. "The first man I talked to was bisexual, and his dream was to find a bisexual woman, fall in love, get married, and have children. That wasn't going to happen with me. He also had what I considered unsafe sex practices. The next guy I talked to was a doctor, and vast class differences came up for me around the way he lived. I grew up poor working-class, and he had a house full of antiques. It just didn't feel right. And he had a lover who lived far away, and I can't fathom that at all."

At the time, Steve was looking for a Jewish woman, preferably one with red hair like his. Steve (an architect who works for the Gap, overseeing the building of new stores) and Dave (who does marketing for the Wells Fargo Bank) had been together for four years. Steve had "always wanted to have a kid. The sad thing about being gay, for me, was that I thought I wouldn't have any." So when he met Dave through a personals ad, it was a plus for Steve that Dave had a son. "Although at first I thought he was this fucked-up guy who had been married and divorced. Actually he was a pioneer" in gay parenting: Dave's son was conceived with a lesbian acquaintance. (He lives with Dave and Steve half the week.) When the men decided to add to their family, they began cruising the Sperm and Egg Breakfast.

Red-haired Jewish lesbians weren't exactly pouring out of the woodwork. But there were other, more crucial values on their shopping list. Dave and his son's mother, for instance, had argued in the past over her affinity with the New Age movement. "I'm experienced at this, and I know what to look for: somebody very grounded, very feet-on-the-ground," Dave told us. Additionally, "I kept seeing Steve going for the more extroverted type, and they were pushing him around, being too controlling. He's kind of controlling, too, and I could see these tremendous battles. He needed someone more introverted to make this mesh a little better, and she seemed more laid-back."

"Sandy's a real goy, and she comes from the Midwest," Steve said in wonderment. "She's the very opposite of me; I come from two very overprotective parents. She's a good balance for me that way. If I got together with a Jewish princess, I can just see too many children in the family!" When he told his parents—to whom he had only recently come out—that he was going to be a father, "one of the first things they asked was if she was Jewish. My mom was upset, at least until she met Sandy, but my dad was like, 'Oh, it doesn't matter.' He did ask if I had talked to any Jewish girls, and when I said yeah, but that it just wasn't right, my dad said, 'Yeah, I can see with Sandy you're in the driver's seat.' As I said to a friend of mine, 'He should know, he's lived with a Jewish girl for forty-plus years.'"

There's only one problem with his parents, he added circumspectly: "I didn't tell Sandy this, but my mom said that she could see problems if we had a girl. With the clothes."

Sandy didn't care about religion (she describes herself as a "recovering Catholic who believes in a Higher Power, but whose religion is really about deciding what's right and wrong"). Nor did she have any particular desire to reproduce a little redhead. "If anything, I wanted a dark man, because I've always grown up with the onus of having to stay out of the sun or risk being horribly sunburned. In fact, I'm pretty much always attracted to dark, curly-haired women who are the opposite of me. Steve looks just like me! But I wasn't going for the genes. I was more watching his interactions with Dave's son, and knowing that he's into processing and that he's a nice guy."

Sandy spent months hanging out with Steve—alone, with Dave, with Steve's best friends—before drawing up a contract specifying their financial and logistical arrangements. The biggest stumbling block was how to proceed if amniocentesis showed a "defective" baby. Steve wasn't willing to do what straight dads have to do— take whatever kid comes along. "I have a sister who's mentally retarded, and I have a real strong belief that you don't kill babies because of stuff like that," Sandy explained. In the end they agreed that "if the baby had genetic problems, Steve would no longer be responsible, and I would raise the baby myself."

Otherwise, they discussed how they felt about everything from circumcision to the Mighty Morphin Power Rangers. Steve was tested to make certain he wasn't HIV-positive. Sandy agreed to move from San Francisco to the East Bay, where the men live, and to give any future child Steve's last name. She got to pick the first and middle names.

After these exhaustive negotiations were completed, Steve began stopping by Sandy's house while she was ovulating. If they had been relative strangers before, the sperm-to-petri-dish-to-syringe-to-ovum dance was a definite icebreaker. "He would come by and do his thing in the bathroom," she recalled, and then she would inseminate herself and lie down for an hour. Sometimes Steve and Sandy took that time to talk. They even made a "date" during the March on Washington—an optimal time for the gay world in general and Sandy's ovaries in particular.

Was it weird to be that involved with male sexuality, given her personal history? Sandy laughed. "When I was a separatist for a while, back in Nebraska, I really believed that guys were from another planet, that it was the Y chromosome that did it. And now . . . well, it's like I've come to be in love with him, in a nonsexual way."

In the end, it took five months and fifteen inseminations before Sandy got pregnant. Sam was born on April 24, 1994, with both Steve and Dave in attendance. The two proud papas dragged out the glossies from the labor and delivery room to show us—and some of them were so up-close and personal that we realized that they had certainly been up to *their* elbows in female sexuality.

Before Sam joined the family, Dave announced to his "very New England, very personally conservative parents" that he and Steve had something to tell them—this after he had come out to them as a gay man, and then as a father himself. "You could see by the look on their faces"—Dave laughed—" 'What *more* could there be?' "

It isn't the Brady Bunch. But not much is these days.

Barbara (Boo) Price, the Oakland attorney who was coproducer of the Michigan Womyn's Music Festival for most of its existence, remembers when things were very different. She was raised in Indiana; "I had my first girlfriend when I was thirteen. I was madly in love with her. And I had a boyfriend in high school. So if it was the nineties, I'd have said I was bisexual." This "one from column A, one from column B" pattern continued in college. "But I didn't think of myself as lesbian, and it had never occurred to me that I wouldn't get married." Indeed, she married a man from Costa Rica;

they moved to Washington, D.C., where Boo worked as consumer counsel in the Justice Department.

When Nixon was elected, she decided it was a good time to get out of public life and have a child. While she was home with her son, Andres, though, "things started crashing in. I called up my girlfriend from when I was thirteen—she was by then living in Pasadena—and told her I thought we had some undone stuff. And it all started all over again. So I thought I'd have a reasonable discussion with my husband. Maybe I was stupid, but we'd been together six years, he was a nice guy, and this was the sixties: progressive politics, nonmonogamy, we were doing the revolution."

To all appearances, Boo's husband took the news well enough. He was about to go on a long business trip; Boo arranged to go to California during that time to see her lover, and to take Andres, who was then two. "And it was, like, 'When you come back, we'll go to a counselor and figure out what we're gonna do, because we love and respect each other, we'll coparent, we'll work something out,'" Boo explains, duplicating the same eminently civilized, reasonable tone she'd used then. "He went 'Uh-huh, uh-huh.'

"In fact he had a hired detective sitting next to me on the plane. Attractive young guy who chatted me up. At the time, wine on planes cost fifty cents. He went, 'Oh no, I don't have any money with me,' so I covered wine." The man insisted on taking her phone number so that he could pay her back. "I thought, This guy's trying to pick me up. But who cares? I'm not going out with him. So I gave him the number."

When he did call to ask her out and she said no, "they hired a woman. She came to the door of my lover's house and said she'd lost her dog, had I seen him? I had a feeling that this wasn't about a dog, but I assumed she was lonely, so I invited her to come in and have some coffee. She said she was getting divorced, this whole story." The bedroom was next to the living room, and, at some point, the "neighbor" put a bug under the bed.

Then Boo's husband showed up, two weeks before he was supposed to meet her in Washington. He barged into the house, "picked up Andres, and was out the door. There was a car with the motor running in the middle of the road." She raced after her ex in time to catch the car's door handle. He accelerated. Boo was left lying in the middle of the road.

She caught the next plane east. "I walked into the house where we'd lived for a couple of years. . . . [It was] six A.M., and there wasn't a thing in the house except my dresses in the closet. All the furniture, the curtains I'd made, everything—swept. My husband and his friends had taken everything and set up a phony house in D.C. so it looked like we'd been living there all the time. At six fifteen the doorbell rang, and there was a guy serving me a process for lesbian custody. They made it look like I'd abandoned the family, the child, and the father was asking for custody because they didn't know how to reach me; but I was dangerous, I was a lesbian, I wouldn't shave my legs or wear dresses. . . . This was all in the papers.

"I went to see an attorney, an older man who was an old friend, and told him everything. We did a very quick search, and there had never been a recorded case of a lesbian mother getting custody, even getting reasonable visitation. The lawyers said, 'Either it's true and you can forget it, or you've been framed and maybe we can get you some kind of visitation.' They sent me to this big shrink. Told me not to tell him I'm a lesbian. But when I explained about the plane, the detective, and the wine, he said: '*You* paid for the wine? That's a very masculine thing to do.' "

During the months she was undergoing psychological testing, Boo was allowed to see her son only once. "He'd been talking before this," she recalls. "I walked into this phony house, and he wouldn't come up to me at first; finally he crawled into my lap and whispered, 'I love you.' He didn't talk again for six months."

By then Boo had been informed by her lawyers that she would lose in court, so an agreement was reached with her husband to reconcile and to continue to "seek psychological help" for her lesbianism. Eventually they separated, and her husband moved to Costa Rica. It was arranged that Andres would spend time with both parents, "and I believed it was especially important for a mixed-culture kid to maintain relations with his father's family. But I was terrified every time he got on a plane. For years, I figured I might have to kidnap him back."

In the era when Boo was raising her son, the fine legal points of lesbian-mother custody cases could pretty much be summed up in one word: cooties. As one 1976 New York decision put it, "Innocent bystanders or children . . . may be affected physically and emotionally by close contact with homosexual conduct of adults." Judges yanked children from their homes on the grounds that they might be embarrassed by having such icky moms (as if there's a child on the planet who isn't sometimes mortified by his or her parents).

Of course, it was also feared that if the children were insufficiently embarrassed, they might turn gay themselves. Although we live in a culture in which Amish and Hasidic parents are presumed to want to inculcate their children with Amish and Hasidic values, funny hats and all, gay parents are put in the position of having to proclaim that they have no secret plans to influence their children. (Not that it works, anyway. We *tried* to persuade Lindsy's kids that the lesbian lifestyle was the way to go, and they didn't listen. Fortunately, they do have excellent taste in boyfriends.)

Today the rhetoric is most likely to be about religion and "The Family." "Every child has the right to be born into a regular family made up of a man and a woman," the Vatican newspaper typically harrumphed in 1994. Far be it from us to put down any man who's a good husband and father (or to pretend that problems don't exist in the lesbian community), but really: Nobody's making U-Haul jokes about heterosexual men. Nor is it usually mothers who abandon and sexually abuse children. If you came to Earth from Uranus and looked at the statistics on abandonment and abuse, you'd end up scratching your antennae over why anyone would think that families with female parents are automatically so terrible.

And the right wing knows all this. In 1995, Jesse Helms had read into the *Congressional Record* an article from a North Carolina newspaper by a doctor who purported to treat the sickness of homosexuality; the article nattered on with every antigay cliché in the book, from the fall of Greece and Rome to the need of gays to "recruit." Then out of nowhere it observed that although all gay people have selfish, sex-obsessed lives, "lesbians tend to have more personal 'caring and committed' relationships of longer duration."

Similarly, in a Reuters interview, former education secretary William Bennett said: "I'm convinced that lesbian relationships more closely resemble traditional male-female relationships than homosexual relationships." Of course, he quickly notes, he doesn't want to let us adopt children or "validate a lifestyle."

We don't like what these straight men are saying about gay men. *We've* certainly never heard any gay man refer to his boyfriend as his "ball and chain." And in any case, what happened to judging couples on their merits? Half of all straight marriages end in divorce, after all.

But their comments about lesbians seem even more bizarre. If they really believe that our relationships are essentially as solid as their own, what do they think would happen if they "validated our lifestyle"? Are they simply panicked at the notion of solid family structures that don't need men?

Talk about recruitment.

What lesbians *are* guilty of is expanding the definition of family beyond the nuclear zone. Many of us have deep, abiding, best-friend connections with our ex-lovers, a phenomenon that's rarely seen in the minefields of heterosexual divorce.

"A lot of our relationships are *based* on friendship," explained political organizer, teacher, and writer Suzanne Pharr. "With us, the initial sexual attraction almost always has a component to it where you feel *seen*." When the sexual part is *finito,* or when two people simply decide that their lives are going in opposite directions, the intimacy remains.

"How can you throw away someone who has your shared history?" Suzanne wondered. "It just doesn't make sense to me that you invest so much emotion and affection and time in another person and then say, 'Well, made a mistake, I'm outta here.' "

Suzanne grew up in northeast Georgia, where "I have twenty-some-odd nieces and nephews. My mother came from a family of seven and my father a family of eight children. I don't lack for family. But with my family I was closeted for the first thirty years of my life, and it's been a very gradual and slow coming out."

So Suzanne has supplemented her family of birth with a half-dozen other lesbian political activists—half ex-lovers, half not—whom she considers "chosen family." In her opinion, some things are thicker than blood. There are, she says, "very deep places that I think you can only go when you share something of a worldview."

One of her earliest chosen family members was her ex-lover Anne Gallmeyer. At the time we met them, they had been living together for several years, ever since it became clear that Anne could no longer function independently. In 1979, doctors at the Mayo Clinic told Anne she was suffering from a rare hereditary neurological disorder known as Marie's ataxia. A form of nerve cell degeneration, it causes progressive uncoordination as muscles become less responsive to the brain. The disease affects basic functions like writing, walking, talking, and swallowing. Anne was already in a wheelchair when we interviewed the two women, and her speech was weak and atonal, so much so that understanding her was difficult.

By the time of her diagnosis, she and Suzanne were already exes, but so close that, though Suzanne was teaching in Arkansas and Anne was working as a librarian in New Hampshire, they would "run new lovers by each other," according to Suzanne. They themselves became lovers in Indiana in the early sixties, when Suzanne was twenty-four and Anne was nineteen. "I was Anne's first woman lover," Suzanne explained. "We really did think it was going to be the rest of our lives. We would have maintained it, but we were so ignorant." What sorts of problems did they have? "I don't even remember," Suzanne admitted.

"Closeted," Anne choked out in a labored voice.

"We didn't know even one other lesbian, that's right," Suzanne added. All they had for a reality check was Radclyffe Hall's *The Well of Loneliness*. They don't even have any pictures of themselves together in those days because "we were too closety." When they had the normal fallings-out that most people in relationships do, there was no friend, relative, clergyperson, or couples counselor they could turn to.

"We didn't think about doing therapy [together]," said Suzanne. "I don't think I even knew that you talked about problems, period. It was in the sixties, and I came from a farm family where my parents got along, but 'relationship' wasn't even quite a word. Later, as we were breaking up, it was the beginning of the women's movement, and this wildly exciting time when people were talking about their sexuality, and what they wanted and what they believed in— things that people now take for granted. But I think we have to be placed in the context of being together *before* any of that."

She turned to Anne: "I think you kind of stuffed it down, and then when it got too stuffed down, you split."

"Right," Anne murmured.

Meanwhile, Anne's very traditional Midwestern parents had (by snooping in Anne's mail) discovered the affair. "They had a fit," Suzanne remembered. They made Anne leave school, and they threatened to put her in a mental hospital if she wasn't "cured" by a psychiatrist they found. Anne's father forcibly took a ring Suzanne had given her and threw it into a lake. It was, Suzanne said carefully, "a time of . . . extreme stress."

"Apple pie . . . motherhood . . . and therapy," Anne chimed in, managing to convey a wry sense of mischief, even though every word was a physical fight.

The women were able to lie low and stay together. They even emigrated briefly to New Zealand in the hopes of finding a new life, but they still felt isolated as lesbians. As they watched the late sixties unfold, they also felt isolated as Americans. In 1968, when Martin Luther King was killed, they knew they had to come home.

Anne's family had disinherited her. "The saddest part of the story," Suzanne continued, "is that at that time her father had the same disease that Anne has now. It was in the early years of it; he had just been diagnosed that year. We were told that his children had a fifty–fifty chance of inheriting the disease, but we weren't able to be close to him, to participate in his deterioration. Nor did he share with Anne what the illness was like."

Anne's dad died of Marie's ataxia. "To me it shows the wretched power of homophobia." Suzanne shook her head bitterly. "That homophobia would be stronger than being with one of your own beloved, who shared the disease you gave them."

After Anne was diagnosed, Suzanne made a commitment that "when the time came that Anne couldn't live with someone else she was going to come live with me." Anyone Suzanne lived with after the diagnosis was told about the pact ahead of time. But the explanation did not assure complete understanding of something so socially radical. "Everybody says, 'Fine,' when you ask. But then when Anne did come to live with the lover I had at the time, it was very hard," Suzanne acknowledged. She and that partner had other problems, but Anne's presence in their home precipitated their breakup.

Suzanne and Anne moved to Portland, Oregon, because Suzanne, who had gone to Oregon to fight an antigay initiative on the ballot in 1993, thought the state's health care delivery system was the best in the country. The house she bought was chosen in part for its proximity to a shopping center; this afforded Anne maximum independence, because she could simply wheel herself across the street.

Suzanne also helped Anne assemble a "care team" of paid nurses and a dozen volunteers—mostly lesbians but also including two straight men. "Someone volunteers physical therapy, someone else keeps her checkbook, someone oversees her social life, and there's emergency backup when anyone's out of town. Anne can do what she damned well pleases with her own life."

And indeed, Anne did seem to lead a more interesting life than many able-bodied people. As we talked with her, she was about to leave on a ten-day tour of Alaska with one of her care team friends. She was also politically active with a disability rights group called ADAPT. "They do direct action, like they took over [Congressman] Dan Rostenkowski's office in their wheelchairs," according to Suzanne. "Nobody ever knows what to do with these people who want to get arrested in their wheelchairs. It's like, 'What the hell do we do with them? The jails aren't accessible! The paddywagons aren't accessible!' "

Do the two women ever get on each other's nerves? "Sure,"

croaked Anne. Simultaneously, Suzanne, with mock horror, exclaimed, "*Never!*" They both laughed.

Suzanne thinks her own Southern roots had a lot to do with her commitment to Anne. "I grew up in a family where if someone's old or ill, they live with you, whoever you are. My sister left her children so she could live with my mother the last three years of her life, so my mother could live at home. It's just the way that you do." She shrugged.

In this instance, her lesbian-feminist roots complemented Southern tradition rather than contradicting it. "One thing that we know now about sexuality that we didn't know thirty years ago, when Anne and I were first together, is that sexuality is very fluid. We can hardly define and pinpoint what is a lesbian, what is a bisexual, and ultimately it's a great thing that's shifted all the norms in this society. I think the same is true of relationships: If you could just see them as fluid, then we wouldn't have to be so mean and cruel and acrimonious and have endings. You wouldn't have expressions like 'breaking up.' You'd have expressions like 'changing.' You would have times when there was a sense of wonderment at how alike you are, and how *seen*, and how discovered, and you'd have other times you wanted to spend totally in solitude and internal growth or with other people.

"But I think where the rubber hits the road is when things are turned upside down and there's a crisis—like with us, now. It's not about saying 'Oh, I'll love you forever the same way I do now,' but 'I'm going to love you forever in many, many different kinds of ways.'"

We wondered how they cope with the sheer heartbreaking *unfairness* of it all. "We don't talk much about our feelings," Suzanne replied. "We do talk about our commitment to have her live here, every day, at home. Because the issue at hand is Anne getting to choose the life and death that she wants, or having her family choose the life and death of a nursing home in Fort Wayne, Indiana, where no one would understand her, away from a whole history and community of lesbian friends. But no, we don't talk about our grief about her disease. It's not our strong suit, individually or together."

"We don't have to talk about it," said Anne.

• • •

There are happy endings, even in Indiana. We began this chapter with the story of Verlann Major and Beth Ernst because there's a myth that some cosmic bowling ball got hurled down the center of the country, scattering all the gay people off to the two coasts. But the girls next door in Middle America might also be lesbians. As a popular button puts it, "We Are Everywhere"—including rural convents in the Hoosier heartland.

Verlann and Beth first met at the Franciscan community in Oldenburg, where Verlann was head of the religion department and Beth was a novice nun. While she had thought about joining a convent since junior high, a love affair with another girl sidetracked Beth until the the breakup of the relationship motivated her to change residence and career, and "made me look at my spiritual life again, too." After a year of commuting from Georgia to Oldenburg on weekends, Beth became a postulant.

However, she wasn't a lesbian yet, despite the five-year duration of her first love affair. "During my first full year of involvement with the community, there was so much spiritual and personal growth work and counseling that I began to admit to myself that falling in love only with women was a pattern in my life, whatever the label was that went with it. But I still never talked about it. And no one asked, even in all these discussions of the vow of celibacy and so on. It was assumed you were heterosexual."

"I remember a meeting just a bit before that, when I was finally confronting my sexuality," Verlann agrees. Not yet able to deal with herself, she nevertheless realized the need to screw up the nerve to act on behalf of others like herself. "I asked, 'What are we doing, as a community, to support lesbian women in our community?' The room became dead silent. Finally one sister said, with great confidence, 'Homosexuality is in men's communities. We don't have to deal with that.' "

Neither Beth nor her first girlfriend had dealt with sexual identity in their relationship, either. "It sounds unbelievably naïve, I know, but I don't think we ever thought about it. For her, she eventually found her identity as a heterosexual; she came from a dysfunctional family and I think I was a way out. For me, I didn't identify myself as lesbian either. I'd grown up in a very Catholic family—my parents had been very supportive of me not pursuing a lot of heterosexual dating and wild stuff; my seven sisters and brothers and I were screened from a lot of things. So I didn't know anything about homosexuality. I don't think I'd even heard the word. I just knew I was in love with that person. I put a box around it. I was denying a lot. I was extremely good at denial."

Verlann was even better at it. Raised in the rural Indiana hamlet of Bath (population: 50), Verlann graduated high school in May 1969 and entered the rural Franciscan sisters' community in September. "I didn't know what else to do, though I really did have a spiritual dimension I was searching out. In retrospect, it may also have been partially a way to not deal with the heterosexual world, where I didn't fit—but that was all subconscious. In a tiny country town in the fifties and sixties, I didn't know lesbian, gay, any of that. It was in many ways wonderful, living in a community of women, but there was nothing sexual about it for me. I'd turned the sex part of myself off, because it didn't fit in with anything else I'd been taught in my life."

Verlann ended up remaining in the order for eighteen years, with sex and sexual identity successfully relegated to the far back burner until half a dozen years before she met Beth. Her denial even survived the probings of therapy. "After a whole year my therapist said, 'You know, we've talked about so many things, I find it interesting we've never talked about sexuality.' I stood up, and paced the room, and said to her, 'You're right. And I'm not going to.' And I quit counseling. My wall was that strong. It wasn't until a year later that I realized, though I didn't have any words, that my sexuality had to be integrated into my life, I had to somehow deal with it, or I'd never be whole. You don't live in a house of prayer, meditate that much on St. Augustine's prayer to God, 'May I know you, may I know myself,' and try to open yourself up to the truth, without hearing things from inside."

Meanwhile, Beth and Verlann had met, but "barely knew each other," according to Beth. "About the whole extent of it was we did music together for mass in the mornings at the convent motherhouse. I played guitar."

"I played bass. And let me show you something." Verlann leaps up from the table eagerly. "This was very romantic! Beth'd be at the music stand here, and I'd be *right here* close in back of her, with my bass." She poses spoon fashion behind Beth, attempting to mug semilecherously. It looks about as convincing as a portrait of the Virgin Mary smoking a cigar.

"She was like a beanpole," Beth says bluntly. "She had *no* sexuality."

At the point right before the two became involved as friends and finally lovers, Beth had gone through the prepostulant and postulant stages of becoming a nun, and was two years past taking temporary vows as a novice. But with one year to go to permanent vows, she was having conflicts, though not about belief or sexuality. "For me, the vow of obedience was the clincher, because it's one thing to dialogue with people, but I still feel in the end I know, for me, what's best. Verlann was a deeply spiritual person. And I was in need of a spiritual director; I'd been told I had to get one."

"Ha, ha, ha," says Verlann.

At one of their first meetings, Verlann, in wise counselor mode, said, "Beth, why don't you tell me a little bit about your life?" And one thing Beth spilled was her relationship with the other woman.

"It was the first person I ever told," says Beth. "It wasn't like I even thought about wanting to flaunt it or anything, but I just thought, If I'm starting with a new spiritual director, I better lay everything out there honestly."

Verlann, at the time in the middle of her own coming out, listened to Beth's story and found herself, "inside, shaking like a leaf. I knew clearly what her story was, almost before it was out of her mouth. And then I knew more clearly for myself, too."

"But I didn't know anything about Verlann's story, because spiritual direction is very one-sided, like counseling," continues Beth. "What happened was, very quickly we developed a friendship. And then finally"—she smiles at Verlann—"it became obvious this was not a spiritual direction relationship anymore."

Regrettably, for recovering Catholic readers swooning for passion in the pews, the pair didn't have sex for a year after becoming friends. "The first time we slept together was terribly frightening for me, even though it was something we grew into gradually just from talking all night in our bedrooms, and it was something we both wanted," Verlann recalls. This time, Beth was the one in the wise adviser role, "and she was wonderful in teaching me how to . . . move into this other kind of closeness. But because of who we were and where we were, there was a lot of guilt."

As a result, they decided to stop being sexually active. "We knew we were at a point where we had to make decisions," Verlann explains, "and sex was going to get in the way of clarity. I mean, it felt great."

The issue was not in being nuns with lesbian identities, but in being nuns with lesbian sex lives they were not willing to be hypocritical about. "The book *Lesbian Nuns* [by Rosemary Curb and Nancy Manahan], many people thought that was a contradiction in terms, because the assumption is if you're lesbian, you must be sexually active," says Verlann. "It's not true. There are a number of women who are lesbian and in the community, who continue to choose celibacy. In fact, one of the Franciscan sisters who led our ceremony yesterday is a lesbian and is even fairly out in the community, but has chosen not to act on her sexuality, so she is neither lying nor in conflict with the church.

"The choice for us was between being sexually active with each other and being in the community—because we could not pretend to be something we were not. I had to separate out my sexual awakening from my sexual identity and say, 'Is this just a gift Beth has given me, the sexual awakening I've been looking for in my life, and now I can just integrate what I've learned and continue as a religious woman, celibate? Or is this going to be a relationship with Beth that goes way beyond sexuality; when the excitement and flames die down, is there going to be something that can last for a lifetime, something that's enough to make up for all I'm giving up in the community?' Because other than the impossibility of ethically acting on my sexuality, it was a great life."

"What she was saying was she was afraid to leave and then have our relationship fall apart after six months or a year," explains the more nuts-and-bolts-sensible Beth. "And she had no model to hope otherwise."

Being marginally more experienced at why lesbian relationships work or don't, Beth already knew what she wanted: Verlann, forever. She also figured that "if [a successful lesbian relationship] is possible for *anybody*, if it can be done, we can do it," even without the emotional and practical benefits that societal approval accords a marriage. So she left Oldenburg for good.

"I had had such a strong wall up, it took me quite a while to allow myself the freedom to even think about wanting that, too," confesses Verlann. But in December 1987, she took a leave of absence from the order, to move to Indianapolis, near Beth. "We had separate apartments on the same street. It was like we were playing house."

By that June, both definitely knew theirs was a life commitment, and Verlann signed the final papers separating herself from the order. "Some people ask, 'Was it like a divorce?' And no, it wasn't. It was like . . ." Verlann hesitates. This is not easy for her to talk about. ". . . like being a child who says, 'Thanks, Mom and Dad, for the way you've raised and nurtured me. But now I've discovered some new things about myself and it's time for me to go out on my own.' I'd grown up. It was time to leave home. So I did. And I remember being happy as I drove away for the last time. But *not* because I'd been unhappy." Tears are now streaming down her cheeks. "I go back there, and it's still a home. And in some ways I still wish I could be there."

Of course, she can't. But many members of Verlann and Beth's former Catholic community have come to All Souls for their blessing ceremony, to be with them in body as well as—abundantly—in spirit. It's just a shame, someone remarks to one of the Oldenburg nuns at the reception, that the union couldn't have been celebrated in a Catholic church. "Sometimes the Catholic Church needs a good kick," the no-nunsense sister retorts, spearing a third piece of lemon cake. (The banquet table, overflowing with the completely nontraditional gooey-rich desserts that Verlann and Beth have substituted for normal shirt-cardboardish wedding cake, has been the only sinful thing in sight all afternoon.)

"The sisters have been so lovely and supportive of this," Verlann sniffles.

Sadly, though, many old acquaintances have not been. The simple act of coming out as a committed couple wasn't without heartbreaking emotional consequences. "This more public process has really been a process of finding out who our real friends are," Verlann explains. "We've lost a number of people who had trusted and loved us for years, and have wiped it all out of their minds—all because they know it's a reality now that we are lesbian, so it's like they have to give up everything they knew previously about us."

Many of the lost friends are from Holy Cross, despite all the couple's care to disconnect themselves clearly from the Church before announcing their relationship—and despite the fact that Holy Cross, though economically poor, is, Verlann says, "relatively politically progressive. What's weirdest is, we've been open as a couple in every sense *except* this formal declaration. Everyone has known for seven years we live together, we vacation together, we bought a house together, we have our finances together. But we do this public thing and it's like, 'Now we know who they *really* are.' "

"Yeah, 'Now we know they have sex!' So everything else is gone," says Beth. "See, I think sexual identity gets misconstrued and reduced to behavior, and that's all they can focus on. I have said to individuals who say to me they just can't imagine the sexual behavior, 'Do you think about what *straight* couples do in bed?' I mean, I personally am very awkward thinking about my sister and brother-in-law making love, because my mind doesn't belong there. We all have that awkwardness the first time we think about what our parents did to make us. There's a certain offensiveness when you contemplate other people's private encounters. And that should be.

"But those private encounters are precisely what people automatically jump into when they think about lesbian relationships—and then they dismiss the whole relationship because they're uncomfortable thinking about something they'd be uncomfortable about even if they were thinking about a straight couple doing it."

"In fact, we've had some people say they felt *betrayed*, because everything good and wholesome they saw before was put out as a smokescreen. Our whole life, to them, had been a lie. They were duped," Verlann adds quietly.

Not everyone in their families reacted well, either. "Some did choose not to come to our union ceremony because they didn't feel they could support it," says Beth, sounding hurt but resigned. "The brother I'm closest to and his wife, who are Seventh-Day Adventists, said they find it difficult to believe in our whole relationship. It's funny, he and his wife and children come and stay with us and seem appreciative of our hospitality, and we stay with them, and they say they love us. But it's a real struggle for some members of our family: How do they show they really love us, and at the same time have reservations about our sexuality and our commitment to each other, particularly when their children are involved"—Beth shakes her head regretfully—"children they want to raise to think homosexuality is sinful and immoral? They don't know what to tell their kids, who have always known us together, 'We love Beth and Annie, we know you love them. . . . But these two aunts who have been nothing but good to you are exactly what we're trying to teach you is wrong.' "

"That's the dilemma in my family, too," agrees Verlann. At the reception dinner, she presents a toast to her family, talking about the many camping trips she and Beth have taken with her grown sibs' eight children (five through fourteen years old). Smiling faces swivel around the room searching . . . and then, in some puzzlement, give up. None of the kids are there. "None of them even know we're a couple. Because their parents, my two sisters and brother, don't know how to deal with it."

It's clear, though, Beth feels, that "it's the family members who have had the least life experience in a diverse environment who seem to be the most afraid. So we talk about it a lot, and try to be as understanding, compassionate, and patient as we can be without sacrificing our own integrity."

With a sigh, Verlann adds: "I've said to my brother and sisters: 'I'll never tell your children. But if they ask I'll not lie to them.' That's about as good as it's gonna get, for now. They have said, 'We hope we can still visit each other and be a part of each other's lives, knowing that we disagree.' We've assured them we can. Because one of the things we're consciously trying to do is to continue to treat with love and respect and care even those people who are not able to accept us. It's gonna take a lot of love, especially after the ceremony. But we don't want to alienate ourselves from these people."

"What we've come to understand is, when you come out, it's a process for other people, too, making them confront their own prejudice and homophobia," Beth explains. "I mean, it's been difficult for *me*, and it's my identity! How much more difficult to understand for someone who doesn't share that identity. I think in terms of the larger picture, bringing society around a little, it has to start with individual people. It's the ripple effect—we have a call to create justice one person at a time, and sometimes that means we have to be willing to sacrifice and stay with the process with people who are angry and bitter toward us."

"So we are going to try as hard as we can to continue to treat them in the same way we always have, and welcome them into our lives," Verlann adds carefully. "Because we don't want to reduce our world to only those people who are comfortable with us, or only gay and lesbian people." She waits a beat and grins. "Not that we haven't talked about moving to Berkeley!"

At any rate, "Some people have reacted very beautifully, too." Among the twenty-five blood relations who attend the ceremony, Beth's mom is a standout in terms of looking perfectly business-as-usual comfortable, in spite of the fact that Beth had been closeted from her until less than a year before. (In fact, neither woman had come out to her family until beginning plans for their ceremony.) "Coming out to my mother was the hardest thing I've ever done," Beth tells us. "I'd distanced myself from her for so long before that on account of my sexuality. Because it's like, if you can't share that, you can't share much of anything else, you know? You're on the surface. And we'd both felt that tension."

While Beth's coming out brought her and her mom closer, "this trip, she told me she actually had had to confront her own prejudices. But she was grateful to me. Because this experience had opened up her world to a whole group of people she'd known nothing about, and had broadened her, and she was glad about that. Both my mom and sister just said how beautiful the ceremony was and how happy they were to be able to participate and be with us for this time."

"I was particularly thrilled that ten or so of my cousins, aunts, and uncles came," says Verlann, "because the invitation was my outing to them. They did not know when they received it in early June that I was lesbian. My cousins especially treated it as completely normal. A young male cousin, about a week before the ceremony, actually sent me a tape of women's music that he'd made himself from a lesbian friend's record collection!"

And many acquaintances to whom the ceremony, and lesbian relationships in general, are not at all normal also reach out, willing to learn. Following the commitment ceremony, a couple from Holy Cross seeks out Paulette Schroeder, the Franciscan nun from their parish who did the gospel reading. "I don't know much about this, or get it," the woman says, somewhat hesitantly. "But if what it means is that Beth and Verlann love each other as much as I love Bill, I guess it's okay."

Sister Paulette replies, "That's exactly what it is, Nancy: just like you love Bill."

"I did get a little worried during the broom thing," Beth confesses the next day.

Verlann beams. "Piece of cake."

"Easy for you to say," Beth mutters, indignant. "I had to jump the fat part."

With a sigh of relief, they also admit to having anticipated the exchange of vows as majorly problematic. "We practiced for months." Beth rolls her eyes heavenward. "We were positive we'd be nervous and forget the whole thing. So around the house we'd be, like, doing the dishes. And Verlann would go, 'Beth?' And I'd go"—Beth adopts a cranky "Can't you see I'm up to my neck in suds" tone— "'Yeah? Whaddaya want?' And she'd go . . ."

Verlann takes her cue. "Just to be with you, Beth, is the most wonderful blessing of my life. Just to live with you allows me to grow in wholeness and holiness. Every day I thank God for the gift of our life together. I promise to love and care for you always, and thus be a blessing in your life. I will live each day with you in a way that allows you to grow in personal wholeness and holiness. And I pray that our life together might always be a blessing for others."

Beth looks into Verlann's eyes. "And I'd say, 'Verlann, sharing life with you has been a blessing which has given me tremendous joy. Each day I am filled with gratitude and a sense of awe at the goodness of God for bringing us together. And as our life continues to unfold, I promise you my covenant love. I will love and care for you forever. I will walk by your side as we both continue to journey in wholeness and in holiness."

"Beth, receive this ring as a sign and symbol of my love for you. As you wear it, may you always be reminded of the happiness that we share."

"Verlann, wear this ring as a sign of my love for you. And may it also remind you of God's invitation to you to always thrive in the love that surrounds you."

The two threats to the family and society smile at each other. Their eyes are radiant with pure love.